The Bush Diaries

The Bush Diaries

A Citizen's Review of the First Term

Largely based on letters and articles submitted
to
The Washington Post, The Wall Street Journal,
and *The New York Times*

Jack Nargundkar

iUniverse, Inc.
New York Lincoln Shanghai

The Bush Diaries
A Citizen's Review of the First Term

iUniverse books may be ordered through booksellers or by contacting:

iUniverse
2021 Pine Lake Road, Suite 100
Lincoln, NE 68512
www.iuniverse.com
1-800-Authors (1-800-288-4677)

ISBN-13: 978-0-595-35898-4 (pbk)
ISBN-13: 978-0-595-80353-8 (ebk)
ISBN-10: 0-595-35898-5 (pbk)
ISBN-10: 0-595-80353-9 (ebk)

Printed in the United States of America

This book is dedicated to
my parents, who provided me the best education that Bombay had to offer,
my wife, who encouraged me to pursue a writing career,
my teenage children, who are already talented writers beyond their years,
and my puppy, who lay curled up at my feet through most of this effort.

Contents

AUTHOR'S NOTE

The inspiration for this book came about after President Bush got reelected. By then, I had amassed probably over one hundred odd letters that I had written to *The Washington Post*, *The Wall Street Journal*, and *The New York Times* during President Bush's first term. Only six of these letters got published—three by the *Post*, two by the *Journal*, and one by the *Times*. Needless to say, I felt that many more of my letters should have appeared in print.

My wife, Raji, encouraged me to take the next step and write a full-fledged book. I was hesitant to embark on a book project, because I kept wondering why anyone would be interested in what I had to say. But then it dawned on me that I already had all this material, which I had written over the past four years on the Bush presidency—letters, articles, and web postings. Since January 1998, I had also maintained a personal web site entitled, "Nargundkar News & Views", which offered my insight and perspectives on contemporary issues ranging from politics and the economy to technology and its management.

Despite being a senior marketing executive in the high-technology industry, I have always had an abiding interest in politics. With the analytical skills of my left-brained engineering side and the creative savvy of my right-brained marketing side working in tandem, I can offer a rather compelling argument. My jobs in the software and telecommunications industries have provided me an opportunity to travel all over the world, meet all kinds of people, and experience various different cultures. So as a first-generation Indian-American author, I bring a different perspective to the subject of government and politics.

Over Thanksgiving weekend 2004 the idea for this book began to crystallize. It became apparent to me that our first MBA president's performance in his first term left much to be desired. Now that he had been returned to a second term in office, I felt the urgent need to revisit his first term and publish a critique. After the 2004 election, the basic tenets of "portfolio theory" had been violated. The American public had allowed the creation of an "inefficient frontier" of Republican-dominated portfolios—in the executive branch and the legislative branch (both, House and Senate) of our government. If we were going to take on such a high level of risk, i.e. an undivided government over the next four years, I thought it was imperative to put out a "caveat emptor" label by scrutinizing what the previous four years had wrought. After all, every financial portfolio comes with the warning label, *past performance is no guarantee of future results*". If the President's past performance itself was suspect, as my detailed analyses throughout this book will point out, what could we expect in his second term?

The Bush Diaries is a compendium of various letters—to the editors of the aforementioned newspapers—that I wrote during the second half of Bush's first term. Other contemporaneous articles that I had written earlier about the President's economic and foreign policy cover the first half of his term. In developing the book, I organized my articles and letters in a chronological order and then inserted a current preface to each one of them, so that the entire narrative reads like a running commentary on the Bush presidency. It is important that the reader keep these "past actions" in mind (the Bush Administration's machinations prior to the Iraq War are an obvious example), while contemplating support for likely "future events" (the crises in Iran and North Korea come to mind). I have also taken the liberty of offering suggestions and making recommendations on a number of economic and foreign policy issues, which I believe will impact the President's second term.

Is there any American who does not believe that the foreign policy of the United States could use a fresh approach? This became rather obvious after Bush's war on terrorism made a diversionary turn into Iraq, soon after the welcome foray into Afghanistan. Although a nobly-intentioned strategy, the Bush Doctrine was executed selectively and badly—thus failing to meet its own stated objectives. Iraq neither had WMD, nor any verifiable links to terrorists prior to the current war. In fact, it is the other two members of Bush's "axis of evil" who possess the WMD and one of them openly harbors terrorist organizations.

As far as economic policy goes, President Bush's blind faith implementation of Reaganomics has produced neither revenues nor job growth comparable to the 1980s. The only common outcome has been a significant upsurge in government spending with the attendant explosion in the budget deficit and national debt, so the much vaunted tax cuts need to be viewed as a tool of fiscal policy, not as its end goal.

This book does not provide a panacea for all our economic and foreign policy problems. However, it analyzes several different issues as they were occurring during President Bush's first term and it also dissects various political pundits' views on these topics at the time. More importantly, this book commits to paper what the hoi polloi have been offering through their blogs online—common sense feedback to an administration that never seems to acknowledge any mistakes. I am hopeful that *The Bush Diaries* will serve as an advance warning primer for possible déjà vu situations in Bush's second term.

The Bush Diaries would never have seen light of day without the support of my family. Raji keeps me from tilting to starboard by occasionally mocking me for being "a closet Republican wanting to come out". My son, Abhi, who is a freshman at the University of Maryland, forwarded me the crucial hyperlink to *The New York Times* article on self-publishing that made this book and its cover a reality. My daughter, Priyanka, a high school freshman, has already had her own letter published in the KidsPost section of *The Washington Post*. They have all been my sounding board for a lot of the content that made it into *The Bush Diaries*.

PROLOGUE

12/29/00: Web article entitled, "Supreme Folly: A Case for Late Night Jollies[1]"

Almost a year ago, on the eve of the New Millennium, I mused about the possibility of a split presidential election. I actually believe that I might have been the first person in the United States to speculate on the possibility of a popular/electoral vote dichotomy in 2000. I wrote at the time, *"In fact, this could turn out to be a squeaker, where the losing candidate gets a slightly higher percentage (possibly within a 1 percent margin of the winning candidate) of the popular vote, but the winning candidate scores a majority of the Electoral College delegates. You read it here first!"*

While my early (and bold, at the time) prescience gives me some comfort, the actual turn of events (i.e., the thirty six day post-election drama) proved to be rather discomforting. OK, so we have had our fair share of jokes—"we are not a banana republic, we only have banana Republicans", which is one that I credit to Paul Begala of MSNBC. But then, I also heard several political pundits allude to the fact that we did not have a bloody military coup, and that "there were no tanks in the streets"—which I heard Tim Russert of *Meet the Press* state on more than one occasion. You weren't serious, Mr. Russert, were you? Personally, I was more relieved that Florida's anticipated post-certification, legislative coup was preempted.

Much to the amazement of the entire planet, however, we instead witnessed the democratic world's first judicial coup d'état. After first abetting in a "running out the constitutional clock", the Supreme Court of the United States, by a narrow majority, then defaulted the presidency of *"Washington, Jefferson, Lincoln, and Roosevelt"* to its ideological soul mate—George W. Bush! Thus the last bastion of truth, honor, dignity, and justice—the U.S. Supreme Court—fell prey to politics by legally appointing the 43rd President of the United States. Among the very first jokes making the rounds of the cocktail circuit following this historic heist was "How could Dubya restore honor and dignity to an office that he effectively stole?"

Since Gore had easily won the nationwide popular vote by a margin of over a half-million votes, Bush had nothing to fear but the vote itself. Throughout the campaign, Republicans constantly suggested that the Vice President would say and do anything to get elected. It is ironical that eventually it was Bush's post-election campaign, led by Jim Baker, which did what it took to secure the Presidency. But what message does the Supreme Court's judicial fiat convey to not only its own citizens, but also to the rest of the world, which looks up to the United States as an exemplary democracy? One explanation—the actual vote, and thus by implication, its intent, is subordinate to the rules under which one votes. Come to think of it, elections are held all over the world, but in our perception of the not so "free-and-fair" countries, it is their rules which sometimes makes us undermine the authenticity of their voter's actual intent.

Under our various U.S. states laws, if election rules happen to be vague and are subject to different interpretations by narrow majorities in our various court systems, the actual will of the people can never be accurately determined. Notwithstanding equal protection concerns, if the contest phase for the most powerful elective office in the world had not been hampered by questionable jurisprudence, the only way to have accurately determined the real will of the people would have been through an actual counting of the votes. This simple fact is what validates our election system as free, fair, and honest as opposed to those other elections that we, as the arbiter of democracy, send observers to, around the world.

Enough already! Despite the T.K.O., Gore graciously conceded and made way for President-Select Bush. Now, a couple of weeks later, we have witnessed the first round of cabinet appointments by Mr. Bush. As I write this, Donald Rumsfeld has been named Secretary of Defense. Talk about déjà vu all over again. So any Democratic misgivings about a purely Papa Bush administration (Cheney, Powell, Rice) have been dashed. We have been further "forwarded to the past" with stalwarts from the Ford era (Rumsfeld, O'Neill) also on George W. Bush's team. Life is full of ironies, and that's what makes it so wonderful. I remember reading a *Wall Street Journal* editorial in the early days of the first Clinton term. It was titled "Stop the Seventies". However, Jay Leno said it better last night on *The Tonight Show*, when he joked that George W. Bush was trying to build a bridge back to the 20th century! And, who would blame Mr. Bush; it was known as the American Century after all.

In any case, as I said in my "Millennium Musings" article a year ago, the new President in 2001 will probably be facing the first economic recession in eleven years. Any attempt to downplay its significance, by claiming inheritance from the previous administration, will not wash with the public. Assuming that the fourth quarter still manages to eke out a small growth in GDP, the earliest that we could officially know, if we are in fact in a contracting economy, would be in July 2001. By then, George W. Bush would be firmly in the saddle, and the public would be looking to him for solutions, and not at trying to figure out who is to blame. They usually do that (look for blame) in an election year, and his father must remember that all too well. Since we all want our President, and our country to do well, I would like to end with an unsolicited piece of advice—defer the $1.3 trillion tax cut—it does not make economic sense at this stage of the economic cycle. Remember those same seventies and stagflation—stagnant growth coupled with consumer inflation—this is what you risk with a huge tax cut at this point of time. Consumers suddenly awash in surplus money, when the economy is not growing, are not a long-term recipe for success. Listening to the Fed chairman and directing Congress towards a fiscally responsible budget hold the key to riding out the next couple of years. A tax cut in early 2003 could set the stage for re-election in late 2004. Happy New Year!

Notes:

[1] The article entitled "Supreme Folly: A Case for Late Night Jollies" was originally posted on my web site www.nargundkar.com/jack.htm on December 29, 2000.

THE FIRST QUARTER: 2001—AN AMERICAN INTIFADA

Despite widespread skepticism, most Americans managed to get over the Supreme Court's folly and George W. Bush was sworn in as the 43rd President of the United States. Upon completion of President Bush's first one hundred days in office, I submitted my first article to the WSJ op-ed pages. Back then 9/11, in everyone's lexicon, was a telephone number for personal emergencies. National tragedy and terror were far from everyone's mind. We all were more concerned with the impending return of trickle-down economics. Little did we know that the prosperity of the "go-go" nineties was soon going to go away?

5/1/01: Op-Ed submission to *WSJ* entitled, "Is This Déjà Voodoo All Over Again?[1]"

Since this is my first article on the George W. Bush presidency, it seems rather apt to be reflecting on the first hundred days of the 43rd president. As far as I can tell, the media and the polls show that Mr. Bush has done a reasonably good job thus far. But my hunch is that the honeymoon is not going to last much longer. Now that first quarter GDP has revealed greater than expected growth, the Bush Administration's excuse of a "Clinton recession" has evaporated? In any case, most other economic indicators suggest that a slowdown is upon us, and Greenspan's recent finagling with monetary policy will take time to work its way through the system. So when President Bush completes his 100th day in office at the stroke of noon on April 30th, should the American public be screaming "Mayday, Mayday, Mayday"! This universal plea for help could serve as a metaphorical reminder that the world's largest economic engine is in need of urgent Presidential attention as well.

In fairness to the President, he has been touting an economic plan—whose centerpiece calls for a $1.6 trillion tax cut over a ten-year period—and, which relies upon non-existent budget surpluses. When Ronald Reagan proposed a tax-cut twenty years ago, he did not even bother with surpluses to finance his tax-cut. President Reagan believed that lower taxes would alter the dynamics of taxpayer behavior, which would result in a net gain in tax revenues. In reality, when it came time to balance the budget, Congress spent even more than what lower taxes returned. Reagan's Vice-President, George Bush, who is the father of our current President, had referred to the Reagan tax plan as "Voodoo Economics" during the 1980 presidential primaries. President George W. Bush is now trying to re-impose a similar tax plan upon the American public with no guarantees of fiscal discipline. With apologies to the great Yogi Berra, one must ask, "Is this Déjà Voodoo all over again?"

President Bush gets high marks for his honesty and integrity, but—having to follow a President who was primarily impeached for lying about marital infidelity that occurred in the sanctum sanctuary of the Oval Office—he does not have a high threshold to cross. Ford and Carter, who appeared like saints after the Nixon era, were not judged to be very successful presidents—so that should serve as a reminder to President Bush. Bush II is paying homage to Bush I more in style, with a similar compassionate conservative message, while adapting more of the Reagan substance, such as Voodoo Economics, Star Wars, anti-abortion, anti-green, etc. While the people may have deemed Reagan the more successful President, Bush Sr. actually laid the foundation for the fiscal sanity of the nineties. By agreeing to a tax hike in 1990, and effectively betraying a campaign promise, Bush Sr. lost his reelection bid in 1992, but he made it easier for Clinton to pass even stricter fiscal measures in 1993, and the rest as they say is history. So while President Bush is attempting to inherit his father's successful foreign policy legacy through Cheney and Powell, he should not distance himself from his father's noble economic motives as well. After all, Bush Sr. did have to pay for the fallout of Voodoo economics, just as the taxpayers have literally been doing for the past twenty years.

Bob Kerrey is in the news these days because the media cannot leave well enough alone, and because the *New York Times* takes itself too seriously on "all the news that's fit to print" stuff. In any case, the same Bob Kerrey as a senator in 1993 made an impassioned speech on the floor of the Senate in hesitant support of President Clinton's historic tax plan. During this speech, Senator Kerrey beseeched President Clinton "to take the high road". The time has come for President Bush to heed those same words and take the high road to a fiscally sound economic plan, which will continue the country on a path to robust growth, low inflation, reduced debt, and low interest rates for several years to come—21st century economic nirvana, if you will!

*   *   *

However President Bush did not take the "high road to a fiscally sound economic plan". With repeated tax cuts and record spending throughout his first term, President Bush managed to turn a budget surplus that he had inherited from President Clinton into massive deficits—a subject on which Vice President Cheney was quoted as saying, "Reagan proved deficits don't matter". In a report dated June 2004, Dr Mark M. Zandi, Chief Economist at Economy.com concluded, "The economy has struggled during Bush's first term. The expansion has gained momentum during the past year, but by many measures has yet to fully rebound from the 2001 recession and weak ensuing recovery. Employment, real median household incomes, and real household net worth are lower today than at the start of the President's term."

Notwithstanding the fact that we did experience "deja voodoo" in President Bush's first term, the Republican Congress appears to be willing to make the Bush tax cuts permanent during his second term. The Center on Budget and Policy Priorities reported in February 2005, "Making permanent the tax cuts enacted in 2001 and 2003 would have a direct cost of $1.8 trillion through fiscal year 2015, based on Congressional Budget Office estimates."

Even before his first tax cut plan was enacted in 2001, President Bush's foreign policy genes started acting up. A saber rattling exercise in the South China Sea went a little awry, and President Bush's diplomatic mettle was tested. Despite the pilot in him, he did not come through with flying colors. If we had known then that 9/11 was barely four months away, this incident would not have been judged a reassuring precursor of the President's ability to handle a crisis. Also, it is apparent that the Bush Administration had decided early in its tenure to reverse the Clinton Administration's policy towards North Korea—which I cautioned against at the time—we continue to experience unintended consequences as a result of that policy reversal.

5/8/01: Op-Ed submission to *WSJ* entitled, "Foreign Policy Faux Pas²"

In my first article on President George W. Bush's first one hundred days in office, I wrote about the likelihood of "The Mummy Returns" with the Bush II neo-voodoo economics? Now I am having second thoughts, not about Déjà Voodoo, but about the foreign policy expertise within the Bush II Administration.

Clinton may have wondered about the meaning of "is", but he apologized so many times in his eight years, even he knew that saying "sorry" is the moral equivalent of an apology while not feeling as much of the pain. So President Bush believed he was offering a "strategically ambiguous" sorry to China to get our EP-3E crew back, but later he decided to shoot from the hip when it came to the question of defending Taiwan. A few hours after his clear cut message crossed the Taiwan Straits and reached the mainland, Bush aides were furiously back-pedaling US policy into the decades-old, nebulous "One China" variety. Then a few days later, the Bush II Defense Department followed with an equally embarrassing flip-flop on high-level military contacts with China.

In football terms, it appears that wide receiver Powell juggled, but managed to hold on to the ball, and complete a short pass from quarterback Bush on the "EP-3E" call. On second down, QB Bush threw an incomplete pass with an impromptu "One China" fake. In a third and long situation, running back Rumsfeld fumbled the ball on the "military contacts" reverse play. So we are now basically in a punting situation on China policy—maintaining the status quo until we get the ball back.

If the faux pas had been limited to China, one would probably not feel so uneasy. However, just as the China strategy was unraveling, the United States got an unceremonious boot of the Human Rights Commission at the United Nations. We did not have a permanent UN Ambassador to make our case, and some of our friends betrayed us. One wonders where Secretary Powell was when the US was being voted out by these traitors. Bush II and some of his Republican colleagues might not give a hoot about the UN, but Bush I used the organization very effectively during the Persian Gulf crisis in 1990–91. It is quite laughable that China, Pakistan, Sudan, Cuba, and Syria are members of a Human Rights panel, when their respective governments do not afford these rights to their own citizens. In any case, it will be interesting to see how President Bush reacts to this affront—because as the old saying goes "You can't demand respect, you got to command it." It is quite apparent that, with this mean-spirited action, the United States is not commanding the respect of its fellow nations as it once used to?

Maybe that is why President Bush is trying to convince the US and its allies about the need for another version of "Star Wars". Given the state of the nuclear world today, I think this might not be such a bad idea. However, if it requires us to abandon our commitment to the ABM treaty, we might want to reconsider the proposition. As the world's only superpower, struggling to command the respect of its fellow nations, we cannot unilaterally dump international agreements when they do not make sense to us anymore. In this regard, President Bush is doing the right thing in trying to get Russia on board. But the piece de resistance would be if he succeeded in bringing China to the party as well. However, this would entail maintaining the Clinton Administration's "strategic partner" relationship with China. On the eve of the new millennium, I had written that the new President would have to conduct *a foreign policy that will need to revisit engagement of communist nations vs. containment of religious fundamentalist ones!*" President Bush appears to be revisiting the engagement of China, so it is unlikely that they will buy into his missile defense plans. However, it is critical that Bush's actions not push China into a strategic alliance with Russia—such collaboration would ironically bring quick domestic support for a missile defense system, but make the world an inherently more dangerous place, and possibly plunge us into Cold War II.

North Korea recently announced that it would continue its moratorium on ballistic missile testing until 2003. President Bush should seize the initiative with this announcement, and re-engage North Korea in discussions along the same lines as the Clinton Administration had been doing. In fact, early in his term, Secretary Powell had indicated, that he would be continuing the Clinton policy on North Korea. However, he was quickly made to do an about-face by the Cheney-Rumsfeld hawks in the Bush Administration. Now might be a good time for the hawks to eat some humble pie and diffuse/eliminate the North Korean threat, while refocusing on suppressing a possible revival of a new "Sino-Soviet" axis.

It might not be evident as yet, but the Bush family karma seems to be playing its hand. Bush I inherited a strong Reagan economy, which was soon to slide into recession. Bush I got unfortunately distracted by a looming foreign policy crisis in the Persian Gulf, and in focusing like a laser beam on this crisis, he ignored the domestic predicament with the economy, and lost his bid for re-election. Now, Bush II has inherited a strong Clinton economy, which also appears to be sliding into a recession. However, Bush II cannot afford to focus solely on the domestic crisis, because of what happened to his father for ignoring a similar one, and delegate foreign policy to his subordinates. The faux pas of the first hundred days on the foreign policy front should serve as a reminder of the diligence that is necessary at all times. On foreign policy, QB Bush is backed up into his own end zone, but fortunately this is only the first quarter. As the "Saturday Night Live" character playing President Bush complains, "Presidenting is hard", but the real President Bush's real challenges are still to come!

*   *   *

After this incident, President Bush pretty much backtracked on his 2000 election year promise to treat China as a "strategic competitor". For the rest of his first term, President Bush continued to regard China as a "strategic partner" which is what candidate Bush had accused President Clinton of doing? Ironically, China seems to have resurfaced as an irritant in the Bush agenda at the start of his second term. However, the current irritation has been caused largely by economic factors, which spiraled out of control during Bush's first term. Consequently, China has a burgeoning trade surplus—a record $162 billion in 2004—with the United States that seems to get further exacerbated by China's refusal to let its currency float. Based on early indications, President Bush seems determined to start his second term with the equivalent of a "trade policy faux pas" with China.

The last line of my previous article seemed almost prophetic after the attacks of 9/11 occurred. In retrospect, President Bush did a terrific job in the immediate aftermath of this great national tragedy. His words at Ground Zero in NYC on September 14, 2001 still ring in my ears, "But I can hear you! And the rest of the country hears you! And soon, the people who did this...are going to hear from all of us!" And, they surely did—with swift and decisive action in Afghanistan—the Taliban was routed. However, the mastermind behind 9/11, Osama Bin Laden, has yet to be found "dead or alive" as President Bush had directed in the wake of this quick victory. As a consequence of 9/11, the economy dragged further and we would soon feel the effects of "war and recession". In this article, I mistakenly referred to the Afghan war as "Operation Noble Eagle". In fact, it was actually called "Operation Enduring Freedom", which the Afghan people seem to be enjoying today with the recent swearing in of a democratically elected President Hamid Karzai.

9/19/01: Op-Ed submission to *The Post* entitled, "War and Recession[3]"

"But the real President Bush's real challenges are still to come!" This was the last line of my article on the Bush II foreign policy back in early May. No one would have dreamed that not only real, but also more surreal challenges would be thrust on a young President this early in his term? On September 11, 2001 for the first time in our history, surreptitious foreign elements launched a vicious and deadly attack on the mainland United States. As the world watched for the most part on television, two hijacked U.S. airliners plowed into New York's World Trade Center—the symbol of American financial prowess, and another hijacked U.S. plane crashed into the Pentagon—an icon of American military power. Some brave American souls sacrificed their own lives in a fourth incident in Pennsylvania thus preventing further carnage targeted at Washington D.C. So we are at war...

Is this déjà vu all over again? Rewind to Bush I—in August 1990 Saddam Hussein overran Kuwait just as the U.S. economy was entering into a recession. Fast forward to Bush II—in September 2001 "prime suspect" Osama Bin Laden has "bombed" New York and Washington just as the U.S. economy is flirting with recession. The Bush I economy dragged on, with inconsequential growth, for 18 more months following a magnificent, though incomplete, Bush I victory in the Gulf War. What is in store now for the Bush II economy, and, more importantly, how complete will the Bush II victory be over this "faceless Intifada" visited upon the U.S. by Bin Laden's and/or associated terrorist networks?

As the Bush II Administration sets about planning Operation Noble Eagle to take on this multi-faceted enemy, I must return to my football metaphors to make a point. This operation is not only going to require great offense, but smart defense, and most importantly—special teams! With a "Michael Corleone" as special teams coach—swift, specific, surgical strikes, need to be conducted simultaneously by Special Forces on "search and destroy, in and out" missions, in several geographic locations across the identified terrorist networks' cells. This anti-terrorist "chemotherapy" should be repeated periodically until the cancer of fear is completely removed. This strategy might sound simple, but we must not forget that they carried out their barbaric acts with an ease, which brought about a shame that was only overwhelmed by the enormity of our grief.

It might also be worthwhile for Bush II strategic planners to benefit from the lessons of history as they set about this "first new war of the 21st century". Afghanistan, and the two countries, Iran and Pakistan, that straddle it on both sides—each of these nations were U.S. allies at some point of time during the Cold War. In fact, Pakistan, notwithstanding its support of the Taliban regime, is still considered as an U.S. ally. Over twenty-five years (1953–1979) of U.S. support to the Shah of Iran culminated in an Iranian revolution and gave us the Ayatollah. Ten years (1979–1989) of U.S. support to the "mujaheddin" rebels in Afghanistan eventually resulted in the Taliban revolution and delivered to us Osama Bin Laden. Why shouldn't fifty years (1947–1997) of U.S. support to Pakistan then not lead to a catastrophe as troublesome as the Iranian experience or more likely as intense as the Afghan one? We cannot easily forget that despite our backing of Iraq during the Iran-Iraq war of the eighties, we were rewarded with a great betrayal by Saddam Hussein, when he walked over Kuwait.

Every father wishes that his sins were not visited upon his sons—so let it be with the Bushes. Bush I ignored the domestic economy after his victory in the Gulf War, he neither saw the recession coming, nor acknowledged—"It's the economy, stupid"—that it refused to grow under his stewardship. So as Bush II engages in Operation Noble Eagle, he cannot fail to recognize being in a déjà vu situation with this perennial "War and Recession" chapter of the Bush presidencies—been there, done that! Only Bush II can't do it like his father did, because it could bring us "Gore in Four"? However, I suspect that Bush II has already laid the groundwork for "voodoo economics"—a pre-Reagan Bush

I characterization for supply-side stimuli—with his budget-busting tax plan, which was passed earlier this year. In the heat of battle, balancing budgets is hardly an option, so we might still end up spending our way out of a shallow recession. But when the dust will have settled, the blame game will begin!

*   *   *

Spend his way out and how? President Bush masterfully steered the public's attention away from a sagging economy in 2002 by milking the terror cow. As we subsequently learned from the likes of former Treasury Secretary Paul O'Neill and counterterrorism coordinator Richard A. Clarke, President Bush had had Iraq on his mind even before 9/11.

If one had to go purely on the basis of GDP growth and not look at budget defi-cits, trade deficits, value of the dollar, job growth in the fourth year of recovery, etc.—then the economy at the start of Bush's second term would appear to be in rea-sonably good shape. From the Bush Administration's perspective, the economy is in even better shape now—so there would seem to be no pressing reasons to engage in another "wag the dog" strategy in 2005–2006 like there were in 2001–2002?

After two denied submissions by the Journal and one rejection by the Post, I real-ized that these national publications were probably overwhelmed with opinions from all manner of experts. Why would they want to put out an opinion piece from an Average Joe, even though he might have something pertinent to say? So I contin-ued my critique of the Bush presidency by publishing essays and reviews on my per-sonal home page (www.nargundkar.com). On the day that we were launching Operation Enduring Freedom against the Taliban and Al Qaeda in Afghanistan, I cautioned the President about not seeing the forest for the trees in his overall approach to the war on terrorism.

10/7/01: Web article entitled, "The 'Stan' Factor: It's a Hard Place for US[4]"

"Tragedy is a tool for the living to gain wisdom, not a guide by which to live."

—Robert F. Kennedy

Robert Kennedy's words of wisdom, following another American heart-break from the sixties, make even greater sense today after the mega tragedy of September 11, 2001. While it is important that we do not let fear and terror rule our lives, it is imperative that we learn the right lessons from this horrific event. It is not sufficient that we try to determine who our friends are after the fact, but more critical that we recognize "who our enemies were before the deed was done?"

Both, the President of the United States and the Prime Minister of Great Britain, have said that this fight against terrorism is, in fact, a war against evil. All the great wars in history have been fought to root out evil—pitching good vs. bad, truth vs. lies, right vs. wrong, etc. When moral values are at stake, the side that will emerge victorious in a protracted war, albeit not in the immedi-ate battle, is the one that stands by its principles. So as the President goes about his task of building a coalition—excluding only those countries that *"continue to harbor terrorists"*—he might soon find our great country allied with almost all the "rogue" and "near-rogue" nations on the State Department's list. We will then soon be engaged in a never-ending guerilla war with an unknown enemy, which will, in reality, continue to be covertly aided and abet-ted by many of these so-called allies in a hodge-podge coalition.

The "Stans" are very much in the news these days—Afghani, Paki, Kazakh, Kyrgyz, Tajik, Turkmen, and Uzbek. Their "Stan" appendage was probably derived from the original Sanskrit word "Sthän", which means, "Place". In fact, after the 1947 breakup of British India into India and Pakistan, the Pakistani media usually referred to India as "Hindustan"—it was their subtle way of demeaning India's preference for a secular constitution, by identifying it as the place for Hindus.

Several of these Central/South Asian "Stans" and a cornucopia of Middle Eastern kingdoms/regimes are now shamelessly climbing aboard the anti-terror bandwagon. "How convenient?" as the Church Lady (Dana Carvey) from *Saturday Night Live* used to say. But then with a simple escape clause, as encapsulated in his phrase "*continue* to harbor terrorists", President Bush has let open the floodgates for overnight outlaw nation transformations, which are ambiguous at best and hard-to-verify at worst.

The President in his desire to placate the larger Muslim population worldwide appears to be striking compromises with Islamic nations of dubious repute, when it comes to their record on the instigating of terror and the harboring of terrorists. This, in and of itself, might not have been an entirely undesirable strategy in our coming to terms with a very complex problem. However, in his eagerness to build a workable coalition, the President seems to be hurting a steadfast ally (Israel) and ignoring a valuable future friend (India). The Bush Administration is determined to rescue an old US ally, Pakistan, which is currently lodged between a rock (of its own creation, the orthodox Islamic government of the Taliban in Afghanistan) and a hard place (as represented by its arch rival, the secular democratic Republic of India). The primary reason for the Bush strategy is the fear of Pakistan's nuclear arsenal, which could easily fall into the hands of the Taliban, thus making the threat of deployment of its "Islamic Bomb" a very real one!

Unfortunately, this is a strategy that is not seeing the forest for the trees. Israel is the only non-Muslim nation on the western tip of an Islamic crescent of countries, which run contiguously towards India, the only non-Muslim nation on the eastern tip of this arc. In 1981, Israel had the foresight to recognize the danger to its existence by Iraq's nuclear ambitions, and took military action to severely cripple a strategic nuclear facility in Iraq. The story goes that Israel had made a similar offer to India in 1977, by requesting landing rights for Israeli air force jets on a comparable mission to neutralize Pakistan's then fledgling nuclear program. As it turned out, Israel's bold actions in 1981 probably altered the overall damage potential of the 1991 Gulf War. Had India been more forthcoming in 1977, the world would not be particularly worried today about Pakistan's self-proclaimed "Islamic Bomb" falling into the hands of an unstable regime?

Notwithstanding the support given by Pakistan and its military dictatorship to the U.S.-led coalition thus far, it is prudent for the U.S. to be wary. History has proven to us that military cooperation, provided to the United States by governments, which are not elected representatives of their people, is a kind of collaboration that has proven detrimental to our interests in the long run. Most significantly our perceived abandonment of such partners in the past, following completion of our military objectives, has only increased the hatred of the United States amongst the people of these "partner" countries. It is quite likely that we have already crossed this threshold with the people of Pakistan, who are not represented by an elected leader today. In the aftermath of the September 11th tragedy, when General Musharraf addressed his nation to explain his reasons for supporting the U.S.-led coalition, he purportedly told them he was choosing "the lesser of two evils". If the leader of the Pakistan considers the United States as "evil", one can only wonder what its citizens might be thinking.

In last fall's election campaign, then candidate Bush had come out strongly against what he termed "nation building". But the lessons of history have shown us that two countries, Germany and Japan, which were devastated after World War II, and which we helped rebuild, are amongst our staunchest allies today. So as President Bush goes about executing Operation "Enduring Freedom", and "lets slip the dogs of war" upon these terrorists and the nations that harbor them, one can only hope that we plan to endure for the people who have suffered under their regimes, and put them on a path to real freedom!

*   *   *

Without ever admitting to his flip-flop on the necessity for "nation-building", President Bush has been attempting to do just that in Afghanistan and Iraq—one can only hope that he will succeed. However, President Bush even today continues to wrestle with the basic dilemma highlighted in this article—how does the United States maintain a delicate balance between continued support for allied Muslim nations helping us in the war on terrorism vs. a compelling need for democratic reforms in those very countries, which are invariably run by dictatorial regimes? Unless the President stops putting convenience before principle—when it comes to allied nations such as Egypt, Kazakhstan, Pakistan, Saudi Arabia, Uzbeki-stan—the rest of the Muslim world will continue to distrust our motives.

Sometimes you are watching a slice of Americana and nostalgia grips you. So on Thanksgiving Day 2001, I got a little sentimental about NYC. This article should be read in that context. In any event, I feel compelled to reflect on a couple of "morally neutral" utterances of that time. Susan Sontag, the cultural maven, had written in "The New Yorker" that the 9/11 hijackers were not cowards. Bill Maher, a comedian extraordinaire that I enjoy, had voiced similar sentiments in the immediate aftermath of 9/11. One would think that taking the lives of innocent, unsuspecting people in so brutal a fashion blurs the lines between courage and cowardice—as it often does in the mentally insane, who epitomize moral neutrality!

11/22/01: Web article entitled, "Ich bin ein New Yorker[5]"

On this 38th anniversary of President John F. Kennedy's assassination, one of his more famous quotes, *"Ich bin ein Berliner"*, came to my mind. But then I happened to be watching the Macy's Thanksgiving Day Parade on TV this morning, and I got to thinking about New York City, once again. It brought back memories of my 500 days as a New Yorker (January 6, 1990 through May 20, 1991), when I was enrolled in the MBA program at the Columbia Business School. This was a pre-Giuliani NYC, and I must admit it was nowhere as appealing as the one I happened to visit on a business trip seven years later in 1998—walking around Times Square at midnight, and not fearing for your life. Thank you, Mayor Giuliani! In any case, I still have fond remembrances of my days as a struggling student in Manhattan—and, taking friends and relatives around the usual NYC sights when they decided to visit. The World Trade Center was always a must-see! So when September 11 happened this year, I was mortified—especially because I happened to watch it all unfold on TV soon after the first plane struck. In a moment of passion, I penned a poem in one continuous sitting the very next day. I was still stoked when I e-mailed it to the editorial page of *The Wall Street Journal* on September 13th with a faint hope that they might publish it. Needless to say, they did not—I consoled myself with the belief that they probably did not subscribe to my political and economic biases? However, this "poem" has been on my mind for the past couple of months. One does not have to actually live in New York City to feel like a New Yorker under these difficult circumstances? Which brings me back to President Kennedy's famous quote in 1963 Berlin—all that any patriotic American has to do today is proudly proclaim in Kennedy-esque fashion, *"Ich bin ein New Yorker"*. So in that same spirit, I present to you my ode to our "freedom from terror"…

INTIFADA—AMERICAN STYLE!

It's hard to imagine the Manhattan skyline
Without its magnificent twin towers
It must send chills down New Yorker spines
Their city has been robbed of its powers

A fringe element filled with so much hate
Destroyed a glorious symbol of Americana
That had withstood Barbarians at its Gate
But crumbled in front of this faceless Intifada

It's time we—Americans Conquered Terrorism—ACT
While the politicians and pundits have their say
Every one of the 100 million US households make a pact
Ten dollars each to Uncle Sam we willingly pay

A billion greenbacks will thus be easily collected
Corporations and philanthropists can put up the rest
Every steel girder and concrete slab must be resurrected
All 110 stories of American pride restored to its best

It's necessary to start this effort right away
So these cowards in hell that wrought its cruel demise
Will by the 5th anniversary of this infamous day
See a new World Trade Center from the ashes rise

Only then will our huddled masses be truly free
Once again to enjoy a complete New York City
And then every citizen from sea to shining sea
Can smile as before whilst thinking of Lady Liberty

*   *   *

I am not smiling and I am deeply disappointed that more than three years after 9/11 no work has commenced on the resurrection of the twin towers—President Bush has shown a lack of leadership in failing to push for the restoration of a significant symbol of America's pride. In my humble opinion, without those towers dotting the Manhattan skyline, New York City is just not the same—and, more importantly, their continued absence is a tacit admission of defeat at the hands of the terrorists, who brought them down!

*"War and Recession Part II" was my year-end article of 2001. While I turned out
be wrong on the threat of inflation, the economic recovery was weak through most of
2002—even threatening a double dip when the corporate scandals unfolded in the
summer of 2002. But there is no denying that Iraq was already on the public radar
as early as December 2001—because even I have alluded to it in this article. So I
have no doubt that Treasury Secretary Paul O'Neill was telling the truth when he
went on "60 Minutes" in early 2003 to state that Iraq was on President Bush's mind
way before 9/11.*

12/28/01: Web article entitled,
"War and Recession Part II[6]"

In my 2000 year-end article entitled, *"Supreme Folly: A Case for Late Night Jollies"*, I had taken the opportunity to offer unsolicited advice to the new President—i.e., to defer any tax cut until 2003. I guess that we will be able to assess
the wisdom of this counsel only by the time that the 2004 elections roll
around? In the same vein, I do believe that the eleven interest rate cuts by the
Fed this year have been excessive—late to start (January 3, 2001), but then too
many, too rapidly and too deep. When the effects of these will get coupled
with some of the Bush tax cuts also going into effect next year, we could witness an unusual inflationary spike in mid-2002? This could then force the
ever-cautious Fed chairman to promptly start hiking interest rates in late
2002, when the economic recovery will probably be barely six months old?
Such a sequence of events could make the 2002–03 economic expansion as
short as the 1980–81 one? Here's something for the Bush economic team to
ponder—despite the 4.75% drop in nominal rates since January, consumers
are not seeing a commensurate reduction in the interest that they pay, only in
the interest that they earn. Any wonder then that we just witnessed the worst
retail sales in thirty years in this holiday season?

With the Congress having recessed for the year without adding more stimuli into the mix, I am wont to quote the concluding lines from my article *"War
and Recession"* of September 19, 2001 (only 8 days after the terrorist attacks):
*"In the heat of battle, balancing budgets is hardly an option, so we might still end up
spending our way out of a shallow recession. But when the dust will have settled, the
blame game will begin!"* It appears that I could be wrong on the depth of this
recession, which is almost ten months old with over 1.8 million job cuts

already announced. However, I take no solace in the fact that the blame game has already begun.

Despite the predicament with the economy, the President has done a remarkable job prosecuting the war on terrorism thus far. Unfortunately, our victory cannot be complete until archenemy, Osama Bin Laden, has been either captured or killed. President Bush (#43), himself, set this as an objective for "Operation Enduring Freedom". Ironically, the President's father (#41) had chosen not to target our other nemesis, Saddam Hussein, during "Operation Desert Storm" in the 1991 Gulf War. Consequently, we have been persistently dogged by an Iraqi threat of terrorism since then.

Even before Bin Laden has been laid to rest, conservatives in this country have been screaming for the blood of Saddam Hussein next. Given that it has been over two weeks since the fall of the Taliban's last stronghold in the Tora Bora region of Afghanistan, and Osama Bin Laden (OBL) is nowhere to be found, this obsession with Saddam needs to be temporarily put on ice. Frankly, when we were "daisy cutting" our way through the Tora Bora mountain range near the Afghan-Pakistan border to smoke OBL out, I had a flashback to *Rambo II*. Only this time it was not Sly Stallone screaming, *"Murdoch, I'm comin' to get you"* into a microphone, but OBL beseeching Allah with these words, *"Musharraf, you American lap dog, I'm going to personally kill you, God willing!"* as he escaped US bombing, and slipped into Pakistan.

The recent attack on India's Parliament by Pakistani terrorists (or freedom fighters, as Pakistan likes to call them) could not have been more ill timed. In fact, I strongly suspect it was instigated by the Taliban to bring about the result it is achieving—a heightening of the tensions between India and Pakistan, and a likely redeployment of a number of Pakistani troops from their western border with Afghanistan to their eastern border with India. Such redeployment would make it easier for OBL and his Taliban entourages to easily slip slide their way from the northwestern frontier provinces southeastward to Islamabad—for their final Rambo-style showdown. Is it any wonder then that General Musharraf has not been in Islamabad for the past week or more?

Even if OBL were not to personally achieve this final act of revenge, the writing is on the wall for Musharraf. By choosing *"the lesser of the two evils"*, as he himself called it, Musharraf made a pact with "the infidel" in the eyes of the orthodox Islamic world. And, the more radical of the Islamists have already proven that they can and will use suicide attacks to achieve their goals. All the more against one that they perceive as a traitor in their midst. It would seem to me that the United States support for Pakistan, as an ally in its war against terrorism, is about to undergo a very rigorous test in the coming months. As we go about prosecuting this war on terrorism, it becomes imperative to stand on the side of truth and justice.

As I mentioned in my other recent article, *"The 'Stan' Factor: It's a Hard Place for US"*: *"It is not sufficient that we try to determine who our friends are after the fact, but more critical that we recognize 'who our enemies were before the deed was done?'"* So let it be with the Caesars of the Islamic world! If we are to really and truly win this war against terrorism, the United States foreign policy will need to be realigned to favor countries with similar ideologies and value systems. Such a revised policy must exclude normal relationships with countries—that are military dictatorships, religious regimes, and diehard communist states—only because they promote our business and economic interests. Respect for the United States will automatically increase worldwide, including in the Islamic countries, if we based our future relationships on steadfast principles and not purely profit motives.

*   *   *

It seems rather obvious that the terrorist attack on India's parliament in December 2001 helped Osama Bin Laden escape from Tora Bora. Also, my fears about an Al Qaeda attempt on General Musharraf's life turned out to be true—he faced two assassination attempts in late 2003. Most importantly, President Bush echoed sentiments similar to those expressed in this article—about the need for a righteous foreign policy based on democratic principles—on November 6, 2003 in a speech he made at the 20th anniversary of the "National Endowment for Democracy". The pertinent excerpt from that speech appears at least a couple of times later on in this book.

Notes:

[1] The article entitled "Is This Déjà Voodoo All Over Again" was originally posted on my web site www.nargundkar.com/jack.htm on April 29, 2001.

[2] The article entitled "Foreign Policy Faux Pas" was originally posted on my web site www.nargundkar.com/jack.htm on May 6, 2001.

[3] The article entitled "War and Recession" was simultaneously posted on my web site www.nargundkar.com/jack.htm on September 19, 2001.

[4] The article entitled "The 'Stan' Factor: It's a Hard Place for US" was originally posted on my web site www.nargundkar.com/jack.htm on October 7, 2001.

[5] The article entitled "Ich bin ein New Yorker" was originally posted on my web site www.nargundkar.com/jack.htm on November 22, 2001.

[6] The article entitled "War and Recession Part II" was originally posted on my web site www.nargundkar.com/jack.htm on December 28, 2001.

THE SECOND QUARTER: 2002—WINDS OF WAR

President Bush survived a difficult 2002—the economic recovery sagged in the second half, the unemployment rate hit 6% in December, and corporate scandals threatened to sink the stock market. Not surprisingly, President Bush deployed a "wag the dog" strategy to redirect the American people's attention to Iraq. By harping on national security issues, the President even managed to pull off a spectacular victory for his party in the mid-term elections.

1/20/02: Web article entitled, "No new taxes...not over my dead body![1]"

"Leadership is a potent combination of strategy and character. But if you must be without one, be without the strategy."

—*H. Norman Schwarzkopf*

When candidate George W. Bush was running for President, he kept promising to restore honor and dignity to the White House. After one full year in office, President Bush appears to be fulfilling that promise by providing ample leadership based on character. However, the President seems to have emulated General Schwarzkopf's advice in the management of his economic policy. Without really considering any of the longer-term strategic implications, President Bush aggressively pushed for and quickly achieved a much-touted ideological objective—tax cuts, which will be implemented in a "trickle-down" fashion over a ten-year period.

While justifying the need for these tax cuts during boom times, Candidate Bush had projected trillions of dollars of budget surpluses, as far as his supply side vision could see. Now in the bust of 2001–02, President Bush continues to defend his already-legislated tax cuts despite a resumption of budget deficits, which can only grow larger each year as more and more of these tax cuts kick-in, and government spending continues to inevitably grow faster and faster. This could turn out to be "That 80's show", requiring us to live beyond our means, all over again? One can only hope that it does not turn out worse than "That 70's show", which produced the nightmare called stagflation. Unfortunately, there is no fearless leader around in 2002 to negotiate a mid-course correction to Bush's fundamentally-flawed 2001 tax plan, much like Senator Bob Dole had done with Democrats in 1982 to rectify the 1981 Reagan tax plan. Majority Leader Tom Daschle, who appeared like he wanted to play the role of the 1982 Bob Dole in 2002, was swiftly vilified by Republicans for his economics, and hence quickly retreated as a likely torchbearer. It remains to be seen whether Senator Kennedy will now assume this "profile in courage"?

For a party that often complained about "Clinton-speak", the Republicans now seem to be engaging in an equally disingenuous form of "Bush-talk". For the President to suggest that a delay in his tax cuts, those of which have still to go into effect, is tantamount to a tax increase—is the equivalent of the Democrats' deception on spending programs of yesteryear, when they often called a reduction in the rate of an increase, as "cuts" in spending. Nevertheless, it is encouraging to hear the new RNC Chairman, Marc Racicot, acknowledge that President Bush's brother, Governor Jeb Bush of Florida, might be thus "semantically guilty of raising taxes" by having agreed to defer his state tax cuts.

It is either plain naïveté, or sheer chutzpah to assume that the goodwill, earned post-9/11 by the President and by association, the GOP, will outlast the larger public's concerns about the economy as it drags on in this election year. All the more, if we happen to be enmeshed in a 1981–82 style recession (long and deep), as opposed to a 1990–91 style dip (short and shallow)? One would have hoped that President Bush (43) might have learned from his father's 1992 experience? It appears that President Bush (43), in trying to avoid a déjà vu situation, albeit mid-term, got ahead of himself by uttering a classic Bushism, *"Not over my dead body, will they raise your taxes."* While he actually meant, *"Over my dead body, will they raise your taxes."* He could use this karmic slip of tongue, to engage in some straight talk with the people on the economy. Bush (41) is said to have lost his re-election bid for having broken a campaign pledge on taxes. The reality is that Bush (41) first put the country on a path to fiscal sanity with his acquiescence to a tax hike in1990, but it was too early for the general public to recognize this in 1992. Following Clinton's bold tax plan in 1993, a determined Republican-led Congress managed to keep a firm lid on government spending after 1994. The mutual distrust between President Clinton and the Republican Congress helped to preserve the nation's fiscal sanity through the nineties.

So will the President risk losing ground for his party in a congressional election in the near term in order to do right by the country in the longer term? Given some of the policy reversals by President Bush in 2001 over Candidate Bush in 2000, it seems to me that a well-informed electorate might actually help mitigate the effects of any likely changes in congressional power after 2002:

- In the foreign policy arena, Candidate Bush had been dead-set against what he termed "nation building". It has now been more or less implicitly acknowledged by the Bush Administration that for Operation Enduring Freedom to succeed in the long term, we will have to help rebuild Afghanistan

- The hot Bush campaign issue, over privatizing a part of social security, seems to have fizzled along with the stock market and the bankruptcy of energy giant, Enron.

- Speaking of energy, it is highly unlikely that the Bush Administration will continue to pursue new oil drilling projects in environmentally sensitive regions of the country, as Candidate Bush had originally proposed in 2000.

- As the details of the accounting scandals at Enron unfold, with even the remotest possibility of these scandals being linked to campaign contributions, one can expect "campaign finance reform", another issue that was anathema to Candidate Bush, to become front and center in 2002

More importantly for the President, who gained wide spread admiration for his candor and straight talk, it is disheartening for us to now hear what I termed before as "Bush-talk". The disenfranchisement of Enron CEO, Kenneth Lay, from "Kenny Boy" status to "Mr. Lay" reminded me of Clinton's reference in that famous finger-pointing TV denial of a "relationship with that woman, Ms. Lewinsky"! This all may be much ado about nothing, but only the truth will tell. Candidate Bush has learned the hard way before when his ancient DWI arrest was revealed a few days prior to the 2000 election. It is quite likely that, that late revelation cost him the votes, which could have avoided a recount in Florida. If anything, the "blue dress syndrome" has proven that it is better to immediately wash your dirty laundry than have it lie in the closet and hope it will clean itself. Finally, as President Bush struggles with the economy, he might just wish that he had put away some of that budget surplus in Al Gore's lock-box, instead of spending it on a tax-cut that is still waiting to happen!!

*   *   *

On a personal level, this article was dead on in predicting the demise of social security privatization and ANWR drilling as first term priorities for President Bush. I also accurately foretold that campaign finance reform would become a "front and center" issue in 2002—in fact, President Bush signed the McCain-Feingold-Cochran Campaign Reform Bill into law on March 27, 2002, albeit in the middle of the night! He rendered unto McCain what was McCain's pet project for a long time, but he denied him the publicity of a White House ceremonial signing.

At the start of his second term, President Bush launched a pretty lackluster 60-day nationwide campaign for Social Security reform. With the AARP aligned strongly against his privatization plan, it looks like the President will end up spending most of his political capital on an issue that might not even muster enough support for a nocturnal signature this time around?

President Bush proved to be not only cocksure of his own wisdom, but also remarkably resilient despite a weak domestic economy in 2002. He established himself as a master politician—performance by numbers did not matter, perception was reality. One did not have to actually be better off; all they needed to do was feel that they were better off. 9/11 made national security the overriding issue for a majority of the people, who believed the President's dire warnings about Iraq. The truth was that Osama Bin Laden, perpetrator of 9/11, was still on the loose. Nevertheless, the President went on record to say that he did not spend too much time thinking about Osama Bin Laden[i]. He was too busy fighting the war on terrorism...

2/2/02: Web article entitled, "State of the World: An Axis of Evil[2]"

"It is unwise to be too sure of one's own wisdom. It is healthy to be reminded that the strongest might weaken and the wisest might err."

—Mohandas K. Gandhi

After listening to President Bush's "State of the Union" speech last Tuesday, I was reminded of the Mahatma's take on wisdom. Frankly, it seems to me that our President could use a dose of humility. For a man, who said that he would not conduct affairs of state based on polls, he sure appears to be behaving that way. Buoyed by stratospheric approval ratings in his execution of the war on terrorism, President Bush now appears to be milking the "terror cow" for what it's worth. At least one got that impression after listening to the President touch briefly on a few domestic issues in the middle of his speech, while devoting most of his attention to the "state of the world". (In the interests of brevity and implied wit, further references to the President's speech will be via the acronym "SOW".)

One would like to give kudos to the President's speechwriters for coming up with a quotable gem like "axis of evil". However, one must wonder if the President and his advisors have really considered all the implications of engag-

---

i.   At a Press Conference in The White House on March 13, 2002 President Bush responded to a reporter's question, "So I don't know where he is. You know, I just don't spend that much time on him, Kelly, to be honest with you." This quote is from official transcript posted at http://www.whitehouse.gov/news/releases/2002/03/20020313-8.html

ing such a disparate axis in protracted, simultaneous, and geographically dispersed wars, if it became necessary? Are we ready to "walk that talk"? Have we already declared a premature victory in Afghanistan without knowing for sure the whereabouts of the Al Qaeda ringleader, Osama Bin Laden, or the Taliban head honcho, Mullah Omar? The President, himself, set the primary objective of Operation *Enduring Freedom* to get Bin Laden "dead or alive". Why would the President want to lose focus of the fact that the mastermind behind the carnage of 9/11 is still at large? He may have brought some justice to Afghanistan, by ridding it of Taliban rule, but he has yet to bring Osama Bin Laden to justice. Only after the supreme leader of Al Qaeda has been secured will justice have been served in the eyes of all Americans.

In my last article, *"No new taxes…not over my dead body"*, I had lamented the birth of "Bush-talk" akin to "Clinton-speak". If President Bush is serious about telling it like it is, why did he avoid mentioning Osama Bin Laden in his SOW speech? Did he really expect us to believe that the "real" state of the Union was strong with its public enemy #1 still on the loose, and with his own Administration issuing a new "terror alert" for likely attacks even worse than 9/11? What's even more baffling is—how could the "real" state of the Union be deemed "strong" when its economy has been on the decline for almost a year? It's hard to imagine Clinton getting away with a whopper as "strong"?

Speaking of the economy, it might appear that I am indulging in Bush-bashing in this election year. I would like to dispel that illusion with some real data, so that in the *Fox* network style, "we report, you decide". Did the President simply do an end run around Enron in his SOW brief, by refusing to mention a scandal that is so fresh in most people's minds? Even if the Administration were to come out relatively unscathed in the unfolding Enron saga, it might do them well to remember that it's still about "the economy, stupid." So without much further ado, let me present you a table with various economic data on the first year of President George W. Bush. The source for this data is the web site www.economagic.com, which gets its information from all the relevant government departments and respected private organizations.

Economic Category	1/2001	12/2001	Comments
Federal Funds Rate	5.98% avg.	1.82% avg.	Down by > 4%
Bank Prime Rate	9.05% avg.	4.84% avg.	Down by > 4%

Economic Category	1/2001	12/2001	Comments
30 year T-bond yield	5.50% avg.	5.47% avg.	Long-term flat
30 year FHMLC rate	7.03% avg.	7.07% avg.	Mortgage rate flat
Housing Starts SAAR	1.66 million	1.57 million	Down slightly
Inflation Rate annual	3.38%	1.55%	Disinflation
Price of Texas Crude	$29.58/barrel	$19.68/barrel	Cheaper Gas
Annual real GDP growth	4.15% in 2000	1.1% in 2001	NBER recession start 3/1
Unemployment Rate	4.2%	5.8%	1.6m jobs lost
Index of Help Wanted	76	46	Down 40%, '87=100
Consumer Sentiment Index	94.7	88.8	U of Mich., '66=100
Total Industrial production	143.93	136.74	-5.8%, 1992=100
Dow Jones Industrial Avg.	10578 (1/22)	10022 (12/31)	Down 5.25%
Nasdaq Index	2758 (1/22)	1950 (12/31)	Down 29.3%

While I confess that a comment column might be construed as my "deciding or interpreting" this economic data, the dispassionate reader will recognize that I have offered only straightforward up or down comments. I leave it up to the reader to really decide whether "cheaper gas" is a good or bad thing from the domestic drilling standpoint, or whether a 4% decline in lending rates not translating into a commensurate decline in mortgage rates and long-bond yields is an indictment on the Bush tax plan? Hey, I am just the messenger, who has already looked into my crystal ball for this year. What I continue to see is that a majority of the people will vote the state of their pocket books in November, and not be overly concerned about an axis of evil? The overriding question at the ballot box for the Average Joe will be a somewhat Reagan-esque, *"Am I better off than I was a couple of years ago?"* Having said that, we will surely be anxious if the perpetrator of 9/11/01 is still unaccounted for by the time the one-year anniversary rolls around on 9/11/02. So let's roll!

*   *   *

While I was wrong about the importance of the economy in a mid-term election, I have been more or less vindicated on the folly of the President's public airing of his "axis of evil" strategy With no WMD being found in Iraq, the other two charter members of the President's axis of evil have flagrantly challenged the United States by insisting on pursuing WMD programs and/or related activities. With our military resources being stretched thin due to concurrent deployments in Afghanistan and Iraq, the President will be hard pressed to "walk the talk" if an Iranian Intifada broke out on the Iraqi border or North Korea conducted a nuclear weapons test in the near future?

The title of this article is meant to be a parody of "The Bush Doctrine" label. In the late spring of 2002, Washington was in a tizzy because of a likely recurrence of "what the President knew and when did he know it"[ii] syndrome—this time relating to pre-9/11 intelligence. Eventually, unlike Watergate, it would turn out to be much ado[iii] about a few things—but the President would survive—and prove yet again that he was a master politician.

5/27/02: Web article entitled, "The Bush Doctorin'[3]"

They say that politics is the last refuge of the scoundrel. Having observed the recent behavior of some Republicans, one would think that patriotism is the private refuge of conservatives. The media nonetheless pounced on the Bush Administration regarding its prior knowledge, or lack thereof, about pre-9/11 intelligence sifting within the White House. Almost simultaneously, the President—who had promised to restore honor and dignity to the White House—has been giving us the impression that he does not always practice his own, often sanctimonious, preaching. During the 2000 presidential campaign, candidate Bush often complained about the abuse of the White House under President Clinton. One would expect that by applying higher moral standards, the GOP's fund-raising use of a 9/11 photograph depicting a Presidential phone call from Air Force One would qualify as "cheesy". However, that money-raker was deemed not to equate on the dishonor scale to the Clinton 'White House coffees' or the Clinton 'Lincoln bedroom sleepovers'?

---

ii.   In 2004 this allegation would take on a life of its own when the knowledge of the famous August 6. 2001 Presidential Daily Brief entitled, "bin Ladin Determined to Strike in US" came to light. The ensuing brouhaha caused The White House to release a Fact Sheet (http://www.whitehouse.gov/news/releases/2004/04/20040410-5.html) on April 10, 2004.

iii. Long after the reelection of President Bush, on February 10, 2005, The New York Times revealed in a front-page story, "In the months before the Sept. 11 attacks, federal aviation officials reviewed dozens of intelligence reports that warned about Osama bin Laden and Al Qaeda, some of which specifically discussed airline hijackings and suicide operations, according to a previously undisclosed report from the 9/11 commission."

One might also wonder about the apolitical nature of a President, using a backdrop of military men on the lawns of the White House to defend himself against all this hyperbole about "*what he knew and when he knew it*" prior to 9/11? Democrats are kidding themselves if they really believe that any President would willfully ignore advance warnings about a 9/11-type attack. They should probably be more concerned as to why the Bush Administration waited (for eight months) until someone (CBS) leaked this potentially devastating information on intelligence failure? In a town where perception is reality, it's naive to expect that the media will go easy on you if they believe that you might have something to hide?

So it did not surprise me that the President would paint an entire town's 'second nature' with the same 'second guessing' brush. It is on such occasions that I am convinced that President Bush is as shrewd a politician as President Clinton used to be—W knows when to play the Washington card. While this might not be an altogether bad thing, it reminds me of Dr. Wayne Dyer's wisdom, "*Your behavior is a much better barometer of what you are than your words.*"

If there had been any doubt in the efficacy of karma, the Bush presidencies of 1991–92 and 2001–02 are providing ample proof—they both wrapped-up a war in the Middle East without getting rid off the madman who started it in the first place, back home the economy was struggling its way out of a recession, millions of Americans had lost their jobs, unemployment was still on the rise, business investments were not picking up despite the Fed's several interest rate cuts to historic lows, energy prices were see-sawing, and their approval ratings had no way to go but down from all-time highs.

We all know that Bush (43) began his term with a dubious mandate, and quickly moved to emulate the last successful Republican president—not his father, but his father's boss—Ronald Reagan. Bush (43) gave us the largest tax cut since the Gipper's budget-defying bonanza in '81. However, in an effort to avoid any later mid-course corrections, Bush (43) staggered his cuts so that any likely major budgetary damage would come largely in the outlying years—more likely than not, on somebody else's watch.

But then, things did not exactly follow the Bush (43) plan...because another madman from the Middle East struck...but unlike in the Bush (41) presidency, instead of an external hit, this time around we took one right in the gut. The events of September 11, 2001 put an already slowing US economy into a tailspin. As a result, if Bush (43) had any hopes of avoiding a budgetary nightmare in his first term, these vanished with the unexpected demands of financing an open-ended war on terrorism, providing for homeland defense, reviving travel and tourism, creating jobs, extending unemployment benefits, etc.

So what options does the President have other than to continue playing the patriotism fiddle. Like father, like son—several in the media thought the son did not have a feel for foreign policy when he was blundering his way through the campaign—it has to be in the genes. But then one would hope that we practiced a coherent and consistent foreign policy based on our core values and democratic principles. We isolate communist Cuba for the same reasons that we engage communist China? We placate a military dictatorship in Pakistan, which continues to support terrorism as a means for pursuing its political goals. We continue to be dogged by Iraq more for personal reasons than political ones—whatever happened to the axis of evil? We are told there are no war plans on the Presidential desk. What do we make of the much-hyped Bush Doctrine—has it been largely a *Bush Doctorin*?

I am not suggesting for a minute that this President is being untruthful with my use of the phrase "Bush Doctorin'". Nevertheless, it was this very President who made a big deal of putting principle before politics, when he was campaigning for our votes in 2000. With his recent approval of tariffs on imported steel to protect the domestic industry, free trader Bush seems to have been blinded by the ferrite deposits of the industrial heartland on his 2004 electoral map. Then again, with a view to keeping rural America voting in the same red column for 2004, the principled President also "compromised" on a farm bill. These actions probably do not get many Democrats blue in the face because they are on the same side as the President on these issues.

As I close out this lengthy discourse on the Bush Presidency, I have to ask—what does one make of all the surfeit of domestic alerts that have been going out in the past week or so? If the Bush Administration thinks that by crying wolf they are playing it safe, they have it all wrong—the public does not care about warnings, they care about safety. The President who said that he would not govern by polls seems to be doing just that—how else can one explain the arrogance of Vice-President Cheney in his handling of the pre-9/11 intelligence brouhaha in the past week? Once the veil of patriotism has been lifted, what will the Administration have to show for itself?

Finally, what's with all the secrecy? Have we become a police state? When I was living in India back in the seventies, the darkest hour for Indian democracy came when Prime Minister Indira Gandhi declared a state of emergency, suspended some basic constitutional rights, and threw opposition leaders in jail—all in the name of patriotism. The day the American people are questioned about their rights to question their government is a day that I pray that the United States of America will never see. Happy Memorial Day!

*   *   *

Memorial Day 2002 marked the beginning of a long, hot summer for the Bush presidency—but the President skillfully doctored the public mindset away from the domestic economy by fanning the winds of war.

In 2005–2006 one can expect President Bush to reverse this strategy by maneuvering the larger public's attention away from Iraq, Iran, and North Korea to the domestic economy. The "axis of evil" already made way for a "nexus of free will" in his second inaugural address. The Bush Administration will try to replace the media's constant focus on the tactical realities of war in Afghanistan and Iraq by highlighting its big picture strategy of "promoting freedom and democracy around the world". Social Security and social issues that are important to his conservative base are likely to dominate the President's second term.

The summer of 2002 was a sizzler from a political and economic standpoint.
Since the proverbial stuff was hitting the economic fan, President Bush and all
manner of neo-conservatives were saber rattling. Iraq had been identified as the first
target on the "axis of evil" list. My concern was that the economy was dangerously
close to double dipping into a recession. The stock indexes had closed at four and five
year lows. Corporate crooks were crawling out the woodwork. What else could a
President do, but "wag the dog"?

7/18/02: Op-Ed submission to *The Post* entitled, "War and Recession III: Gore in Four?[4]"

The blame game for our hapless economic circumstances has begun. The
political situation has been further compounded by several concomitant corporate crimes, which Congressional leaders are focusing on with the upcoming mid-term elections at the back of their minds.

Four consecutive years of balanced budgets have become history, and we
have resumed spending money that we don't have—"cashing hot checks" is
how former VP candidate Lloyd Bensten had described this phenomenon
back in 1988 while associating it with the 1980's prosperity—so whatever happened to the Clinton surplus of the late 1990s? This is, indeed, "Déjà Voodoo
all over again".

The markets seldom lie—both, the S&P 500 and the Nasdaq stock market
indexes, hit four and five-year lows respectively in the past couple of
days—they are suggesting a stinging rebuke of the Bush economic policy,
which has undoubtedly been further aggravated by corporate mismanagement
on a grand scale. Recent revelations, in *The New York Times* and *The Washington Post*, relating to President Bush's own past behavior as a lax corporate
manager does not help the current morass that we seem to be in. More importantly, economic theory tells us that the stock market is usually a leading indicator of the nation's economic health—so we could be "double-dipping" by
the time the November 2002 elections roll around?

My fear is that if any more major, negative, and unexpected corporate
announcements are made in the second half of this year, this bear market that
began in March 2000 could "celebrate" its third anniversary early next year. I
don't think the US stock markets have ever been down for three consecutive
years—at least, not since the Great Depression?

Sometimes I wish that President Bush had not made such a big deal about honor and dignity. Talk around office water coolers these days centers around how the poor inner city juvenile gets locked up for holding up a 7-11, while the white collar executive makes out like a bandit despite having run his company into the ground and deprived his employees and shareholders of their life savings. The bigger scandal, it seems to me, is the looting of the national treasury by misguided economic policies? We got all bent out of shape with President Clinton's personal foibles, but don't appear to be fazed by President Bush's professional performance.

Dana Milbank of *The Washington Post* has been reporting in the past week about how President Bush has been going around the country telling people, and I quote from Dana's story in the July 2nd issue of the *Post*, *"that he promised during the 2000 presidential campaign that he would allow the federal budget to go into deficit in times of war, recession or national emergency, but he never imagined he would 'have a trifecta.' Nobody inside or outside the White House, however, had been able to produce evidence that Bush actually said this during the campaign."*

Wow! We got ticked off with Clinton because he lied about his sordid personal behavior, but I don't see a ground swell of public outrage at this alleged professional whopper from President Bush? Dana Milbank then goes on to add that the candidate who actually spoke about this "trifecta" was in fact Vice President Gore in 1998. I know that much of this will be dismissed as the rough and tumble of politics.

What about our war against terrorism? It seemed to be going so well until Osama Bin Laden vanished around Christmas time. Shortly after, President Bush made his rather bold, if not bombastic, foreign policy statement on the "axis of evil". There was general concern that the United States would make a military strike against Iraq with an objective of getting rid of Saddam Hussein. However, other world events—notably, Pakistan stepping up its campaign of terror against India, and a renewed wave of suicide bombings by Palestinian terrorists in Israel—appeared to have derailed the first phase of President Bush's overall plan based on the "axis of evil" philosophy? With a few "friendly fire" incidents in Afghanistan, including the recent mistaken bombing of Afghan civilians, coupled with the increasing militancy against western interests inside Pakistan (Danny Pearl's death, the church bombing, French citizens killed on a bus, and a car bomb driven into the American consulate)—all of these events are likely to soon sour the American public on a prolonged war, not going anywhere, against terrorism.

Every American knows that fifteen of the nineteen terrorists, who participated in the 9/11 attacks, came from Saudi Arabia, one of our closest allies. So would it be too unpatriotic for us to sacrifice our never-ending dependence on Saudi oil? I would imagine that all of us would be gladly willing to pay more at the pump, in order that we can pursue life, liberty, and happiness without compromising our core principles.

Al Kamen, who writes a column called "In The Loop" for *The Washington Post*, is running a contest for readers to guess which high-level cabinet member of the Bush team will be the first to resign. My speculation is that Treasury Secretary Paul O'Neill will resign before the end of the year, if the US economy does a double dip, as is being currently indicated by stock market trends. The other distinct possibility is that Secretary of State Colin Powell will try and salvage what is left of his pride, if he continues to be undermined by the "axis of evil" hawks in the Bush Administration. Of course no such resignation will happen, if we are scheduled for an "October surprise", which seems to be a convenient time, in more ways than one, to initiate the action against the "axis of evil"? In any case, going into 2003, if we have neither the war on terrorism satisfactorily resolved, nor the recession out of the way, Gore in Four could become a reality?

*   *   *

While my rhetorical suggestion of "Gore in Four" turned out to be redundant, my speculation on Treasury Secretary Paul O'Neill's resignation was on the money—although the economy didn't actually double dip. He was apparently fired via a phone call from his friend, Vice President Cheney. I only wish that Secretary of State Colin Powell had also resigned in December 2002, when the American public would have reacted with a startling "Why?" Following President Bush's reelection, we are shrugging off Mr. Powell's resignation with a "Why not?" It's a small price for him to pay for his February 5, 2003 presentation at the United Nations, where Secretary Powell convinced the world that Saddam Hussein possessed WMD!

One can only hope that the new Secretary of State, Condi Rice, will give diplomacy a fairer shake, which necessarily means using the United Nations more effectively and not arriving at the negotiating table with one hand on the holster.

The sad truth, about the corporate scandals that erupted in the summer of 2002, is that none of the really big fish had been fried as of early 2005. Prior to the 2004 Presidential Election, the only CEO that the Bush Justice Department was able to convict and send to jail was a woman, Martha Stewart—who was actually convicted about lying and obstructing justice in a comparatively small, personal "insider trading" case.

7/18/02: Op-Ed submission to *The Post* entitled, "War & Recession IV: 'Road to Perdition'[5]"

"Integrity is like oxygen. The higher you go, the less there is of it."

—Paul Dickson

This is the first time since 1984 that the Dow Jones Industrial Average has fallen for seven consecutive trading days (July 8th through July 16th). It has also given up almost 900 points in the process. The average American investor seems to be metaphorically following a "Road to Perdition", which happens to be the name of the brilliant Tom Hanks movie that coincidentally opened around the country this past weekend (July 13–14). President Bush must have believed that he was headed for another triumphant speech in New York City last Tuesday (July 9th), but nervous traders on Wall Street were not as kind as FDNY personnel had been last September at Ground Zero. Even Chairman Alan Greenspan of the Federal Reserve did not succeed in providing much succor to the markets with his testimony to Congress today (July 16th). What's going on?

In a damage control exercise, GOP talking points appeared to have been circulated across the board over the "Perdition" weekend, because everyone from the President on down was using similar language yesterday (July 15th). President Bush sounded like he had had one of his bad weekends from a distant past, *"America must get rid of the hangover that we now have as a result of the binge—the economic binge—we just went through."* Rush Limbaugh, the GOP attack dog of the 1990s, sounded a trite defensive with, *"The Clinton economy was an orgy. The Clinton economy was nothing but a drunken spree, and now we must pay the bill…"* Surely, we have already paid a big part of the bill, as the stock market has given up about $7.7 trillion since the halcyon days of the 1990s—the decade, which Mr. Limbaugh derisively refers to as the "Decade of Fraud and Deceit"—why else would there be such a big hullabaloo? It seems like the Average Joe screamed loud enough about his retirement savings to scare the United States Senate to hastily pass a new corporate auditing standards bill by a 97-0 margin!

Incidentally, WorldCom executives pleading the Fifth at a congressional hearing last Monday (July 8th) were the trigger for this current market slide. This has to be true because on the Friday (July 5th) before their Monday testimony, the DJIA had soared over 300 points. In case, no one has noticed, it should be pointed out that WorldCom's fraud and deceit began in the first quarter of 2001 and not during the "binge" or "orgy" of the 1990s.

In my article entitled "The Clinton Legacy" dated October 8, 2000 I had lamented, *"Thus an important post-Watergate era statute has expired because of misuse by partisans on both sides of the political spectrum. This could be a Clinton legacy, which might come back to haunt the Congress of the United States."* Barely three years after Congress allowed the Independent Counsel law to lapse, a fallout of its politically motivated impeachment of then President Clinton, we are faced yet again with various financial scandals, including a couple possibly affecting the President and the Vice-President of the United States. As a consequence of its past haste, Congress is now missing out on some "Starr" appointments that could have investigated Enron, Harken, Halliburton, WorldCom, Global Crossing, and Qwest. It might seem uncanny, but it is true that the common thread in all of these companies has been their use of the outside auditing firm of Arthur Andersen LLP.

In this 30th anniversary year of Watergate, Deep Throat's advice to "follow the money" seems even more profound than ever. But alas, the Independent Counsel that Deep Throat spawned is dead. Who knows where these various money trails would have led? After all, Dick Cheney, then CEO of Halliburton, did say in a 1996 promotional video that the advice provided by Arthur Andersen was, *"over and above the, just sort of the normal by-the-books audit arrangement."* It might have been an entirely innocent statement then, but Halliburton's subsequent financial troubles don't make the Vice President look good now.

So what does all of this have to do with this being the fourth article in my series on "War & Recession"? Everything! Despite the 6% GDP growth in the first quarter of this year, and an anticipated 2.5% growth in GDP for the second quarter, the economy might not be out of the "double dip" woods. I had alluded to this possibility in "War & Recession III" barely two weeks ago, even before the DJIA began its precipitous seven-day, 900-point decline—again, the stock market is usually a leading indicator regarding the future health of the economy. Notwithstanding Greenspan's testimony today, I wouldn't be surprised if the NBER (the National Bureau of Economic Research, the official agency that dates US economic cycles) waits until early 2003 before deciding when this recession actually ended? But eventually, these declarations don't matter as much as consumer sentiment, which took a serious dive last month.

More importantly, NBC news reported yesterday that in the new Zogby poll, President Bush's latest job approval rating had fallen to 62%. This is a direct reflection of the public's fading interest in the war on terrorism, which had been instrumental in keeping the President's job approval ratings in the stratosphere. As the mid-term election draws closer, the American public is going to get more and more focused on the economy. The fact that the number of unemployed American workers has increased by almost two million since President Bush took office does not help the defenders of the President's domestic policies. Also, since the dollar reached parity with the Euro recently, those cheap European imports and inexpensive continental vacations have become history. We thus have a disgruntled public, pretty much across the economic spectrum, suffering a long, hot summer—eventually leading into the fall elections. Stay tuned, folks. Like the great Yogi once said, "It ain't over, till it's over!"

*   *   *

Unbelievably, the GOP pulled off a surprise victory in the mid-term election of 2002. The economy turned out to be an insignificant factor, both, in 2002 and 2004. With apologies to James Carville, it wasn't the economy, stupid—and President Bush even managed to avenge his father's 1992 reelection loss by largely disregarding the economy in his 2004 campaign.

While I continued my critique of the Bush Administration with more articles through the end of 2002, I slowly began to respond to editorial page opinions in leading national newspapers. Among my first such letters, I reacted to a piece in The Wall Street Journal, wherein Holman Jenkins had suggested that the media needed to be focused on "real priorities" as opposed to what they perceived as a brewing scandal involving Bush and Harken Energy. So I asked them an important rhetorical question—could 9/11 have been avoided if Ken Starr had left Clinton alone?

7/31/02: Letter to *WSJ*—Re: Holman Jenkins' "Reviewing the Records of Two Politician CEOs"[6]

Mr. Jenkins ought to realize that as far as the common man goes Bush-Harken is akin to Clinton-Whitewater. Having made that analogy, I must ask Mr. Jenkins whether it would have been "impossible to find any harm" if Clinton had waited eight months to file the required forms in a similar situation? More importantly, did anyone on the editorial board of *The Wall Street Journal* give President Clinton the benefit of the doubt when he had "bigger fish to fry"—like Osama Bin Laden, whose "fifteen dollar tent he tried to destroy with a million dollar cruise missile" a few days after his testimony to a grand jury, which had then been investigating Clinton's veracity regarding an extramarital liaison? Maybe if the press had let the Clinton White House get "back to talking about real priorities" at that time, Osama could have been pursued more vigorously and possibly eliminated, and the subsequent tragedy of 9/11/2001 might never have happened?

Before the Bush Administration settled in on the "inherited a recession" excuse, they had us believe that 9/11 had caused it. Through the summer of 2002, Iraq was used to divert the American public's attention from a weak economy and unfolding corporate scandals. I had written then, "The President might do well to focus on the problem at hand instead of being distracted by the 'axis of evil' in the bush" and further warned that "with the ongoing violent Intifada in the Middle East, no Arab or European ally will support a military strike against Iraq."

8/2/02: Web article entitled, "War & Recession V: The Courage to Continue[7]"

"The new President will probably have to deal with an economy slipping into its first recession in eleven years, a stock market whose indexes won't crash as hard as its ".com" components, and a foreign policy that will need to revisit engagement of communist nations vs. containment of religious fundamentalist ones!"

—"Musings for the New Millennium", an article posted on my web site on 12/31/1999

Exactly thirty-one months after I first wrote about the possibility of a new President having to deal with an economy slipping into recession, the Commerce Department has finally validated my old speculation as fact. It turns out that the Bush Administration's oft-repeated claim, that the current recession was brought about by the tragic events of 9/11/2001, has proven to be false. In fact, the Administration's self-acknowledged chief economic spokesman, barely three days prior to the release of the Commerce Department's latest economic data on July 31st, was crowing on NBC's "Meet the Press" and I quote Treasury Secretary, Paul O'Neill's remarks to moderator, Tim Russert, *"And when I said I didn't think we were going to have a recession, I would tell you if people count as a recession one quarter of negative growth and the National Bureau of Economic Research says that's a recession, God bless them. I don't care. We've never had—at least, I think, for 35 years, we've never had a one-quarter recession before."*

It so happens that the U.S. economy, starting in the first quarter of 2001, suffered three quarters of negative growth, and finished with 0.6% negative growth for the year. It's no wonder that the first Republican President, Abraham Lincoln, said a long time ago, *"Better to remain silent and be thought a fool than to speak out and remove all doubt."* Unfortunately, Mr. O'Neill did not stop with a rather Hoover-esque reference to *"the economic fundamentals are good and strong"* he went on to predict that we would close out this year at 3 to 3.5 percent real growth. A surfeit of bad economic news has been released since Mr. O'Neill's pompous comments on several of last Sunday's talk shows—the Commerce Department revised first quarter 2002 growth downward from 6.1% to 5%, and said that in the second quarter the economy grew only 1.1%, which was less than half the consensus estimate; the ISM index of manufacturing activity sank to 50.5 in July from 56.2 in June; and, the Labor Department reported that the four-week average of first-time claims for state jobless benefits rose to 386,000, barely above a 14-month low—all of which makes one wonder whether the Treasury Secretary is seeing the same data as the rest of us?

Washington is abuzz right now with the talk of a war with Iraq. The President might do well to focus on the problem at hand instead of being distracted by the "axis of evil" in the bush. *The Washington Post* reported this morning (8/2/02) of an NBC News investigation into several attempts by Pakistani Intelligence and the Taliban in the years 1998–2001 to illegally purchase arms and nuclear materials through brokers in the United States. Taped phone conversations between Pakistani nationals and their U.S. decoy reveal that their intentions were to inflict harm on U.S. citizens and property. Even now, Pakistan continues to be a breeding ground for anti-Western sentiment, as has been proven through several acts of terrorism since the beginning of this year. Most of the actions taken by President Musharraf do not bode well for democracy in Pakistan, and its history with military dictatorships has never been good.

Thus it would seem more appropriate for us not to lose focus of the immediate region, which was responsible for the 9/11 tragedies. Making sure that Pakistan remains stable and secure does not imply that we tolerate or support its current political structure indefinitely. Also, the process of "nation-building" in Afghanistan is going to take several years. More than a half-century after World War II we still maintain troops in Germany and Japan, where our last successful nation-building efforts occurred. More importantly, with the ongoing violent Intifada in the Middle East, no Arab or European ally will support a military strike against Iraq. Saddam Hussein might possess nuclear, chemical, and biological weapons, but he will most likely deploy these against Israel before he tries any misguided "dirty bomb" attack against the United States. President Bush might therefore want to seriously consider warning

Iraq that any nuclear, chemical, or biological weapon launched by it against Israel would be interpreted as an attack against the United States. During the Cuban missile crisis, President Kennedy effectively used a very similar strategic admonition against the Soviet Union. However, in the ultimate, it's imperative that the United States plays a leading role in resolving the Israeli-Palestinian crisis before we mount any unilateral strike against Iraq.

The theme of this article is yet again—War and Recession—and this is the fifth in a series that began shortly after September 11, 2001. On the Fourth of July, barely a month ago, I had warned in my third article of this series, *"More importantly, economic theory tells us that the stock market is usually a leading indicator of the nation's economic health—so we could be "double-dipping" by the time the November 2002 elections roll around?"*

Frankly, I would hate for this to happen. In fact, any American with a job and a 401K would most certainly be praying that the economy does not tank again—but the "double dip" fear has surely entered the average Joe's lexicon after the latest market slide began on July 8, and which has yet to abate. The sight of corporate CxOs being paraded away in handcuffs has not alleviated investor fear. One hopes that after August 15th, which is the deadline for the Top 1000 or so U.S. corporations to certify their books, the markets begin to recover. If the President is serious about igniting a concomitant economic recovery, he might want to reconsider his "déjà voodoo" economic plan? Again, it was the same Abraham Lincoln, who had cautioned, *"You cannot escape the responsibility of tomorrow by evading it today."* But then, it might be reassuring for President Bush to know that another of his favorites, Winston Churchill, had offered these words of wisdom, *"Success is not final, failure is not fatal: it is the courage to continue that counts."* If President Bush wants to continue for a second term he better start mustering that courage sooner than later!

*   *   *

Not only did the economy manage to avoid a "double dip" in 2002, but also President Bush managed to get reelected in 2004. Notwithstanding those dual miracles, and with the luxury of hindsight, I still believe that the President should have shown the courage then to continue on his original post-9/11 path. The Iraq War is proving to be a costly diversion—both, in human lives lost and in the open-ended burden of reconstruction that is largely a US responsibility—which could still derail the war on terrorism. The foolproof way to prevent that from happening is to get the

United Nations involved in the peacekeeping and reconstruction efforts—but this also means that we need a UN ambassador post-haste.

If you talk to the Average Joe, he will tell you that after toppling the Taliban government in Afghanistan, Saudi Arabia should have been our next logical choice—Iraq did not even register on Average Joe's radar until the Bush Administration started ranting about Saddam Hussein and Iraq's alleged ties to 9/11.

8/12/02: Letter to *WSJ*—Re: Simon Henderson's "The Saudi Way"[8]

After reading Simon Henderson's "The Saudi Way", one really begins to wonder why there aren't any war plans on President Bush's desk. When Japanese planes struck Pearl Harbor in 1941, we went to war with Japan. Sixty years later, fifteen Saudi citizens—belonging to a Saudi-financed terror network, Al Qaeda, commanded by a Saudi-born terrorist, Osama Bin Laden—commit hara-kiri by guiding American civilian airliners into the World Trade Center and the Pentagon killing over 3000 American citizens. And, one year later, we are planning to go to war with Iraq? Am I missing something? Mr. Henderson is only partly right when he states, "the House of Saud is not our 'ally' in the war on terror". Saudi Arabia is not our ally. Period! Saudi actions over the past several years have spoken louder than its words. The Saudis confirm an old adage—with friends like these, who needs enemies!

Mr. Henderson's article was probably written before last Sunday's "Meet the Press" interview with Adel Al-Jubeir, a Saudi Foreign Policy Advisor, who had the gumption to tell Andrea Mitchell of NBC News, "We are countries that have vastly different cultures, but we have very similar values." When I heard that preposterous comment I almost fell of my chair! It was like rubbing salt into our wounds…but Andrea Mitchell let it pass. Even more befuddling to me is the lost opportunity, post-September 11, by the Bush Administration to enforce the President's own anti-terrorism directive (*"you are either with us or against us"*) as far as the House of Saud goes. One would have expected that, as a champion of democracy, and as a witness to recent Middle Eastern political history, the United States would be not only more vigilant with regards to the increasingly militant nature of this entire region's people, but also be less fawning of its dictatorial and arrogant leaders, who rarely ever represent the true will of their populace.

On the first anniversary of 9/11, I wrote about a "silent war" alternative to the Bush Doctrine—fearing its impending application in Iraq. I still believe this would have been an appealing option—Iran-Contra style activity as opposed to a Gulf War II to topple Saddam. Congress has already appropriated over $150 billion towards the cost of the Iraq war, and 1364 Americans troops have been killed in Iraq as of January 20, 2005[9]. In retrospect, this article turned out to be very prescient on Iraq?

9/3/02: Op-Ed submission to *The Post* entitled, "The 'Silent War' Doctrine[10]"

The US economy refuses to reveal its hand, and one of its leading indicators, the US stock market just completed its fifth consecutive down month. One could debate that we are probably ready to take a double dip into the receding waters of an economic tide, which has so far barely come in with three quarters of erratic growth? While business sentiment seems to have picked up, consumer spending appears to have stalled—it's the latter that makes up a sizeable two-thirds of US GDP. With an election around the corner, what's a President supposed to do? Maybe try wagging the dog!

So with the war on terrorism not going exactly as he had planned—Osama Bin Laden is still out there somewhere, and we don't know for sure whether he is "dead or alive"—the President's stated post-9/11 objective will likely remain unfulfilled a year later? This is not a reassuring anniversary message to report back to the American people, and therefore an Iraqi diversion surely makes for an appealing substitute. However, the road to Baghdad has already been littered with "friendly fire" from within the Administration—not as much from the President's own men, as those of his father's Administration. Score one for open democracy, if not one against presumed loyalty, which is allegedly a trademark of this President.

It would seem to me that, if we did have to go to war with Iraq as the next step in our global war on terrorism, someone in the Bush (43) Administration would have done the math? Even at 1990–91 prices, the war alone would cost us $60 billion. Unlike the three-day ground offensive of 1991, we would have to engage in a longer, more-protracted war to take control of Iraq. The loss of American lives would be far greater than the 293 casualties of 1990–91. In addition, we would need to occupy a post-war Iraq for far longer than we would ever desire. And yet, all the President's men, save Colin Powell, want to take on this tremendous burden without even being 100% certain about the true current status of Saddam Hussein's weapons of mass destruction. Notwithstanding all the Allied covert intelligence since 1998 (when the UN inspectors were last in Iraq), we would be hard-pressed to accurately verify the real state of Saddam's biological, chemical, and nuclear weapons programs without a fresh round of inspections.

It's quite possible that the Bush Administration has some hard intelligence—which for national security reasons cannot be divulged to the American people—about Saddam Hussein planning to unleash an imminent terrorist attack on the United States? In such a case, there would be no time for new UN inspections, and my article ends right here…let's roll! However, Colin Powell's recent interview with the BBC tends to belie this possibility. The Secretary of State wisely held out the possibility of trying to get the UN inspectors back into Iraq. This is a wise strategy, which has even been endorsed by the wiser men of the Bush (41) Administration. In a bygone era, Nehru's ambassador to the UN had made this prudent observation to its General Assembly, "*The more we sweat in peace the less we bleed in war.*" Why would our President want to shed costly American blood without making our Allies sweat the details of the peace with the UN, and our enemies really sweat the threat of war? In the latter regard, increased saber-rattling below the 33rd parallel and above the 36th parallel in Iraq seems a good way to keep Saddam on his toes.

Now would be an appropriate time to revisit the Bush Doctrine. In hindsight, the President should never have drawn his "axis of evil" line in the sand without consulting our NATO allies. He now appears to be in a hurry to prove that he is a man of his word, and in the process comes off like a schoolyard bully itching for a fight. Inexcusably, the war on terrorism seems to have lost its punch at home, and faded even more significantly in the minds of our European allies. Meanwhile, we continue to generate anger and hatred in the Islamic world. An episode on CBS' "60 Minutes" last week, about a Muslim school in Brooklyn, brought some very disturbing facts again to the forefront. If our own American teenage children, of the Islamic faith, believe that suicide bombings are justified, and represent "holy martyrdom" what can we expect of the Muslim psyche in the rest of the world? This ingrained nature reflected by these young impressionable minds did not surprise me for a minute. It reminded me of my business school days a dozen years ago, when Iraq had occupied Kuwait. This Muslim anger has been seething for a long time at all levels, not only abroad but also at home. Back then, during the school-sponsored Thursday "happy hour" with fellow MBA students at the Columbia Business School, a prestigious Ivy League institution, I often heard in rather colorful language from Muslim students, both domestic and foreign, about how wrong-headed they felt US foreign policy was, towards not only Iraq but also towards the larger Islamic world. In those days, prior to even the first World Trade Center attack of 1993, one tended to dismiss such ardor as healthy dissent. Now, twelve years later—with watered-down versions of "madrassas" in our own backyard, where a Muslim teenager feels she would "do the same" and even refers to blowing up a naval station for the cause—that is cause for worry, and a reason to reevaluate our overall foreign policy.

If we have been practicing a foreign policy that has succeeded in alienating even our staunchest allies—the European Union—that, in of itself, would be a reason to start over. It's not the possibility of a United States of Europe, which worries most Americans—as a matter of fact they probably welcome it. It's not even the likelihood of a United States of Africa, which Libyan leader Gaddafi strongly covets, that we need to be concerned about. It's the birth of a new post-9/11 USA that has me on edge. And, it's not the good old domestic USA that I refer to; it's a foreign USA that is in the making. The seeds of this new country were planted post-9/11, and the Bush Doctrine is fertilizing its growth at a rapid clip. Yes, I refer to the eventual evolution of a new United States of Arabia. If anyone had any doubts about the possibility of all the Middle Eastern countries coalescing into a federation of Arab states, one has to look no further back than the past couple of months. All our Arab coalition partners from the last Gulf War—Egypt, Saudi Arabia, Jordan, Syria, and "Et tu Brute" Kuwait—have chosen to slam the door on President Bush's current Iraq initiative. It's quite apparent that the common Arabian blood has proven to be thicker than its desert oil, which is what they see America really lusting after.

So where do we go from here? The Bush Doctrine needs to be modified, not only to incorporate the realities of the post-Cold War era, but also to reflect the dynamics of the post-9/11 age. On the surface, it appears that the President attempted to do this with his "axis of evil" speech earlier this year, and with a quick follow-up on a more meaningful engagement with Russia. However, our successful Cold War strategy of containing the communist threat continues to be needlessly extended to Cuba, an ally of the now-defunct Soviet Union. Meanwhile, the other Cold War strategy of engaging the enemy (China) of my enemy (the then Soviet Union) needs to be revisited simply because the parameters in the equation have changed. Having said that, President Bush's "axis of evil" strategy is fraught with danger, because it makes a quantum jump beyond containment—it advocates offensive action to achieve a short-term military objective—regime change by removal of an "evil" head of state. However, achieving a short-term military objective is only a part of what should logically become our longer-term, over-arching goal, which would be to transform the vanquished evil-doer's entrenched power structure into a functioning democratic government with a respect for the rule of law. We have done this successfully in the past in post-WWII Germany and Japan. Our then commitment to nation building and our consistent support in restoring the economies of these nations is what contributed to America's prestige around the world. This era was not only marked by the sacrifices of our "greatest generation", but also by the noble actions of a victorious, yet humble United States government.

It has become apparent that post-9/11, we have entered a new phase in our history, which one could call the "Silent War" era. If the Cold War was marked by the descent of a symbolic Iron Curtain around Europe, the Silent War era will be remembered for the ascent of a silent, faceless enemy network around the world. This transnational network knows no borders and pursues its ambiguous goals by the terrorizing of innocents, which it plans in quiet secrecy and justifies through an even more dubious interpretation of its religious faith. By contrast, during the Cold War we were faced with a very visible "evil empire", which wished to propagate its communist ideology to second and third world nations by debunking the very notion of a religious faith.

The Silent War cannot be won from without—through an aggressive implementation of the Bush Doctrine—but it needs to be won from within. While I did have concerns about the Bush Administration's unseemly reliance on secrecy in our open society, this apprehension related more to the habeas corpus rights of ordinary US citizens, then to any cloak-and-dagger operations in the war on terrorism. In any case, it has become imperative for us to counter this silent, faceless enemy with enigmatic "Iran-Contra" style operations instead of large-scale public warfare such as a "Gulf War II". Although Saddam Hussein is not a silent, faceless enemy we are more or less certain that he will engage with Al Qaeda sooner than later. We should preempt this union by toppling Saddam through a new, under the radar "Iran-Kurdi" operation. This would necessarily imply that we immediately mend our fences with non-Arabic Iran, using the same engagement (enemy of my enemy) strategy of the Cold War. Re-engaging Iran would also help us with resolving the terror aspects of the Israeli-Palestinian conflict.

In the ultimate, for the war against terrorism to succeed, it needs to be a Silent War. So any strategic considerations that need to be made would need to be kept under wraps. Thus it would be foolish of me to spell out options that can only be ruled out because they have been discussed publicly. The larger point is that we need to be thinking out of the box. The bigger deal is that we need to convert an archenemy from the orthodox Muslim world into a close and reliable friend. In this regard, it is important for the United States to take a lesson from this Peter Farquharson quote, *"Relationships of trust depend on our willingness to look not only to our own interests, but also the interests of others."* During the Cold War, this attitude was a key difference cited by third world nations that were allied with the Soviet Union—it looked out for their interests. Maybe it was more perception than reality, but the Silent War will not be won on perceptions, it can only be won for real!

*   *   *

"The Silent War" option is too late for Iraq, but it certainly is not a moment too soon to deploy a strategy that will foment a new kind of people's revolution in Iran. An Osirak-style surgical strike within the fiefdom of Kim Jong Il might be necessary to get North Korea back to reality. The point is that it has been over three years since President Bush designated three countries as belonging to an "axis of evil", and he has done nothing significant to change that status in the case of two of those three nations. At some point of time, he has to take some action—even if it means jettisoning the Bush Doctrine and negotiating in good faith for a diplomatic solution—or the United States continues to lose face within the international community? President Bush either needs to "walk the talk" that he adopted at the 2002 State of the Union or modify that talk accordingly.

The euphoria of victory in the mid-term election was soured when presumptive Senate Majority Leader, Trent Lott, committed a classical gaffe—which quickly cost him his leadership position in the Senate. Shortly after Xmas 2002, I posted my customary year-end piece on my web site. After this entreaty, I took a deliberate eighteen-month sabbatical from writing articles. We had entered half time of the Bush presidency and I was hoping for peace and recovery. However, peace was not to be, and I found myself hard-pressed to second guess the President's actions during a time of war.

12/29/02: Web article entitled, "The Bush Enigma: Peace and Recovery[11]"

The mid-term election results made it quite apparent that President Bush and his team successfully redirected the minds of a majority of voters from the struggling economy to the prospect of war. Meanwhile without a coherent message from the Democrats, the average voter did not have any difficulty in rejecting the Democratic messenger in several key races around the country.

In any event, with the Democratic Party's repeated failure in the past eight years to regain a clear majority in the House and the Senate, it is quite obvious that they need to revisit Politics 101. One of its fundamental political equations states that the sum of the parts (blacks, women, labor, and environmentalists, et al.) can never be greater than the whole, unless it includes the biggest missing part—which, in this case, is the average white guy (AWG). The AWG represents a plurality of Americans, and the Democratic Party is not "talking" the AWG's language. It just so happens that in a number of instances on the "left" and east coasts, the AWG's spouse is neutralizing the AWG's vote, and therefore in many of these coastal states the "sum of the parts" is helping Democrats win, especially when these parts turn out in large numbers. However, this feminine power does not manifest itself in much of the heartland, save for a few states in the industrial Midwest. The AWG was largely responsible for the swathe of Republican red across the electoral map of the country even in 2000.

Democrats have also been losing ground due to the gradual disempowerment of the "liberal media establishment". With the ascent, over the past fifteen years, of conservative talk radio and a conservative broadcast TV network, the AWG has finally found an alternative voice. However, even if this alternative voice is providing Republican candidates an edge in many local congressional elections, its full impact has yet to be felt at the state or national level. Liberals can draw some satisfaction from the fact that the king of conservative talk radio, Rush Limbaugh, who has been hosting a nationally syndicated, three-hour daily "advertorial" for the conservative cause since 1988, could not prevent Bill Clinton from getting elected in 1992 and 1996. Having said that, it is the Limbaugh wannabes—such as Bill O' Reilly, Sean Hannity, Oliver North, Gordon Liddy, Michael Savage, etc.—that are now engaging the AWG at different levels.

Unfortunately for the Republicans, their "stealth" engagement of a powerful bloc of southern conservatives was recently exposed at the 100th birthday party celebration for Strom Thurmond. In the brouhaha that followed, Trent Lott was more or less forced out as the incoming Senate Majority Leader. Surprisingly, while Mr. Lott was struggling to save his job, someone in Lott's office actually defended his faux pas by claiming that Mr. Lott had been speaking from the head (i.e. logically) as opposed to from the heart (i.e. emotionally). There's a 2004 election TV ad campaign in the making, *"I didn't mean what I actually said…I only said what I have always meant."*

On a more serious note, for the Democratic Party to become an effective voice for all Americans in 2004, it needs to carefully hone its core message. If they get the message right, Democratic voters will automatically choose the appropriate messenger to run against President Bush. A cursory look at the Bush record of the first two years provides ample ammunition for the Democratic charge on, both, the domestic and foreign policy fronts. In fact, this is precisely what I have been trying to highlight in my five-part *"War and Recession"* series, which began shortly after 9/11.

Let me try again by revisiting Bush foreign policy, which began to really take shape following the tragic events of 9/11 and culminated in the public enunciation of the Bush Doctrine, including the delineation of an Axis of Evil, at the President's State of the Union address earlier this year. This doctrine called for preemptive action against rogue states involved not only in the proliferation of weapons of mass destruction (WMD) but also with known links to terrorist activities. By targeting Iraq as the first nation to test the validity of its doctrine, the Bush Administration managed to focus the American public's attention on national security. As a by-product of this well-timed strategy, President Bush's party bucked historical trends to gain seats in the mid-term election. However, by initially stressing style (unilateralist) over substance (proof of Iraq's WMD arsenal vs. its linkage to terrorist activity) in the implementation of this policy, the Bush Administration turned off several of our allies. Consequently, the people of two leading allied nations, Germany and South Korea, voting in their respective elections around the same time, elected leaders by casting largely anti-US votes. If the citizens of allied nations can harbor such strong anti-US sentiment, it boggles the mind to think what the citizens of the rest of the world think about America? These sentiments matter because they could lay the seeds for future terrorist activity against US interests worldwide.

As we inch closer to war with Iraq, President Bush is being flagrantly challenged and defied by a second member of his Axis of Evil—North Korea. The North Koreans have openly acknowledged that they already possess some WMDs, have proceeded to kick out UN inspectors, and even resumed nuclear fuel enrichment at one of their previously defunct reactors. Defense Secretary Donald Rumsfeld has gone on record recently to assure the world that the United States could engage Iraq & North Korea in simultaneous conflicts, if required. However, would such a turn of events, God forbid, actually help us in our global war on terrorism? It might seem ironical that of the three nations that constitute President Bush's Axis of Evil, only Iran has acknowledged links to terrorist activities (i.e. through its support for Hezbollah).

There is an old adage that proclaims "charity begins at home". One would hope that President Bush, having witnessed the rapid decline in his father's political fortunes following his successful execution of the 1991 Gulf War, would begin to address a similarly affected domestic economy on a war footing? If one were to make a comparison of the Bush economy of 2001–02, it would have to be with the Reagan economy of 1981–82. The good news for President Reagan was that after an eighteen-month recession, the economy soared and helped him get reelected in a landslide in 1984. The real question is will the Bush economy turnaround in 2003–04, and help President Bush get reelected in a landslide in 2004?

President Bush's defense that he inherited a recession might have earned him a pass in the mid-term elections, but he now has barely twenty-two months to reverse a loss of almost two million jobs, three consecutive years of stock market declines, and what by 2004 could become four consecutive years of growing budget deficits. If there is a single lesson that every President since WWII should have learned, it is that while "War and Recession" may define a presidency, it is the President who must define the nation's "Peace and Recovery". The Bush enigma was born out of 9/11, which will permanently define his presidency, even if that is destined to last a single term. However, a Bush legacy can only be established if he is reelected to witness a new World Trade

Center arise from the ashes. There could be no greater symbolism of winning the war against terrorism, and setting the nation on a road to peace and recovery!

*   *   *

Actually, it was the "War on Terrorism" that pretty much defined the entire Bush first term. Peace was never given a chance and Recovery did not seem to matter as much to the American public like it once used to—"Are you better off?" became an irrelevant question in the post-9/11 era. Amidst the trumpets of impending war, I turned my focus to commenting on editorials and news items relating to the Bush presidency in major national newspapers.

Notes:

[1] The article entitled "No new taxes…not over my dead body!" was originally posted on my web site www.nargundkar.com/jack.htm on January 20, 2002

[2] The article entitled "State of the World: An Axis of Evil" was originally posted on my web site www.nargundkar.com/jack.htm on February 2, 2002.

[3] This is an edited version (two non-contextual paragraphs were deleted) of the article entitled "The Bush Doctorin'", which was originally posted on my web page www.nargundkar.com/jack.htm on May 27, 2002.

[4] The article entitled "War and Recession III: Gore in Four?" was originally posted on my web site www.nargundkar.com/jack.htm on July 4, 2002

[5] The article entitled "War & Recession IV: 'Road to Perdition'" was originally posted on my web site www.nargundkar.com/jack.htm on July 16, 2002

[6] Holman W. Jenkins, Jr. writes the "Business World" column for *The Wall Street Journal*. This column entitled "Reviewing the Records of Two Politician CEOs" appeared in *The Wall Street Journal* edition of July 31, 2002.

[7] The article entitled "War & Recession V: The Courage to Continue" was originally posted on my web site www.nargundkar.com/jack.htm on August 2, 2002.

[8] Simon Henderson, an adjunct scholar of the Washington Institute for Near East Policy, runs saudistrategies.com, a consulting firm. This op-ed piece entitled "The Saudi Way" appeared in *The Wall Street Journal* edition of August 12, 2002.

[9] The Washington Post publishes a daily count of American casualties in Iraq as reported by the Pentagon. This was the number per its January 21, 2005 edition.

[10] The article entitled "The 'Silent War' Doctrine" was posted on my web site www.nargundkar.com/jack.htm on the first anniversary of 9/11 (September 11, 2002), eight days after I submitted it to *The Washington Post*.

[11] The article entitled "The Bush Enigma: Peace and Recovery" was posted on my web site www.nargundkar.com/jack.htm on December 29, 2002.

THE THIRD QUARTER: 2003—MISSION ACCOMPLISHED...*WITHOUT WMD!*

In early 2003 there was a feeling of invincibility within the Bush Administration—a relatively easy military victory in Afghanistan in late 2001 was followed by the GOP's historic mid-term election performance in late 2002. Defense Secretary Donald Rumsfeld's lack of diplomacy seriously set back U.S. foreign policy. More importantly, a respected Secretary of State, Colin Powell, began to lose credibility because he was hard-selling the world on a war with Iraq without really sharing all his convictions that we had a hard and fast case.

If there was a single attribute, that riled not only our friends but also ticked off our enemies, it had to be the one to do with the Bush Administration's style of diplomacy. The United States, under President Bush's leadership, had not been wearing the mantle of sole superpower with humility. This was all the more astonishing given that President Bush had specifically invoked the need for humility during his presidential campaign. It was quite apparent that by the summer of 2002, an air of arrogance had settled in amongst various members of the Bush Administration. No other person in the Bush Cabinet got more carried away with his "media darling" status, then the Secretary of Defense! In his enthusiasm to get other nations to climb on board the "let's get rid of Saddam" bandwagon, Secretary Rumsfeld not only offended neutral countries but also trashed our long-standing allies. It began with a barb about Germany and France constituting "Old Europe"[i], and then worsened when the Secretary listed Germany along side Cuba and Libya, among the few group of nations not supporting U.S. policy on Iraq. Bush foreign policy was then further egged along this confrontational route, by the participation of the editorial page of The Wall Street Journal, which published a letter, signed by the leaders of eight European Union countries, pressuring the United Nations' Security Council to act on Iraq[1]. This endorsement became a big issue in Europe because none of the signatories belonged to "Old Europe".

On the political punditry front, I realized that I needed to switch my own tactics, in trying to get my voice heard. So, going forward, I decided to focus my efforts on critiquing the experts, who write political columns for the major national newspapers. I had been a subscriber to The Wall Street Journal for over sixteen years, and they had previously published my letters on a few occasions. I had also been reading

---

i.   During a briefing at the Foreign Press Center on January 22, 2003, in response to a reporter's question, Defense Secretary Rumsfeld said, "Now, you're thinking of Europe as Germany and France. I don't. I think that's old Europe." The entire transcript of this briefing can be viewed on the Defense Department's web site at http://www.defenselink.mil/transcripts/2003/t01232003_t0122sdfpc.html

The Washington Post on a daily basis, since moving to Maryland in 1998. What better way to have one's opinion heard then by taking on the big boys?

With President Bush's attention focused like a laser beam on Iraq, the folks at The Wall Street Journal, whose editorial pages had been strongly advocating his Iraq policy, decided to give him a boost on the domestic front as well. At the dawn of 2003, they editorialized that the Bush economy had performed in a stellar fashion in 2002. I had facts that indicated something quite to the contrary—thus began a couple of years of furious letter writing...

1/4/03: Letter to *WSJ*—Re: Economy of the Year[2]

It warmed the cockles of my heart to see you designate the 2002 Bush economic record as the "Economy of the Year". So now 3% GDP growth—in the first full year after a recessionary year (2001), in which we had a record eleven interest-rate cuts by the Fed—is worthy of a TIME magazine "Person of the Year" award in your supply side judgment? Let me take you back to 1995, when real GDP grew at a mere 2.67%, thanks in large part to a paranoid Fed! Fed Chairman, Alan Greenspan, who had yet to anticipate "irrational exuberance", nevertheless raised interest rates over half-a-dozen times beginning in early 1994 and ending in mid-1995.

At the time, you had run a series of editorials chastising the tepid growth of the Clinton economy—"Is this growth?" was a recurrent theme of your "Review & Outlook" columns. Needless to mention, an economy that was taking a mid-course breather, then saw real GDP growth rates of 3.6% in 1996, 4.4% in 1997, 4.3% in 1998, 4.1% in 1999 and 3.75% in 2000. As a matter of record, the Reagan economy grew at 4.3% in 1983 (in its first full year after the recession of 1981–82). Coincidentally, the last time we saw 3% GDP growth in the first full year (1992) after a recession (1990–91) was when Bush (41) occupied the White House. Maybe that should be a wake-up call for Bush (43) and his "Economy of the Year"!

It might seem strange that after that initial letter to the Journal, I actually did not write another for a couple of months. Frankly, I was rattled with the gale force "winds of war" that had been blowing through the Washington firmament. On February 20, 2003 I had an opportunity to spend "An Evening with Bob Woodward" at the George Mason University in Fairfax, VA. This event was organized by The Washington Post to enable its readers to hear first hand from the renowned author on his new book, "Bush At War" and other contemporary political issues.

Prior to his talk, Mr. Woodward conducted an informal poll (by a show of hands) among the audience numbering approximately 800 local area residents. The audience appeared to be equally divided between Democrats and Republicans, and hence equally split between those who had voted for Bush and those that had voted for Gore in 2000. Interestingly, when Woodward asked how many in the audience supported the Bush tax cut plan—only a fourth of the audience raised their hands. Not surprisingly, the support for going to war against Iraq showed a third for, a third against, and a third as undecided.

During the Q&A session, I asked Mr. Woodward a rather long-winded question, which boiled down to this—foreign policy is as much a matter of style as it is of substance, and I thought that the Bush Administration had gone about it the wrong way? With little or no consideration for style (diplomacy), they had tried to unilaterally (at least, initially) force the substance (a need to disarm Iraq of its weapons of mass destruction) down the world's throat? More importantly, by pursuing a "my way or the highway" attitude they had soured our allies against what seemed to be a noble cause—ridding the world of evil? Mr. Woodward replied in an equally long-winded manner, and surprisingly addressed only how strongly the President believed in the substance of what he was undertaking without providing any clarity on the matter of the Administration's style?

In any case, as we built up to what seemed like an inevitable war, I wrote to one of its leading proponents—pleading for more diplomacy from the President? In hindsight, it would have been better for Secretary of State Powell to have resigned after the mid-term election. Now, he will have to forever answer for his February 5, 2003 presentation to the United Nations[3], where he made the case—largely unsubstantiated, as we later learned—for "disarming" Iraq.

3/5/03: Letter to *WSJ*—Re: The Bush Doctrine & Iraq: a classic dilemma

In the post-Westphalia era, no moral imperative gives us the right to play God, but the sanction of world opinion comes pretty darn close to ensuring that we do the right thing. The dilemma faced by the President in his implementation of the Bush Doctrine is that he wants to do it his way, even though its application involves a restructuring of the international community, which naturally will want to have its say? It is not too late for the President to recognize that "the more we sweat the peace, the less we will bleed in war."[4]

In the ultimate, Robert Novak had it right all along about "everything riding on Iraq"—it helped reelect the President. But I clearly had it wrong, despite an early military victory in Iraq, and a raging insurgency to follow; the American economy still did not become the deciding factor in the 2004 election.

3/6/03: Letter to *The Post*—Re: Robert D. Novak's "Everything Riding On Iraq"[5]

The underlying assumption of the "Texas Poker" gambit that military victory in Iraq will "unleash the American economy" has been proven false before. In Gulf War I, President Bush Sr.'s remarkable victory over Iraq in the spring of 1991 was followed by a humiliating electoral loss in the fall of 1992 due to a languishing economy. There is no guarantee that a victory over Iraq in the spring of 2003 will help reelect President Bush in the fall of 2004 because the cost of this victory will further burden our economy, not only in the long term (nation building) but in the short term (oil price gyrations, revenge terror attacks at home, instability in the Middle East) as well.

Clinton continued to be the favorite punching bag for the WSJ editorial pages. I made an early call on the need for a secular democracy in Iraq—however, in December 2004 with the Sunni insurgency raging and a Sunni call for a boycott of the January 2005 elections—this might have been wishful thinking on my part.

4/8/03: Letter to *WSJ*—Re: Paradox of your editorial pages

You can call it the paradox of your editorial pages that they can make one laugh and cry at the same time. Henry I. Miller is lamenting in his letter (re: WSJ dated April 8, 2003) about how "environmental extremists in the Clinton Administration" are responsible for the numerous "accidents and mishaps resulting from insufficient training and battlefield-simulation exercises" in Afghanistan and Iraq. Only a day earlier, in your editorial entitled "The Future of Iraq", you had touted the efficacy of the very same U.S. forces, which were "moving with impunity in Baghdad" barely two weeks into the conflict. So when things go wrong, it's still the Clinton Administration's fault (no surprise), and when everything is going according to plan, it's plainly the Bush Administration's virtue (again, no surprise). Now, for the "real humor" in today's editorial pages—doesn't Noah Feldman[6] recognize that "Islamic democracy" is an oxymoron? The only three functioning democracies among the world's Muslim nations—Bangladesh, Indonesia, and Turkey—are secular republics. Let's not kid ourselves about the task that lies ahead—if we want to succeed in rebuilding Iraq, we would be better off in seeking that separation between church and state, which has served all of the world's great democracies in good stead.

This was the first of my letters actually published by The Washington Post in its editorial pages on April 12, 2003. The letter that appeared in print, under the heading "Next Steps on Iraq", had a few minor edits, which included dropping of the last sentence in the letter that appears below.

Although Saddam Hussein was captured eight months after this letter appeared, remnants of his Republican Guard and foreign jihadists continue to fuel an insurgency in Iraq today. More than twenty-one months after Baghdad fell, we are far from "winning the war" that I wrote about below.

4/11/03: Letter to *The Post*—Re: Michael Kinsley's "No Quagmire, but Still Some Questions"[7]

In support of Michael Kinsley's brilliant analysis ("No Quagmire, but Still Some Questions"), it is worth pointing out that the top three objectives for the pre-emptive war with Iraq were as follows:

1.   Disarming Iraq of its weapons of mass destruction (WMD)

2.   Toppling the regime of Saddam Hussein

3.   Killing Saddam Hussein

The first objective is far from being met; in fact, we have still to find any significant WMD to actually even worry about getting rid of them. The second objective has been largely achieved, with the last pocket of resistance in Tikrit to be overcome. It's the uncertain outcome of the third objective, the death of the dictator that can prove to be the most troubling. As the ghost of Osama Bin Laden continues to haunt us in Afghanistan, the last thing we need is the myth of an invincible Saddam Hussein to dog our rebuilding efforts in Iraq. So it might behoove the Bush Administration to refrain from popping the cork on the champagne right now, because as the classic saying goes, "we might have won the battle (for Baghdad), but we have yet to win the war (rebuilding a safe, modern, democratic Iraq)." In the long run, the world community will forgive us not meeting all of our original objectives, if the afore-mentioned war is won.

*   *   *

True to form, the Bush Administration could not resist "popping the cork on the champagne" and barely three weeks later committed one of the biggest blunders of the Bush presidency. On May 1, 2003 President Bush donning a pilot suit landed in a Navy S-3B Viking aircraft on the deck of the USS Abraham Lincoln and proceeded to address the nation a short time later. In what was designed to be the "mother of all presidential photo-ops", President Bush spoke from the deck of the aircraft carrier with a prominent red, white and blue "Mission Accomplished" banner in the background for all to see. He went on to declare that "major combat operations" were over in Iraq. Prior to this declaration, 114 U.S. soldiers had been killed in combat in Iraq—by the end of the President's first term, we had lost a total of 1364 American troops!

Barely two weeks after the fall of Baghdad, the media began to realize that they had been largely suckered into supporting a war, which had been launched on bogus evidence for the most part. With no trace of WMD in these initial weeks, the rationale for the preemptive strike on Iraq quickly began to disappear.

4/22/03: Letter to *The Post*—Re: William Raspberry's "Hokum From the Prosecution"[8]

Upon reading William Raspberry's "Hokum From the Prosecution" in yesterday's Post, I couldn't help wondering whether we are letting American power (as demonstrated by an easy military victory in Iraq) trump American justice (as manifested in the truth, the whole truth, and nothing but the truth, so help me God)! The rationale for future pre-emptive military action, i.e. the Bush Doctrine, will suffer a significant setback if our original objectives in Iraq are not met in a timely fashion. It's imperative that we find at least some weapons of mass destruction soon, and even more critical that we locate the Ace of Spades even sooner!

*   *   *

The long term implications for the Bush Doctrine from the Iraq WMD fiasco were not good. In fact, by early 2005 the persistent defiance of Iran and North Korea, regarding the true state of their respective nuclear programs, had already rendered the Bush Doctrine passé.

My writing stars were ascendant in April 2003. After a lapse of more than five years, the editorial page that I love to debate published one of my letters again. This letter appeared, under the heading "Don't Let Conservatives Define Liberals' Views", almost verbatim in the May 2, 2003 edition of The Wall Street Journal. They only deleted the phrase "but also located its chief executioner—the Ace of Spades, Saddam Hussein" in the second to last sentence.

The WSJ editorial page often disparages liberalism by interpreting it in slanted terms. So I used the Iraq war and the elusive WMD to set the record straight. By publishing my letter, they seemed to acknowledge an implicit threat to the Bush Doctrine, if Iraq's WMD were not found.

4/24/03: Letter to *WSJ*—Re: Letters to the Editor

Why is it that you often let conservatives define what liberals stand for, what they think liberalism means, and now let them "examine liberal unhappiness" on the outcome of the war in Iraq (re: today's "Letters to the Editor")? Notwithstanding the couple of "equal opportunity" liberal voices in today's letters, I must say that as a subscriber of almost seventeen years, I rarely see a prominent liberal piece opining on conservative ideology.

As a person of moderately liberal leanings myself, I would like to caution that we cannot afford to equate short-term military victories into longer-term policy triumphs. Yes, I am unhappy because the President's premier objective for invading Iraq (finding and disarming Iraq of its weapons of mass destruction) remains unfulfilled a full two weeks after the fall of Saddam Hussein's regime. If Iraq was so urgent a threat that it necessitated pre-emptive military action over the objections of most of our allies and both our neighbors, we should have not only found some evidence of that threat by now, but also located its chief executioner—the Ace of Spades, Saddam Hussein! Anything less is going to be a serious setback for the Bush Doctrine!

*   *   *

I don't want to read too much into this, but my letter was written a week prior to the "Mission Accomplished" stunt, but it appeared the day after President Bush pulled it off—it felt like that they were trying to pass my message of restraint up the chain of command.

Defense Secretary Rumsfeld had supplied the most provocative quotes during the run-up to the Iraq war, and continues to "shock and awe" the world with his comments every so often. Shortly after the fall of Baghdad, which was accomplished in a record three weeks from the start of the war, Rumsfeld crowed, "Never have so many, been so wrong, about so much?"[ii]

4/29/03: Letter to *The Post*—Re: Richard Cohen's "Baghdad Bait and Switch"[9]

It's three weeks since the fall of Baghdad, and President Bush is ready to announce the end of the "combat phase" of Operation Iraqi Freedom. Meanwhile Defense Secretary Rumsfeld is crowing in Qatar, "Never have so many been so wrong about so much." Along comes Richard Cohen's "Baghdad Bait and Switch" in today's Post to remind us that we could well be equating our short-term military victory to a longer-term policy triumph. With each passing day, the ghost of Saddam Hussein and the pre-eminent threat that his weapons of mass destruction posed hangs over our heads like the sword of Damocles. It's not only our credibility but also the Bush Doctrine itself that is at stake, if the original objectives for this war are not met.

*   *   *

No WMD were ever found and an insurgency is still raging almost twenty-one months later, one wonders if Secretary Rumsfeld has had second thoughts about his braggadocio? The "sword of Damocles" turned out to be a hoax, which seriously damaged the credibility of the United States in the eyes of so many around the world, who turned out to be so right after all.

---

ii.   During a visit to U.S. Central Command in Doha, Qatar on April 28, 2003 to thank service members for the job they did on Operation Iraqi Freedom, Defense Secretary Rumsfeld said, "Never have so many, been so wrong, about so much." American Forces Press Service's Jim Garamone's report on the visit can be viewed on the Defense Department's web site at http://www.defenselink.mil/news/Apr2003/n04282003_200304281.html

We are still living down the repercussions of the Bush Administration's whoppers on Iraq—amazingly, a majority of the American people reelected President Bush despite these lies—I guess honesty and integrity is not what it used to be?

5/7/03: Letter to *The Post*—Re: Richard Cohen's "Never Mind the Weapons"[10]

Richard Cohen's "Never Mind the Weapons" in today's Post provides interesting food for thought. Isn't it ironical that we recently impeached a President for lying about his personal foibles? Yet, we are now hailing a President and his troika (Cheney, Rumsfeld, and Powell) that has delivered more professional whoppers on serious policy matters in the past nine months than I care to recall! Nothing succeeds like success, so maybe the struggling economy might be a wake-up call?

*   *   *

The struggling economy did not amount to a hill of beans in the eyes of the electorate. The moral of the lesson is that you can screw up on your job, but you cannot screw around in your job!

Nixon used Vietnam to defeat McGovern and Bush used Iraq to beat Kerry. While wars may help Presidents to win elections, they do not guarantee desirable foreign policy outcomes. The Vietnam War did not prevent the spread of communism in South East Asia—in fact, Vietnam is still one of the few communist hold-outs (like Cuba and China) despite the end of the Cold War and the break-up of the Soviet Union.

5/12/03: Letter to *The Post*—Re: George McGovern's "A More Constructive Internationalism"[11]

Upon reading George McGovern's "A More Constructive Internationalism" in today's Post, one gets a feel for how unfairly this man has been demonized by conservatives in this country? Unfortunately, we live in a time when being anti-war is equated with being unpatriotic or inexplicably "against the troops". We live in an age where giving heed to international opinion is misconstrued as subjugating our foreign policy to the United Nations? And, we are led to believe that a pre-emptive application of military power, irrespective of our larger policy goals, will provide us security at home and bring peace abroad. Only time will expose the truth as it did with Mr. McGovern's nemesis, President Nixon.

*   *   *

The Iraq War has thus far not contained terrorism—in fact, it has augmented it. Nevertheless, the Bush Administration would have us believe that the Afghan and Iraq Wars have prevented another terror attack on American soil—their answer to the 9/11 commission findings was about how the United States had become "safer but not safe" since 9/11? Well, safer is not good enough; every citizen wants to be safe within his own country. I would imagine that ought to be the goal for the second term—getting us back down to code green!

Five weeks after the fall of Baghdad, there were still no signs of WMD anywhere in Iraq. WMD had been the rai·son d'ê·tre for President Bush's preemptive strike against Iraq. Now, these elusive WMD had become fodder for late night talk show hosts. So I decided to get into the act with my very own semi-humorous yet quasi-serious discoveries of WMD.

5/15/03: Letter to *The Post*—Re: FREE FOR ALL[12]

In the weeks since the fall of Saddam Hussein's regime, we have had a number of WMD discoveries in Iraq. Here they are listed "David Letterman" style—my Top 10 list of WMD discoveries in Iraq:

10. Washington Moscow Disagreement

9. Wahhabi & Mujaheddin Decoys

8. Western Muscle on Display

7. Waiting on Meaningful Democracy

6. Wide Media Disbelief

5. World's Masses Duped

4. Worldwide Muslim Dissatisfaction

3. Wholesale Memory Degradation

2. W. Mandated Disorder

1. Winning for My Dad[13]

*   *   *

This list might seem facetious on my part, but it reflects all the feelings and events surrounding Iraq during that time. In fact, most of these "WMD discoveries" are valid even today.

While it didn't seem likely back in May 2003, CIA Director George Tenet did eventually bite the bullet in July 2004 for his "slam dunk" assessment of Iraq's WMD program. However, despite two major intelligence strikeouts (9/11 and WMD) eighteen months apart, President Bush honored Mr. Tenet with a Presidential Medal of Freedom in December 2004.

5/29/03: Letter to *The Post*—Re: Richard Cohen's "Victory per Rumsfeld's Say-So"[14]

Richard Cohen's "Victory per Rumsfeld's Say-So" in today's Post brings to mind the brouhaha from a year ago regarding the inability of our various intelligence agencies to "connect the dots" with respect to the events leading to 9/11. I suspect that the Bush Administration is already looking for an "intelligent scapegoat" to absorb the fallout from the thus-far non-existent WMD in Iraq? It would be ironical, if the countries that might actually possess WMD and pose a clear and present danger to the free world will now get a free pass to avoid any further embarrassment to our government!

*   *   *

As could be expected, Iran started acting really belligerent in 2004, and its nuclear ambitions surged following President Bush's WMD fiasco in Iraq. North Korea, which did not like being ignored, kept up a steady drumbeat of pressure and has been threatening to conduct an underground nuclear test. At the start of his second term, President Bush did not appear to have a coherent plan to deal with either of these charter members of his "axis of evil"?

*It wouldn't be far from the truth to suggest that the WSJ editorial page was the
key driver from the media of the Bush Administration's Iraq policy. So its editors
naturally defended their "incredible" position—and, as usual, I had Words of Major
Disagreement with their rationale.*

6/2/03: Letter to *WSJ*—Re: Weapons of Mass Distortion[15]

Your lead editorial, "Weapons of Mass Distortion", misses an important
point. Of the several post-war justifications cited by you, namely, "a tyrant and
his psychopath sons have been deposed", "mass graves have been uncovered",
"torture chambers have been exposed", and "Saddam's victims can speak freely
for the first time in 30 years", only the first reason qualifies as a pre-war argument from the Bush Administration. In fact, the major thrust of the Bush
Administration's pre-war case was based on Saddam's weapons of mass
destruction, and his links to Al Qaeda—neither of which have been proven to-
date. The real "credibility gap" is going to be our future inability to convince
even our strongest allies of real threats to our collective security, if the pre-war
case is never proven.

*   *   *

*A little over a year later, the 9/11 Commission[16] would conclude that there were
no "operational" links between Saddam Hussein and Al Qaeda. However, the Bush
Administration's constant reference to such a link would permanently sear it in the
minds of a majority of Americans. What Mass Distortion, indeed! Coincidentally,
the Bush Administration stopped making references to such a link after the President
had been reelected.*

The WMD thing stuck with me for a while. I could not fathom how the main-stream media refused to catch on to the fact that Saddam Hussein's government had actually been telling the truth about its WMD program in the months leading up to the war. More importantly, we would soon learn that the UN inspections had, in fact, worked—there were no WMD to find[iii]!

6/11/03: Letter to *The Post*—Re: Harold Meyerson's "Reaping The World's Disfavor"[17]

Harold Meyerson's "Reaping The World's Disfavor" in today's Post is a chilling reminder of the intoxication of power. The Bush Administration has used a national tragedy (9/11) to redefine the meaning of fear within this nation of immigrants, while simultaneously alienating friends abroad through a misguided application of its doctrine of preemption. If indeed, we are unable to find any weapons of mass destruction in Iraq, the sad irony will be that the dictator Saddam Hussein was telling the truth! So one can only hope that as Congress sets about to investigate the truth behind "WMD-gate", the Democrats don't get tricked into a public "Ollie North"-style "Iraq-Contra" sideshow—that Would be Masterful Deception!

*   *   *

The unfortunate part is that there have been no real Congressional investigations into the entire Iraq-WMD affair. More importantly, since the Republicans control both chambers of Congress, there is no likelihood of any hearings taking place until 2007 at the earliest—by which time it will be too late. President Bush has been essentially unencumbered of Congressional oversight, which might be a reason why a mission can appear accomplished when it has barely begun? Congress must take its

---

iii.   Charles Duelfer, Head of the Iraq Survey Group, completed his final 1000-page report on September 30, 2004. The Washington Post in a front page story headlined, "U.S. 'Almost All Wrong' on Weapons", on October 7, 2004 quotes Mr. Duelfer telling the Senate Armed Services Committee in a hearing the day before, "We were almost all wrong" with reference to Iraq's WMD. Mr. Duelfer's final report can be viewed on the CIA web site at http://www.cia.gov/cia/reports/iraq_wmd_2004/

oversight role more seriously during the President's second term so that mission creep does not set in.

The last time I had been a regular subscriber to the New York Times was when I lived in New Jersey (1986–89). Maureen Dowd used to be a correspondent in the Times' Washington bureau back then—but I didn't realize she was such a terrific writer until I came back east to Maryland from Reagan country.

6/19/03: Letter to NY *Times*—Re: Maureen Dowd's "Bushworld and Hillaryland"[18]

Maureen Dowd got it only half right when she concluded that Hillary Clinton is running—because, like everyone else, Maureen probably meant "running in 2008"? All the parameters, for "the mother of all déjà vu's", have been in the making throughout the Bush II presidency. One does not have to point out the obvious ones like Gulf Wars, Recessions, and Budget Deficits. However, it is those events still in the making that bring an air of excitement. So will the Clinton-Gore express of '92 be replicated with a Gore-Clinton juggernaut in '04? If the W. Mandated Disorder (WMD) is not resolved by the time primary season concludes next spring, I expect all of us will be "reliving history" starting November 2004!

*   *   *

My imagination ran a little wild with this one. However, this is one instant where Maureen Dowd got it wrong as well. And, the American people proved once again that they are as unpredictable as the polls that allegedly reflect their opinions.

George Will, the conservative columnist, finally picked up on the Bush Doctrine
@ risk proposition—something that I had been alluding to since the fall of Bagh-
dad—unlike the WSJ editorial page editors, who only three weeks earlier had
claimed that it was the media that had been distorting the facts on Iraq?

6/22/03: Letter to *The Post*—Re: George Will's "The Bush Doctrine At Risk"[19]

Finally, the first honest and incisive analysis from a conservative (George Will's "The Bush Doctrine At Risk") on the imperative for us to find those elusive WMD in Iraq. In addition to putting the Bush Doctrine and U.S. credibility at risk, the WMD is our raison d'être (pardon, my French) in Iraq—our soldiers aren't still dying everyday, only because we wanted to take out a dictator and free a people? If that were true, instead of George Will's rhetorical "on to Burma?"—I'd posit "one down, two to go on the axis of evil?" Unlike Iraq, North Korea defiantly boasts about resuming its nuclear weapons program, while Iran continues to be bashful about its real nuclear intentions. So it's refreshing that George Will recognizes why we need to find the real WMD, even as several of his ideological soul mates blame the mainstream media about "Weapons of Mass Distortion".

*   *   *

When this entire brouhaha about WMD was going on, a conservative colleague
said to me in a rather nonchalant fashion, "Oh, don't worry, Jack. We'll find WMD
in Iraq even if we have to plant it there ourselves?" I must confess that I was relieved
when the Duelfer report came out without any cause for suspicion to its authenticity.

As an Indian-American, who grew up in India, I am wary of Pakistan's military dictators—they have been not only bad for India, but also worse for Pakistan. The Muslim world sees a lot of double standards in U.S. foreign policy as it pertains to Muslim nations. This letter pointed out the need for consistency in our dealings with Muslim countries.

6/24/03: Letter to *WSJ*—Re: George Melloan's "Bush Wades Into Some of The World's Worst Messes"[20]

George Melloan states in his article, "State actually undercuts the president's policy through its willingness to coddle dictators" and also, "the president wants to inspire people with a principled foreign policy." I am loath to point out that President Bush's policy with respect to South Asia defies both of these observations. Pakistan has helped us greatly in our war against terrorism on its western border with Afghanistan, and President Bush is therefore rewarding General Musharraf with a visit to Camp David. Meanwhile, Pakistan has done very little to deter terror on its eastern border with India. President Bush could have killed two birds in one stone by inviting Pakistan's Prime Minister Mir Zafarullah Khan Jamali to Camp David instead of Gen. Musharraf. Firstly, President Bush's actions would have been consistent with those he employed in the Middle East peace process—in not dealing with a terror-supporting President of the Palestine Authority (Arafat) but meeting with its peace-making Prime Minister (Mahmoud Abbas) instead. Secondly, he would have dealt with an elected representative of Pakistan as opposed to a military dictator, who usurped power through a coup. President Bush could have sent a strong message to the world that the United States is as serious about democracy as it is about the war on terrorism.

Coincidentally, only a day earlier, the leader of the world's most populous country, Prime Minister Wen Jiabao of China welcomed the leader of the world's largest democracy, Prime Minister Vajpayee of India. If President Bush were following a truly principled foreign policy, which actually saw the forest for the trees, he would recognize that our long-term interests are not being served by sacrificing our democratic ideals at the expense of our security needs? Pushing India, a close ally of Russia, into the arms of China—creates a triumvirate with far-reaching influence across the globe! How long before Germany and France jump on that bandwagon?

*   *   *

The third world power play that I first alluded to in June 2003 came to the fore again recently, when China and India decided to kiss and make up. They jointly represent a third of humanity, both are nuclear powers, and they have been the world's two fastest growing economies for the past few years. India has been a vibrant democracy for all but two years (1975–77) since its independence (1947). China has been a communist state since 1949. President Bush had promised during his 2000 campaign to treat China as a "strategic competitor" and not a "strategic partner". He should begin to fulfill that promise in his second term, while simultaneously engaging India as the "strategic partner" in Asia.

It was neither Clinton-phobia, nor Reagan-nostalgia that did the trick for Bush in 2004. It wasn't even the economy, stupid! It weren't the elusive WMD or the shadowy Osama Bin Laden. It wasn't the Bush karma, either—war and recession did not translate into peace and tangible recovery. And yet, President Bush won! Notwithstanding the tenuous moral values argument, I have still to read a plausible explanation for this phenomenon from the pundit class.

7/1/03: Letter to *The Post*—Re: Dana Milbank's "As 2004 Nears, Bush Pins Slump on Clinton"[21]

President Bush might still be able to fire up donors with his statement, "Two-and-a-half years ago, we inherited an economy in recession." However, he will need to account to the entire American public for what he has done to rectify that situation since then? Despite the Fed's extended monetary priming with 13 interest rate cuts on Bush's watch, and despite Bush's own fiscal stimulus with annual tax cuts, the economy continues to flounder in a jobless recovery. Sixteen months from now, President Bush might find it very difficult to measure our national well-being with the classic Reagan test, "Are you better off than you were four years ago?"

Even from a national security standpoint, in the fall of 2004, the American people will want definitive answers to the whereabouts of Osama Bin Laden, Saddam Hussein, and those elusive WMD? Clinton-bashing might have narrowly elected President Bush in 2000, but more Clinton-phobia will not do the trick in 2004. In fact, by then we all might be pining for those go-go nineties?

*   *   *

In hindsight, I would venture to guess it was that one message, which we heard consistently throughout 2004, "I will choose to defend America every time." Now, which patriotic American would not want to vote for someone, who put that priority above all else?

Barely three months after the fall of Baghdad, I questioned the President's use of "bring 'em on"[iv], which the militants did—and, an insurgency still rages on today, nearly two years after the fall of Baghdad.

7/3/03: Letter to *The Post*—Re: Dana Milbank & Vernon Loeb's "Bush Utters Taunt About Militants: 'Bring 'Em On'"[22]

With reference to Dana Milbank & Vernon Loeb's front page story, "Bush Utters Taunt About Militants: 'Bring 'Em On'", it might be worth pointing out that Saddam Hussein issued a similar challenge to the U.S. military prior to the start of the recent war in Iraq. The events that have unfolded in Iraq, since President Bush announced the end of major combat operations on May 1, probably reflects what Saddam Hussein had in mind when he issued his own "bring 'em on" threat? President Bush might also recall that the Afghan Mujaheddin, with tacit support from our own CIA, used a similar guerilla (i.e. militant) warfare strategy to push the Soviet military out of Afghanistan in 1989 after a ten-year occupation. Given this history of the region, it would behoove the President to let his actions speak louder than his words!

*   *   *

As the saying goes, "Be careful what you wish for?" The insurgents in Iraq did "bring 'em on" and how? President Bush now has only one option in dealing with the insurgency raging in Iraq. He has to cajole our Sunni Muslim allies such as Egypt, Jordan, Pakistan, Saudi Arabia and Turkey to provide up to 50,000 additional ground troops in Iraq that will be used largely in peacekeeping operations. U.S. coalition and Iraqi forces can then be redeployed to more effectively fight the insurgency.

---

iv.   See report dated July 2, 2003 of a press conference in the White House that saeme day posted on the USA Today web site at http://www.usatoday.com/news/world/iraq/2003-07-02-bush-iraq-troops_x.htm. President Bush said, "There are some who feel like that the conditions are such that they can attack us there. My answer is bring them on".

The WSJ editorial page politicized the debate on the investigation into our Intelligence failures so blatantly that I was not amused. These guys did not give President Clinton time of day when he was trying to go after Osama Bin Laden—most likely based on similar faulty intelligence. Now they seemed all concerned about the damage to a "vital tool of U.S. security"—what chutzpah?

7/14/03: Letter to *WSJ*—Re: Lack of Intelligence[23]

Now that the shoe is on the other foot, I am quite amused by your pleading for a de-politicization of Intelligence (Re: Lack of Intelligence in today's WSJ). When the same George Tenet's CIA alerted then President Clinton back in 1998 about the possibility of hitting Osama Bin Laden in an obscure location in Afghanistan, all manner of conservatives made hay with the "million dollar missile into a $15 tent" story! Now, President Bush is burning $4 billion a month in Iraq and has yet to rid the world of Saddam Hussein. In fact, President Bush even directed more firepower into the Tora Bora Mountains of Afghanistan in December 2001 than Clinton had with his selective hit on Osama in 1998. Osama might be still around, too! These are facts and the American public is smart enough to determine President Bush's credibility based on his various utterances before and after these facts occurred. However, your feeble attempt to associate any investigation of the attendant intelligence lapses with "the potential to damage a vital tool of U.S. security in the war on terror" is pathetic.

*   *   *

The difference between their two approaches was that President Clinton was trying to do a preemptive strike on an individual, who had long ago declared "Holy War" on the United States; while President Bush made a preemptive strike on a country, which had made no overt threats against the United States. In the meantime, the individual, Osama Bin Laden, who was responsible for the most deadly terrorist attacks on the United States, still eludes capture more than three years after those attacks. And, the country, Iraq that was preemptively attacked by President Bush wallows in an insurgency, which is being fueled by a leader, who also eludes capture nearly two years after the fall of Baghdad.

President Bush should realize that he cannot achieve his strategic objective (which he has cleverly revised from the pre-election "defending America every time" to a post-election "spreading of freedom and democracy abroad") without key tactical successes (eliminating Osama Bin Laden to secure Afghanistan and Abu Musab Al-Zarqawi to stabilize Iraq) along the way. He needs to do what it takes to ensure these critical tactical successes, before any further tinkering with the strategic objective.

A couple of days later I picked up the drumbeat with The Washington Post. I even tried what I thought was a catchy phrase "where the lies lie?" to associate with the behavior of the Bush Administration in this matter. However, it was apparent that the media on both ends of the political spectrum was more hung up on these sixteen words from President Bush's State of the Union speech on January 28, 2003[24] "The British Government has learned that Saddam Hussein recently sought significant quantities of uranium from Africa." These sixteen words became the topic of international debate, following Ambassador Joseph C. Wilson's op-ed piece entitled "What I Didn't Find in Africa" in The New York Times dated July 6, 2003.

7/16/03: Letter to *The Post*—Re: Michael Kinsley's "…Or More Lies From The Usual Suspects?"[25]

As usual, Michael Kinsley in his inimitable style (re: "…Or More Lies From The Usual Suspects?" in today's Post) has exposed that age-old fact—truth and politics don't mix! Clinton asked us to ponder "what the definition of is is"? The Bushies, as Michael Kinsley is wont to call them, are now suggesting it does not matter "where the lies lie?" President Clinton got impeached for wagging his finger at us on national television and lying about sex. President Bush gets a pass for lying about a threat to our national security on national television and then sending us into a never-ending pre-emptive war? Also, every conservative I have read or heard in the past couple of days seems to be hung up on the sixteen "innocent" words in Bush's State of the Union speech. So for the record, Clinton's lie took only eleven words, "I did not have sexual relations with that woman, Miss Lewinsky." I am surprised Michael Kinsley missed that fine detail.

I sincerely believe that this letter largely answers the question "Why do they hate us?" However, the WSJ editorial page, in its infinite wisdom, chose not to run it. I am convinced that as long as the "politics of convenience" continues to trump our core values in the implementation of our foreign policy, we will never get them to stop hating us.

7/20/03: Letter to *WSJ*—Re: Letters to the Editor

Saleem Javaid's letter in the WSJ dated July 17, 2003 actually isolated the key reason as to "why they hate us"? He interpreted Prof. Ajami as saying that, "the anguish of the Arabs in particular and Muslims in general is rooted in corrupt regimes that were propped up by the West." This has been our "problem of convenience" in the past: Shah of Iran from 1953–1979, Generals Ayub, Yahya & Zia of Pakistan from 1958–1988, General Suharto of Indonesia from 1966–1998, President Saddam Hussein of Iraq during the Iran-Iraq War from 1980–1988, even maverick Osama Bin Laden in Afghanistan while it was under Soviet occupation from 1979–1989, and of course currently the various oil-rich kingdoms of the Middle East since their independence from colonial powers. We espouse our values—life, liberty, and the pursuit of happiness—only when it is convenient to us. This sad truth can be evidenced even today as we continue to support non-democratic regimes in allied nations such as Jordan, Kuwait, Pakistan, Saudi Arabia, and the various Muslim nations of the former Soviet Union. It is insulting to assume that the ordinary Muslim on the street does not recognize this duplicitous behavior for what it is—inconsistent, irrational, and self-serving. If we are serious about propagating our values across the Muslim world, it is time we started matching our actions to these values—I am confident that the Muslim street will follow!

*　　　*　　　*

President Bush appears to have acknowledged our "politics of convenience" problem, when he addressed the United States Chamber of Commerce at the 20th Anniversary of the National Endowment for Democracy in November 2003. Unfortunately, commensurate actions did not follow in 2004 to match the rhetoric of that speech. Hopefully, President Bush will live up to his words with appropriate deeds in his second term.

The Bush Administration has yet to satisfactorily address four of the five national security issues listed in the letter below.

7/24/03: Letter to *The Post*—Re: William Kristol's "Gephardt's 16 Words"[26]

Bill Kristol is the last neocon that I expected would spin "Gephardt's 16 Words". How could we be safer today when George Bush has still not delivered on the following items relating to our national security:

1. Osama Bin Laden, whom he wanted taken "dead or alive" nearly two years ago, is still around to threaten us with another 9/11?

2. Saddam Hussein, whose Elvis-like omnipresence continues to influence the killing of American soldiers almost on a daily basis in Iraq.

3. Iraq's Weapons of Mass Destruction—if the President won't admit that Iraq does not have any WMD, he better find them real fast because every minute that he doesn't, surely make "us less safe and less secure".

4. Kim Jong Il, who after the President went on record with the Post's Bob Woodward in August 2002 as a person he "loathes", has been become an increasingly dangerous threat to the United States.

5. Iran's recent acknowledgment that it is holding Al Qaeda members within its borders poses a "grave and gathering" danger to our "nation-building" efforts in Iraq.
    Gephardt could have sugar-coated it but the facts are on his side.

*   *   *

Although Saddam Hussein was subsequently captured, it appears that he will not go on trial for a long time to come. President Bush could easily take the WMD issue off the table for good, by gracefully acknowledging that Iraq's WMD had, in fact, been eliminated by the various UN actions since the end of the 1991 Gulf War. In any event, Osama Bin Laden, Kim Jong Il of North Korea, and the Ayahtollahs in Iran continue to pose an ongoing threat to our national security.

The Sunni Arab insurgency that has engulfed Iraq, since the capture of Saddam, should put to rest the myth that the Arab populace respects and responds to "real power". The primary lesson coming out of Vietnam was that nationalism takes precedence over everything else—insurgencies thrive because the local population rarely ever betrays its own.

8/5/03: Letter to *WSJ*—Re: Francis Fukuyama's "The Real Intelligence Failure"[27]

Francis Fukuyama's article, "The Real Intelligence Failure", is a better-late-than-never attempt by your editorial page to come to terms with some of the overarching problems we have encountered in the execution of the Bush Doctrine. However, with respect to the possibility of Iraq having destroyed its WMD prior to the current war, Mr. Fukuyama fails to recognize the Arab psyche, when he wonders "why did Saddam not reveal this, and save himself from an invasion?" There are several possibilities:

- He could never really admit to his Arab neighbors and the larger Muslim world that he no longer possessed the power that these WMD had bestowed upon him?

- He was actually telling the truth, but he anticipated that Western nations would mistrust him, and presenting a continued defiance of their will made him appear as a hero to his Arab neighbors and the larger Muslim world?

- He probably believed that as long as the United Nations remain engaged in the WMD saga, he would never be prematurely attacked by the United States and its Western allies?

Notwithstanding the prevailing myth that the Arab psyche respects and responds to "real power", it is incumbent upon us now as an occupying power to inculcate our true values in Iraq. For, in the long run, we might be forgiven our intelligence failures only if we don't fail to perform intelligently!

*　　　　*　　　　*

Performing intelligently implies that we execute Plan C—which is to bring in a multinational Sunni Muslim peacekeeping force, while we focus on tactical successes as enunciated previously and also address "root cause" issues in parallel. This is obviously more easily said than done, but it is the price we have to pay for not having had a Plan B to secure the peace in Iraq. As soon as we realized that we were, in fact, not being "greeted as liberators", Plan B should have been deployed. It's a moot point now—so a Plan C on the fly will have to do.

In the long run, the Iraqi elections could turn out to be the equivalent of a rather transient regime change—we will probably end up having traded Saddam Hussein for the Ayahtollahs in Iran. In a long-term geopolitical context, this might not be an altogether bad thing—since it will bring about a balance of oil power between the Shias (Iran and Iraq) and the Sunnis (Saudi Arabia, Kuwait, Qatar, and the U.A.E) in the Middle East? The key for us would lie in balancing our long-term interests between Riyadh and Tehran—neither of which is in a hurry to embrace democracy, as we know it.

8/19/03: Letter to *The Post*—Re: George Will's "The Shah and Us—and Regime Change"[28]

Upon reading George Will's "The Shah and Us—and Regime Change", I could almost sense a case of buyer's remorse for "Regime Change", which by extension implies Mr. Will is probably having second thoughts about the wisdom of the Bush Doctrine? In fact, he ends his article almost wistfully with reflections on our great American values put forth by eminent American statesmen of yesteryear—Woodrow Wilson, Abraham Lincoln, and Benjamin Franklin. It brought to my mind the thunderous outburst in an Indian courtroom during the British Raj, by the great Indian patriot, Lokmanya Tilak, who told a British judge, "Freedom is my birthright and I shall have it!"

The success of the Bush Doctrine seems to be predicated on the equivalence of freedom and democracy. We are learning from our experience in Afghanistan and Iraq that it is relatively easy to bring freedom to a people, but not quite simple to impose a democracy upon them. The latter gets even more complicated because people don't even to have to be free to exhibit a fierce nationalism. We are thus faced with the burden of being presently viewed as an occupying neocolonial power instead of a liberating nation-builder. The bottom line is that the yearning for freedom has to come from within, only then will democracy flourish as we are witnessing in several Eastern European nations today.

*   *   *

I am almost tempted to suggest that there is a proportional relationship between literacy and democracy, which would seem to explain why a number of Eastern Europe countries have succeeded with democratic reforms. But then, India, despite its high illiteracy rate, has also thrived as a democracy for over fifty years. The key to being a successful democracy in a globally interconnected world is to adopt a secular constitution, which gives one the freedom to practice any religion.

This is the challenge for President Bush—he has to be able to convince at least our Muslim allies that it should be possible for people of different faiths to live without fear of persecution within their countries. In that respect, Saddam Hussein might have been an evil dictator, but he was a secular minded one; whereas Crown Prince Abdullah, a seemingly benevolent dictator, is a theocrat.

Notwithstanding the war in Iraq, every now and then, the domestic economy would also grab the attention of the pundits. Outsourcing of jobs was to become a hot button issue in the election year of 2004. My point here was that interdependence of capital and labor had to be viewed in the context of the global economy.

8/29/03: Letter to *The Post*—Re: E.J. Dionne's "Do Jobs Not Matter Anymore"[29]

Upon reading E.J. Dionne's "Do Jobs Not Matter Anymore", I would like to point out that a purely domestic "capital vs. labor" argument has become passé in the global economy. Not only have our manufacturing jobs migrated to sources of cheap labor in China, but also our services sector jobs have now begun to take flight to inexpensive labor in English-speaking countries like India. Capital outflows, i.e., "foreign direct investments" by U.S. businesses into these countries, go hand-in-hand with this labor flight.

A newer phenomenon is the flight of "investment capital" as opposed to capital investment. It has been reported that the 2003 stock market boom in countries such as India, South Korea, and Taiwan has been fueled not by their local investments but largely by "investment capital" flowing in from capitalist havens like the United States. Only after China and India finally convert to a truly free economy with a floating currency, unrestricted stock markets, and free flowing capital—only then will their labor advantage start getting neutralized. Until then Mr. Dionne's perceived interdependence of capital and labor within the domestic U.S. economy is not going to make a huge difference to our "transient" jobs and the entrepreneurial investors who create them?

*   *   *

The test for President Bush in his second term is going to be job creation. So far he has been primarily replacing jobs that were lost in the last recession. With manufacturing jobs migrating to China and service jobs going to India, what's the future for the average American worker? If we need to create more knowledge-based jobs, it means giving even more priority to education at the under-graduate and graduate levels. I remember growing up in India at a time when education was valued more than anything else—we were taught at a very young age that one could always lose wealth, power, and fame; but knowledge was something that nobody could take away from you.

In the short term, President Bush needs to provide incentives for American multinational companies to enable them to repatriate their profits, which can then be "incentivized" for job-creating investments in the American economy. He should also change our tax laws such that it makes it harder for American companies to be incorporated in "offshore islands" for the primary purpose of U.S. corporate tax avoidance—especially when these companies do most of their business in the United States. They too should be given incentives to write off a portion of those U.S. corporate taxes against domestic business investments that create jobs. After all, the Bush economy has been largely fueled by consumer spending, which is now over 70% of GDP. Ironically, it is business investments that have been lethargic during the business-friendly Bush Administration's tenure.

*By positioning Iraq as the "central front" in the "war on terror", President Bush
transformed the mindset of not only his regular base of supporters among the American public, but it also won him fresh converts—who would in 2004 supply him his
margin of victory for reelection. The media never really fully grasped the significance
of this back in 2003, but his attendant message ("I will choose to defend America
every time") played consistently throughout 2004. The Average Joe actually believed
that President Bush was defending America when he invaded Iraq, which then
became the central front in the war on terrorism because of its links to Al Qaeda and
possibly 9/11?*

9/9/03: Letter to *WSJ*—Re: The Central Front[30]

At the outset, let me state unequivocally that we now need to do what it takes
to ensure success in building a safe, secular, and democratic Iraq. Having said
that I almost gasped when I heard the President tell us on Sunday that "Iraq is
now the central front" in the war on terrorism! It most certainly was not that
way, prior to his launching of the war on March 19. In fact, our own intelligence found it difficult to establish proof of any connection between Saddam
Hussein and Al Qaeda. In the five months since the fall of Baghdad, we have
also been unable to locate any weapons of mass destruction. This makes it all
the more difficult for the average American to understand how Saddam could
have shared "a common goal of killing Americans"? This goal thus became
feasible only after our troops invaded Iraq. Most people that I have talked to
since 9/11 think that Saudi Arabia should have been our next target, after
Afghanistan, in the war on terrorism. In any case, one can only pray that we
prevail in Iraq because failure is not an option given the catastrophic implications it would have on our larger strategic objectives in the Middle East and
on the war on terrorism worldwide.

∗ ∗ ∗

*President Bush's diversionary foray into Iraq was primarily responsible for the
introduction of Al Qaeda into Iraq—its Jordanian-born leader Abu Musab Al-
Zarqawi has wreaked havoc by fueling an insurgency that has proven hard to con-
tain. The longer it takes for us to eliminate this man, the greater the possibility that
he will spawn more and more surrogates to keep the insurgency alive. One can only*

hope that President Bush has a Special Forces operation targeted solely at getting A.M.A.Z.

Pesky "old Europe" insisted on "unless this, and unless that". Well, "unless" got new meaning after our invasion of Iraq. We are living the consequences of the UN-less occupation everyday.

9/24/03: Letter to *The Post*—Re: Coverage of UN speeches in today's Post

When will the bull-headed foreign policy hawks in the Administration realize that the Bush Doctrine is on life support? If post-combat phase reconstruction in Iraq does not get the imprimatur of the United Nations, either our solo efforts at an Iraqi renewal get bogged down in the short term, or the UN is doomed in the long term. In the meantime, the other two members of the axis of evil can get away with either trying to acquire WMD (Iran) and/or actually testing WMD (North Korea)?

If this is not enough of a nightmare scenario, President Bush should imagine what if the proverbial shoe was on the other foot? What if Russia decided it wanted to occupy one of the oil-rich "Stans", that was a part of the old Soviet Union, to counter "surging Islamic terrorism"? What if China made a pre-emptive strike at Taiwan to deter "terrorist designs on the mainland"? Despite our skepticism, the UN does serve a purpose—its very existence is a deterrent to unprovoked aggression by any of its member nations. No matter how we slice it, in the eyes of the world, our actions in Iraq while abiding with the letter of UN resolution 1441, has broken its spirit!

*　　　　*　　　　*

My fears about Russia or China attempting an UN-less action have not diminished since I wrote this letter to the Post over fifteen months ago. President Bush better be prepared for a serious foreign policy crisis in his second term that might not have anything to do with the "axis of evil".

I was remembering all the various Independent Counsels that were deployed during the Clinton years, when I wrote this letter to the Post. A couple of these issues probably still do merit the attention of at least some sort of special counsel?

10/3/03: Letter to *The Post*—Re: An Independent Counsel[31]

If the Independent Counsel law were still in effect today and this had been a Democratic President, we would probably have at least six cases under investigation:

1. Administration's failure to prevent 9/11/01 attacks on the United States

2. Administration's failure to capture Osama Bin Laden two years after the Afghanistan War

3. Administration's failure to find the perpetrator of the Anthrax attacks two years later

4. Administration's failure to capture Saddam Hussein six months after the fall of the Iraqi regime

5. Administration's failure to find any WMD after six months of unfettered access in Iraq

6. Administration's leaking of an undercover CIA operative's name

*   *   *

With a Republican Congress still in control, I don't really expect any serious "checks and balances" on the executive branch at least through 2006, by which time one hopes that most of these issues become redundant.

It was naïveté on my part to even write such a letter, but then hope springs eternal in the human breast. I thought that if President Ronald Reagan could accept responsibility for the 1983 bombing of the Marine barracks in Beirut[32], President Bush could at least acknowledge being wrong about WMD in Iraq. No one was suggesting that he pull out of Iraq, like Reagan did from Lebanon—which is often cited by conservatives as having sent the wrong message to terrorists about U.S. resolve under pressure. But when the President of the most powerful country on earth is so wrong about his primary justification for launching a war—a preemptive strike, nonetheless, without the sanction of an explicit UN resolution—some sort of redress can only help the cause.

10/5/03: Letter to *WSJ*—Re: "All the Candidate's Women"[33]

It is easy enough to appreciate Arnold Schwarzenegger's candid apology (re: "All the Candidate's Women") to the women he might have offended in his past. In fact, many of us can be magnanimous when we aren't the aggrieved party. If one of the offended women came forth and accepted Arnold's apology, then we could say that he had been at least partly redeemed? Speaking of apologies, would it at all be possible for the Wall Street Journal editors to advise President Bush to admit that he was wrong on Iraq's weapons of mass destruction (WMD)? Now that David Kay has issued his preliminary findings and revealed that six months of unfettered access in Iraq has turned up no WMD, shouldn't you, the WSJ editors, take the advice of fellow conservative, George Will, and issue a mea culpa to your readers for having actively pursued a hawkish policy on Iraq? Are the WSJ editors willing to recognize that their leading role for a pre-emptive war with Iraq has resulted in a serious setback to the Bush Doctrine, as can be evidenced by the growing threats from the other two members of the "axis of evil"? Sadly our hands are now tied as both, North Korea and Iran, pursue WMD programs with gay abandon!

*　　　　*　　　　*

I would imagine having prematurely declared the "mission accomplished", President Bush could not get himself to admit that there were no WMD to be found in Iraq. Hence my flagging of this third year in the Bush presidency as "Mission Accomplished...Without WMD!" However, the larger point to be made here is that if

President Bush cannot acknowledge that he had made a mistake[34], how is he going to fix the problem in Iraq? More importantly, this posture of perfection pervades the Bush Administration—an approach that is not very conducive to diplomacy on the world stage. One hopes that they will make an "attitude adjustment" in the second term.

A couple of days later I tried to get the Post to see my point of view. I was hoping that somebody in the Bush Administration would at least listen to what George Will, an old line conservative, had to say about the WMD fiasco? Meanwhile Secretary of State Colin Powell continued to embarrass himself and his fans from the liberal side of town.

10/7/03: Letter to *The Post*—Re: Colin Powell's "What Kay Found"[35]

When are Administration officials going to realize that it is not "What Kay Found" (Re: Colin Powell's op-ed piece today) but what he did not find in Iraq that is uppermost on the average American mind? Undoubtedly, this fear is being reflected in all the recent polls on the subject, and is causing a spurt of rather defensive op-ed pieces from senior Administration officials in the national media. Nevertheless, it is rather sad to see the Secretary of State scraping the bottom of the barrel to look for "strains of organisms", and tell us "one of the strains could be used to produce biological agents"? I remember quite distinctly being told by Secretary Powell before the war that, in fact, the barrel would be overflowing with WMD. One would imagine after having six months of unfettered access to Iraq that Mr. Kay and his team would have produced more desirable results than the much-maligned UN inspectors? It isn't too late for the Bush Administration to come clean with the American people and admit that it was wrong about WMD in Iraq, as one of their own conservative stalwarts, George Will, has suggested. Such an act would make all of us re-focus and support the larger task at hand—the rebuilding of Iraq!

The following month, Republican Senator Pat Roberts of Kansas wrote an op-ed piece in the Post in a valid defense for keeping his "panel above politics". I just thought he did not do it in a very "intelligent" way by defending flawed pre-war intelligence on Iraq.

11/13/03: Letter to *The Post*—Re: Senator Pat Roberts' "A Panel Above Politics"[36]

With all due respect to the Chairman of the Senate Select Committee on Intelligence, when he makes a statement such as, "Ultimately it was used by this administration and this Congress to present a case to the world that Hussein had to be disarmed once and for all." The "it" being the "intelligence"—coming out of our various agencies—which has made us the laughing stock around the world. Six months after major combat operations were declared over by our President, we are still unable to determine if Saddam Hussein has, indeed, been "disarmed"? In the meantime, we as a nation have been "disarmed" of our international reputation and dignity, as an always fair-minded, and yes, usually "intelligent" people!

*   *   *

A little over a month later, Saddam Hussein was finally found hiding in a hole in the ground just outside his hometown of Tikrit. His capture helped alleviate some of our embarrassment over intelligence gaffes relating to WMD.

When a U.S. judge brings god into the courtroom, we might as well amend the constitution and make it legal. Let's then stop complaining about "Islamic fundamentalism", and let the "neo-crusades" begin!

11/14/03: Letter to *The Post*—Re: Alabama Judge Is Removed[37]

It was heartening to read that the decision to remove Chief Justice Moore was a unanimous one. Following the Court's decision, I heard Justice Moore on the TV news saying, "God is above the law." A similar sentiment is expressed throughout the militant Islamic world, as its radical clerics proclaim "Jihad" and order their rabid followers to kill in the name of God. It's all these conceited interpreters of religion who give God a bad name. No wonder that our astute founding fathers made that wonderfully prescient distinction between church and state. With apologies to American Express, we all should leave home without them (i.e. our religious beliefs)!

*　　　*　　　*

President Bush could have seized the initiative here to make a strong statement about the need to keep our faith outside of our government—if not for domestic consumption, it would have helped his standing in the Muslim world at a time when he was directly responsible for preemptively attacking and occupying a sovereign Muslim nation. However, I suspect with his reelection bid less than a year away, he could not afford to antagonize his conservative base.

In President Bush's second term, this issue of separation of church and state at home is going to be even more closely monitored abroad as long as our military is in Afghanistan and Iraq. The freedom of religion issue is critical to the success of President Bush's call for greater "freedom and democracy" in Muslim countries—and, he needs to remember that perception is often times mistaken for reality, so we need to be extra cautious at home.

This was the second letter that The Washington Post published with minor edits in its December 5, 2003 edition under the heading "'Cut and Run' and the Right Approach in Iraq". If President Bush had followed a similar strategy back then, our troop strength in Iraq would probably be going down right now?

11/19/03: Letter to *The Post*—Re: Eliot A. Cohen's "If We Cut and Run"[38]

Eliot Cohen makes an interesting case for persisting in Iraq, but while he reiterated the objective (winning our war), he "cut and run" on the strategy that could achieve this difficult goal. The strategy is quite simple really, but it requires courage to execute:

1. We eat a little humble pie and admit ASAP in a speech to the UN General Assembly that one of our foremost objectives for going to war has not panned out (i.e. Iraq possesses no WMD and we were wrong about that, but Iraq and the world is still better off without Saddam Hussein).

2. We take the initiative in patching up with "Old Europe" by supporting a joint French-German UN Security Council resolution on Iraq, which transfers peacekeeping operations to the UN within six months, and reduces US military presence in a staggered fashion until a freely elected Iraqi government takes over.

3. We continue to keep administrative and political control of Iraq until UN-approved elections are conducted nationwide in Iraq within the next 12 to 18 months. During this time we dedicate our major resources to rebuilding Iraq with some of that $87 billion President Bush got from Congress recently.

This is the kind of strategy that post-WWII Germans and Japanese experienced under the United States, and this is the only type of strategy that will also work in Iraq!

*   *   *

In January 2005, the Bush Administration was pushing ahead with its plan to conduct elections for an interim Iraqi government, which was to then draft a consti-

tution by August 2005. From a U.S. standpoint, there were no indications about troop reductions in the near future.

This letter was sent directly to Post columnist, Richard Cohen. When I wrote this letter, I believed it had an element of "conspiracy theory" behind it, so I did not submit it to "Letters to the Editor". We have since learned about the famous August 6, 2001 Presidential Daily Brief headlined, "Bin Laden Determined to Strike in US". We have also since learned about ex-CIA Director George Tenet's famous "slam dunk" assessment regarding Iraq's WMD program[39]. When this letter is read with all of this hindsight, it might not appear all that conspiratorial?

11/25/03: Letter to *The Post*—Re: Richard Cohen's "The Patriotism Refuge"[40]

Has it occurred to you that there might be a "quid pro quo" situation between our various Intelligence services and the Bush Administration? President Bush received bad intelligence on Iraq but has not let any heads roll as you rightly point out. Now why would a President, who had no qualms in firing his first economic team (O'Neill & Lindsey) for doing a lousy job, not do the same with his intelligence team for repeated failures such as the events leading to 9/11, the post-Afghan war hunt for Osama Bin Laden, finding the perpetrator of the anthrax attacks, the pre-war WMD estimates in Iraq, and the post-war insurgency in Iraq? Gives one pause to wonder—whether our intelligence really "failed" us on 9/11?

Remember that the CIA was hot on the Al Qaeda trail after the attack on the USS Cole in October 2000. From the time President Bush took office on January 20, 2001 until September 11, 2001, there is no public record of the Bush Administration actively pursuing Al Qaeda. There have been reports since 9/11, of an issue between the Bush Administration and the 9/11 Commission, over the release of the Presidential Daily Briefs (PDBs) leading up to 9/11. Is it possible that these PDBs show that the CIA was greatly concerned about an imminent attack on the United States? I have even read about Condi Rice having allegedly seen intelligence briefs, as late as 9/10/01 that alluded to terrorist attacks on American soil? If all this is true, did the Bush Administration ignore these warnings? Is it the reason why the CIA is now being forgiven for its post-9/11 lapses? In the interest of the future security of our nation we must get to the truth behind the "real" intelligence situation going back to the closing days of the Clinton Administration. Let the chips fall where they may.

*   *   *

Despite the "slam dunk" performance, President Bush recently awarded the Presidential Medal of Freedom to ex-CIA Director George Tenet.

I still believe the Presidential visit to Baghdad on Thanksgiving Day 2003 was a reckless act of showmanship—whoever suggested it should have been fired?

11/28/03: Letter to *The Post*—Re: Dana Milbank's "An Indelible Moment in A War and Presidency"[41]

My instinctive reaction was like almost everyone else and I thought it was an absolutely fabulous, heroic, and symbolic thing to do—a surprise visit by the President to our troops in Baghdad on Thanksgiving Day! In fact, when I saw that tear well up in President Bush's eye as he basked in the applause from the troops, I even had goose bumps myself. Then reality set in—is this guy completely insane? As my rational mind took stock of the pros and cons, I concluded that the risks to the United States far outweighed any gain that might have accrued as a result of this reckless trip. If, God forbid, anything had happened to the President, we would have lost everything: stock markets would have crashed worldwide, our freshly growing economy would have buckled, a chaotic rebellion would have immediately engulfed Iraq, and, most importantly, the war on terrorism would have been lost forever. Fortunately, the President is home and we are none the worse off for it. Dana Milbank wonders, "The visit's impact on U.S. public opinion and on the Iraqi public is not yet knowable." My opinion is quite bleak—the President should immediately fire the wise guy or gal, on his national security staff, who came up with this turkey of an idea!

*   *   *

The safety concern has gathered even more significance in recent months as the insurgency in Iraq continues to rage. President Bush should understand that Iraq cannot be deemed a success as long as there is just one small secure section in Baghdad, which we call the "green zone". Under Saddam Hussein, the average Iraqi citizen probably lived in fear but felt safe. Under U.S. occupation, the average Iraqi citizen probably does not live in fear any longer but cannot feel very safe.

President Bush has no other alternative but to aggressively push reconstruction efforts and extend the green zone to all of Iraq during the course of his second term.

*Business Week published one of my letters in its December 29, 2003 issue. I have
included it here because of its relevance to the "outsourcing" issue, which was to
become a campaign issue in the presidential election of 2004. The letter that
appeared in print had a few minor edits and the last sentence was deleted.*

12/7/03: Letter to *Business Week*—Re: "The Rise of India"[42]

As a first generation Indian-American, it made me proud to read about "The
Rise of India". However, I am alarmed by the perception that this rise is coming at the expense of the United States. Whenever our economic model
undergoes a transformation, as we witnessed with "Japan's manufacturing
prowess in the 1980s", we appear to go through some sort of a "xenophobic"
phase initially. Eventually, the Japan that could say no ended up enduring a
recession that lasted through most of the 1990s, while the US that kept saying
yes witnessed record economic growth during the same period! Some of your
(re: BW editorial) policy recommendations on education, academic research,
startup funding, and immigration would go a long way towards re-modeling
the US economy, yet again, to meet these offshore cyber challenges to our
New Economy.

*　　　　*　　　　*

*The letter in no way meant to imply that a similar fate as befell Japan might
transpire with my native land. I was suggesting that when the economic paradigm
changes, we tend to adapt in innovative ways so that we always come out on top. In
any event, in a 24/7 global economy connected via a high-speed telecommunications
infrastructure today and a high-speed transportation infrastructure tomorrow, "outsourcing" will no longer be a major issue.*

*Even in the short term, I believe that outsourcing is a zero sum game. Thanks to
the afore-mentioned high-speed telecommunications infrastructure, software engi-
neers from India don't need to physically work in the United States like they had to
in the past. A lot of the reasons that Indians had for migrating to the U.S. have
gradually disappeared. So American jobs that were being lost to Indians coming over
are now being lost to Indians staying behind.*

*There is, however, one aspect that is often overlooked and that has to do with
Indian-American entrepreneurs—Silicon Valley has a surfeit of them—that have*

gone on to start high-tech companies, which have been very successful and created thousands of American jobs. Without doubt, most Indian-Americans feelings are reflected in a remark the Russian-American comedian, Yakov Smirnoff, made famous, "What a country!"

Towards the end of the year, the Journal editorialized about the tenuous nature of our relationship with Pakistan as far as the war on terrorism was concerned. Despite the Journal's reservations, President Bush went on to award Pakistan with the status of "major non-NATO ally" in June 2004[43].

12/29/03: Letter to *WSJ*—Re: Our Man in Pakistan[44]

Your observation that "Our Man in Pakistan" is "the world's weakest link" in the war on terror should serve as a wake-up call that capturing Osama Bin Laden cannot remain dependent on this fragile partner. When President Bush addressed the United States Chamber of Commerce at the 20th Anniversary of the National Endowment for Democracy in early November, he made this brilliant remark, "Sixty years of Western nations excusing and accommodating the lack of freedom in the Middle East did nothing to make us safe—because in the long run, stability cannot be purchased at the expense of liberty. As long as the Middle East remains a place where freedom does not flourish, it will remain a place of stagnation, resentment, and violence ready for export. And with the spread of weapons that can bring catastrophic harm to our country and to our friends, it would be reckless to accept the status quo" If we replace "Middle East" with "Pakistan" in the President's remarks, one would have to conclude as your editorial did, "The status quo looks increasingly perilous, both for General Musharraf and the U.S"!

*   *   *

"Our Man in Pakistan" later returned President Bush's favor, by announcing on the last day of 2004 that he would not relinquish his military uniform and title as promised. This would be an early setback to President Bush's impending second term agenda for freedom and democracy. If the President is not going to be able to get our Muslim allies to bite the bullet on democracy; it's certainly going to be no picnic in the Middle East.

Notes:

[1] The letter entitled "United We Stand" was published by The Wall Street Journal editorial page on January 30, 2003, and signed by seven European Prime Ministers: Jose Maria Aznar of Spain, Jose-Manuel Durao Barroso of

Portugal, Silvio Berlusconi of Italy, Tony Blair of Great Britain, Peter Medgyessy of Hungary, Leszek Miller of Poland and Anders Fogh Rasmussen of Denmark; and President Vaclav Havel of the Czech Republic.

[2] *The Wall Street Journal* editorial entitled "Economy of the Year" appeared in its *Review & Outlook* section of January 4, 2003.

[3] The entire transcript of Secretary of State, Colin Powell's presentation to the United Nations Security Council on February 5, 2003 can be viewed on the official web site of the White House at http://www.whitehouse.gov/news/releases/2003/02/20030205-1.html

[4] This quote is attributed to India's ambassador to the United Nations, Vijaya Lakshmi Pandit. She had said, "The more we sweat in peace the less we bleed in war."

[5] Robert Novak is a syndicated columnist for the *Creators Syndicate*. This column entitled "Everything Riding On Iraq" appeared in *The Washington Post* edition dated March 6, 2003.

[6] Noah Feldman, a Fellow at New America Foundation, is an Assistant Professor of Law at New York University School of Law.

[7] Michael Kinsley, Editorial and Opinion Editor of *The Los Angeles Times*, writes a weekly column for The Post. This column entitled "No Quagmire, but Still Some Questions" appeared in *The Washington Post* edition dated April 11, 2003.

[8] William Raspberry has been a Post columnist since 1966. His column generally appears on Mondays and Fridays. This column entitled "Hokum From the Prosecution" appeared in *The Washington Post* edition dated April 21, 2003.

[9] Richard Cohen has been a Post columnist since 1976. His column generally appears on The Post's opinion page on Tuesdays and Thursdays. This column entitled "Baghdad Bait and Switch" appeared in *The Washington Post* edition dated April 29, 2003.

[10] This Richard Cohen column entitled "Never Mind the Weapons" appeared in *The Washington Post* edition dated May 7, 2003.

[11] George McGovern was the Democratic Party candidate for President in 1972. This op-ed piece entitled "A More Constructive Internationalism" appeared in *The Washington Post* edition dated May 12, 2003.

[12] *The Washington Post* publishes a special "Free For All" section of its "Letters to the Editor" on Saturdays. My attempt at parodying the WMD fiasco did not make it to "Free For All" to see.

[13] *TIME Asia* in its "Starting Time" section for the week of October 7, 2002 quotes President Bush verbatim, "After all, this is a guy who tried to kill my dad" in a reference to Saddam Hussein's attempt to assassinate George Bush Sr. in Kuwait in 1993. The quote was also featured in Michael Moore's documentary "Fahrenheit 9/11".

[14] This Richard Cohen column entitled "Victory per Rumsfeld's Say-So" appeared in *The Washington Post* edition dated May 29, 2003.

[15] *The Wall Street Journal* editorial entitled "Weapons of Mass Distortion" appeared in its *Review & Outlook* section of June 2, 2003.

[16] *The National Commission on Terrorist Attacks Upon the United States* released its final report on July 22, 2004.

[17] Harold Meyerson is editor at large of the *American Prospect* and political editor of *L.A. Weekly*. His column appears on Wednesdays in *The Washington Post*. This column entitled "Reaping The World's Disfavor" appeared in *The Washington Post* edition dated June 11, 2003.

[18] Maureen Dowd has been a columnist on *The New York Times* Op-Ed page since 1995. Her column generally appears in The Times Op-Ed page on Thursdays and Sundays. This column entitled "Bushworld and Hillaryland" appeared in *The New York Times* edition dated June 18, 2003.

[19] George F. Will is a columnist, television personality and author. His column generally appears on Thursdays and Sundays in *The Washington Post*. This column entitled "The Bush Doctrine At Risk" appeared in *The Washington Post* edition dated June 22, 2003.

[20] George Melloan writes the "Global View" column for *The Wall Street Journal*. This column entitled "Bush Wades Into Some of The World's Worst Messes" appeared in *The Wall Street Journal* edition of June 24, 2003.

[21] Dana Milbank was a White House correspondent for *The Washington Post* until December 2004. This report entitled "As 2004 Nears, Bush Pins Slump on Clinton" appeared in *The Washington Post* edition dated July 1, 2003.

[22] Vernon Loeb is a *Washington Post* staff writer who covers the Defense Department. This joint report with Dana Milbank entitled "Bush Utters Taunt About Militants: 'Bring 'Em On'" appeared in *The Washington Post* edition dated July 3, 2003.

[23] *The Wall Street Journal* editorial entitled "Lack of Intelligence" appeared in its *Review & Outlook* section of July 14, 2003.

[24] The full text of President Bush's 2003 State of the Union speech can be viewed on the White House web site at http://www.whitehouse.gov/news/releases/2003/01/20030128-19.html

[25] This Michael Kinsley column entitled "…Or More Lies From The Usual Suspects?" appeared in *The Washington Post* edition dated April 11, 2003.

[26] William Kristol is editor of The Weekly Standard, chairman and co-founder of the Project for the New American Century, and a political contributor for the FOX News Channel. This op-ed piece entitled "Gephardt's 16 Words" appeared in *The Washington Post* edition of July 24, 2003.

[27] Francis Fukuyama is a professor of international political economy at Johns Hopkins University in Maryland. This op-ed piece entitled "The Real Intelligence Failure" appeared in *The Wall Street Journal* edition of August 5, 2003.

[28] This George Will column entitled "The Shah and Us—and Regime Change" appeared in *The Washington Post* edition dated August 19, 2003.

[29] E.J. Dionne Jr. is a senior fellow in government studies at the Brookings Institution. A Post columnist since 1993, Mr. Dionne's column appears on The Post's opinion page on Tuesdays and Fridays. This column entitled "Do Jobs Not Matter Anymore" appeared in *The Washington Post* edition dated August 29, 2003.

[30] *The Wall Street Journal* editorial entitled "The Central Front" appeared in its *Review & Outlook* section of September 9, 2003.

[31] *The Washington Post* editorial entitled "An Independent Counsel?" appeared in its October 3, 2003 edition.

[32] At a news conference held on December 27, 1983 President Ronald Reagan said, "If there is to be blame, it properly rests here in this office and with this president. And I accept responsibility for the bad as well as the good."

[33] *The Wall Street Journal* editorial entitled "All the Candidate's Women" appeared in its *Review & Outlook* section of October 3, 2003.

[34] At a news conference held on April 13, 2004 President Bush was asked by John Dickerson, White House correspondent for TIME Magazine, "After 9/11, what would your biggest mistake be, would you say, and what lessons have you learned from it?" To which President Bush, in part replied, "You know, I just—I'm sure something will pop into my head here in the midst of this press conference, with all the pressure of trying to come up with an answer, but it hadn't yet" and concluded his long answer by saying, "I don't want to sound like I've made no mistakes. I'm confident I have. I just haven't—you just put me under the spot here, and maybe I'm not as quick on my feet as I should be in coming up with one." The full text of this press conference can be viewed on the White House web site at http://www.whitehouse.gov/news/releases/2004/04/20040413-20.html

[35] Colin Powell was Secretary of State during President Bush's first term. This op-ed piece entitled "What Kay Found" appeared in *The Washington Post* edition dated October 7, 2003.

[36] Senator Pat Roberts (R-KS) is the Chairman of the Senate Select Committee on Intelligence. This op-ed piece entitled "A Panel Above Politics" appeared in *The Washington Post* edition dated November 13, 2003.

[37] *The Washington Post* editorial entitled "Alabama Judge Is Removed" appeared in its November 14, 2003 edition.

[38] Eliot A. Cohen is professor of strategic studies at Johns Hopkins University's School of Advanced International Studies. This op-ed piece entitled "If

We Cut and Run" appeared in *The Washington Post* edition dated November 19, 2003.

[39] Bob Woodward in his book, "Plan Of Attack", tells of a meeting held in the Oval Office on December 21, 2002 with President Bush, Vice President Cheney, National Security Advisor Rice, and Chief of Staff Card in attendance, where CIA Director George Tenet responds to President Bush's query on the case for Iraq's WMD by saying "It's a slam-dunk case!"

[40] This Richard Cohen column entitled "The Patriotism Refuge" appeared in *The Washington Post* edition dated November 25, 2003.

[41] This report by Dana Milbank entitled "An Indelible Moment in A War and Presidency" appeared in *The Washington Post* edition dated November 28, 2003.

[42] "The Rise of India" was the Cover Story in the *Business Week* issue dated December 8, 2003.

[43] On June 16, 2004 the White House Office of the Press Secretary released a memorandum for the Secretary of State designating the Islamic Republic of Pakistan as a Major Non-NATO Ally. The full text of this memo can be viewed on the White House web site at http://www.whitehouse.gov/news/releases/2004/06/20040616-3.html

[44] *The Wall Street Journal* editorial entitled "Our Man in Pakistan" appeared in its *Review & Outlook* section of December 29, 2003.

THE FOURTH QUARTER:
2004—"FEAR MORE YEARS"

"Fear More Years" encapsulates my perception of what four more years under President Bush would entail, if he lived up to the words of his 2004 campaign. Since fear was a primary component of his reelection effort, the title of the chapter represents a cynical way to put out a "caveat emptor" label on his second term—a warning to all Americans that they will have to contend with another four years of fear mongering?

In any event, the foreign policy "PAIN" that I was experiencing at the start of 2004 was largely instigated by the two assassination attempts on President Musharraf's life in December 2003. I feared that if the terrorists quickly got lucky, a third time around, Pakistan and Afghanistan would displace Iraq as the "central front" in the war against terrorism. Fortunately, the dictator survived—but he would conclude a year later that real democracy did not help his longevity.

1/1/04: Letter to *The Post*—Re: Robin Wright's "Bush Faces a Challenging Year: The Turn From War to Peace"[1]

Robin Wright has it right on the money regarding the foreign policy challenges faced by President Bush in this election year. However, if I had to rank them in order of importance, I would characterize these in the acronym "PAIN" (Pakistan, Afghanistan, Iraq, and North Korea). Pakistan, the creator of the Taliban, is the number one crisis brewing in the war against terrorism. The elimination of President Musharraf will re-energize Al Qaeda and practically install a surrogate Taliban regime in Islamabad with control of Pakistan's prized nuclear assets. Can anyone imagine how long it would take Osama Bin Laden to pull the trigger once his Al Qaeda has its hands on the "Islamic Bomb"? It is quite apparent that the Taliban/Al Qaeda brain trust has recognized that it would become easier for them to recover Afghanistan, if they first toppled Musharraf in Pakistan. In fact, they probably view it as a double play—Pakistan and Afghanistan—in one strike? Ironically, the Iraq problem for Bush in 2004 is more a nation-building one now that Saddam and Iraq's WMD have been put to bed. The real PAIN point of 2003—North Korea—will fade as an "imminent" threat in 2004 only because the perpetrator of 9/11 will once again loom large if the Pakistan situation really gets out of control.

*   *   *

I was frightfully wrong about Iraq—assuming that with Saddam's capture on December 13, 2003 and the WMD issue receding into the background—all we would be faced with is a nation-building problem? But then Abu Ghraib had still not surfaced, and the insurgency was still a relatively minor issue in early 2004.

As the year progressed, North Korea appeared to fade as an "imminent" threat but then resurfaced as a "grave and gathering" danger to our national security soon after the elections. Afghanistan successfully conducted elections in October 2004—giving President Bush something to be proud of on the foreign policy front. Osama Bin Laden would reappear after a prolonged absence in a rather silly attempt to influence the outcome of our presidential election.

The Post editors were concerned about a lackadaisical Congress allowing the executive branch to willy-nilly make policy while wearing the cloak of national security. I was rather perturbed by the erosion of our civil liberties at the expense of allegedly enhanced security—the comparison to communism was meant to alarm—but the Post didn't run it, anyway. How quickly the cold war memories have faded?

1/5/04: Letter to *The Post*—Re: Silence on the Hill[2]

"The balance between liberty and security" is in reality a classic dilemma wherein the ends (guaranteeing security) don't necessarily justify the means (sacrificing liberty). Judith M. Brown reveals in her recent biography of India's first prime minister that at the peak of his political power, Jawaharlal Nehru wrote, "it is more important to adopt the right way, to pursue the right means, than even to have the right objectives, important as that is." Democracy, like happiness, is not a destination but a continuous journey, which encounters bumps in the road every now and then. It's only through the vigilance of the executive, judicial, and legislative branches of our government, can we remain true to the core beliefs enshrined in the Declaration of Independence, "that all men are created equal, that they are endowed by their Creator with certain unalienable Rights, that among these are Life, Liberty and the pursuit of Happiness." If liberty is a right granted to me by my Creator, why would my government expect me to sacrifice even a part of it to make me feel more secure? Isn't this what communism was all about?

*   *   *

If there were any doubts about how ridiculous our "democracy" had become by the start of President Bush's second term, one only needs to look at the farcical stage show that the President has been putting on in his current sixty day, sixty city tour for Social Security reform. His so-called "town hall meetings" have crowds that are rigorously pre-screened by GOP organizers to weed out likely dissenting voices. Notwithstanding genuine security concerns, which are presumably being handled by the Secret Service, what does this practice say to the world about our democracy, freedom of speech, and freedom of assembly?

Thus our "Pravda President" gets a "first-hand impression" that he has a Social Security plan, which the heartland loves and any polls indicating anything to the contrary are just a concoction of the "liberal media establishment". It would serve this nation well, if the Republican Congress and the GOP at large did a refresher course on the Constitution of the United States and the Bill of Rights.

Ex-Treasury Secretary, Paul O'Neill—who probably took that refresher course soon after leaving the Bush Administration—began a year of revelations about President Bush's real foreign policy priorities from the day he took office.

1/11/04: Letter to *The Post*—Re: Mike Allen's "O'Neill: Plan to Hit Iraq Began Pre-9/11"[3]

Paul O'Neill's startling revelation "that President Bush began planning to oust Saddam Hussein within days of taking office and before the attacks of Sept. 11, 2001" exposes "What Massive Deception (WMD)" has been perpetrated on the American people. It is quite apparent now that President Bush entered office with a mind set on avenging his father's would-be assassin. Iraq's WMD stockpile, its links to Al Qaeda, and other "yellowcake" lies were fed to us in order to justify a pre-emptive strike on Iraq. With nearly 500 U.S. soldiers having sacrificed their lives so far and the price tag for the war exceeding $100 billion, President Bush has uncovered the only WMD that really mattered to him—Winning for My Dad! It's no wonder we saw the "Mission Accomplished" banner way back on May Day (a symbolic cry for help?), even though Saddam was to crawl out of his hole almost seven and one-half months later? Ironically, Paul O'Neill's "kiss and tell" book will probably pre-empt any future applications of the Bush Doctrine.

*   *   *

Unfortunately, a majority of the American public didn't seem to care about these "little white lies" that seemed to pepper the Administration's post-facto explanations about anything. One can only hope that President Bush will bring back the "honesty and integrity", which was promised in the first term, before any more damage is done to our democracy?

Fed Chairman, Alan Greenspan, had little or nothing to do with Bush's reelection. The Fed did eventually commence interest rate hikes in June 2004 and bumped up the Federal Funds rate five times before the end of the President's first term.

1/13/04: Letter to *WSJ*—Re: Susan Lee's "Will Greenspan Seal The Bush Re-Election?"[4]

The simple answer to Susan Lee's question is "No". At the outset, I must confess that Ms. Lee did a thorough job analyzing the impact of monetary policy on the economy. However, there are some variables, which Ms. Lee chose to ignore on the fiscal side of the equation, beyond Mr. Greenspan's control. Even if deficits don't matter, at some point of time in the very near future, the effect of simultaneous tax cuts and runaway government spending of the past few years is going to catch up with the continuously low interest rates that have been in effect during this same period? It would be tragic, if Mr. Greenspan would be forced to push the brakes hard on his easy money policy with half-a-dozen rate hikes before the end of this year. If you don't believe it, just look at your favorite barometer of inflation in days gone by—the price of gold! The price of gold went up 20% in 2002 and then another 20% in 2003, and is now hovering at a 14-year high of $425. Ms. Lee was on target with her speculation that "a weaker and weaker dollar might also bring higher and higher oil prices." It already has—with oil prices reaching their pre-Iraq war high of $35 a barrel today. Given his cautious nature, we shouldn't be surprised if Mr. Greenspan makes a "preemptive strike" on inflation sooner than later. How that might affect the economic recovery is as unpredictable as the Bush re-election?

*   *   *

Greenspan chose to be cautious with quarter-point increments, which did not bring in a flood of foreign investments in U.S. treasury securities. Consequently, there was no commensurate lift in the value of the dollar. The greenback reached an all-time low ($1.36) against the Euro at year's end, and was near five-year lows with most major currencies. I am not certain that the weak dollar contributed to the tremendous hike in crude oil prices, which reached an all-time high ($55 per barrel) in mid-October. Gold was also trading at a sixteen-year high ($440 per ounce) towards the end of 2004. Despite this turmoil in commodity markets, the Bush econ-

omy grew at an annualized real growth rate close to 4% in the first three quarters of 2004, while inflation crept up to 3.5% during the same period.

This letter turned out to be my winning entry in a contest run by Al Kamen of The Washington Post's "Federal Page". Mr. Kamen is popular with the Beltway crowd for his "In The Loop" column. In this particular contest, Mr. Kamen wanted readers to choose a contemporary TV show or movie, whose title best represented the character of the Bush Administration. My entry explains why I believed that there could be only one clear choice. The ten winning entries in each category appeared in Al Kamen's column in The Washington Post on February 4, 2004. We all received one of those coveted "In The Loop" T-shirts.

1/14/04: Letter to *The Post*—Re: First In the Loop contest of 2004

There can be only one TV series that truly reflects the character of the Bush Administration. It runs on CBS on Thursday at 10 pm: "WITHOUT A TRACE"

The Bush Administration has seen the loss of nearly 3 million jobs, which don't seem to be coming back. They have vanished—WITHOUT A TRACE!

The Bush Administration has been unable to find Osama Bin Laden for almost 2 and 1/2 years. He seems to have vanished—WITHOUT A TRACE!

The Bush Administration has been unable to find any of Iraq's weapons of mass destruction (WMD). They seem to have vanished—WITHOUT A TRACE!

You get the picture!

*   *   *

By the start of President Bush's second term, the jobs seemed to be coming back, albeit at a measured pace. However, Osama Bin Laden and Iraq's WMD seemed to have vanished forever!

President Bush's proposal for a manned mission to Mars came out of left field. Some conservatives, like Charles Krauthammer, thought it was a good idea? I thought Bush's "indecent proposal" neither made economic sense, nor survived scientific scrutiny.

1/16/04: Letter to *The Post*—Re: Charles Krauthammer's "A Modest Proposal"[5]

What Charles Krauthammer calls "A Modest Proposal" appears more like "An Indecent Proposal" after all the budget math has been done. Irrespective of the relatively minor "election year" funding proposed for this grandiose venture by President Bush, one would have expected Mr. Krauthammer to do his homework. The Apollo program back in the sixties cost us $25 billion—I don't know what that translates to in today's dollars, but the senior President Bush received an estimate of $400 billion for a Mars program back in 1989.

Even if the current President Bush's "moon-hop to Mars" mission was fully funded, has anyone analyzed its scientific feasibility? I did a quick back-of-the-envelope calculation on the proposed "manned-station-on-Moon-first-and-then-onto-Mars" project. The Moon is about 240,000 miles from Earth, and Mars is about 49 million miles from Earth. So what do we achieve by stopping at the Moon, which is 0.8% of the distance to Mars? Nothing, but burn more rockets and fuel, and incur more risk. Besides, the Moon—been there, done that! As for Mars, let's see how the current unmanned missions perform, before we try to determine if "Men are really from Mars"?

*   *   *

This "indecent proposal" was all the more surprising because President Bush has been the most profligate spender since President Lyndon B. Johnson. He had just signed a $400 billion Medicare Plan in December 2003. The Iraq war was last estimated to cost over $200 billion. In addition, he had been pushing through massive tax cuts every year. So it amazed me that President Bush chose this particular period in his presidency to announce what appeared to me as a fulfillment of another of his Daddy's dreams—Bush Sr., who as President had proposed that we land a man on Mars by 2010. Some believed that it was an election year gimmick to portray President Bush as "visionary"—I guess only time will tell.

*Not surprisingly, The Wall Street Journal editorialized about the "GOP Spend-
ing Spree" barely a few days later. I took it as an opportunity to warn President
Bush that he needed to stop spending money like there was no tomorrow. The WSJ
published my letter, under the heading "Hey, Big Spender, Spend a Little Less" in its
January 27, 2004 edition. However, they truncated it in the middle of the third last
sentence, to make it end very effectively with, "I hope this is a wake-up call for President Bush".*

1/20/04: Letter to *WSJ*—Re: GOP spending spree[6]

Notwithstanding the fact that the Democrats controlled Congress for forty
years until 1994, I found your "domestic discretionary spending" table incredi-
bly revealing. With the exception of Ronald Reagan, the four Republican
presidents (Nixon, Ford, Bush I, and Bush II) have out spent the three Democratic presidents ("Big Society" Johnson, "stagflation" Carter, and "the era of
big government is over" Clinton) by wide margins. Even more enlightening is
the fact not one of those three Republican presidents completed two full
terms. I hope this is a wake-up call for President Bush, who can ill-afford to
have the domestic economy out of control at the same time as his foreign policy. Come November, the people are going to ask that illuminating Reagan-
esque question "Are we better off than we were four years ago?" I am not sure
that the answer is very obvious to a majority of the people today!

*   *   *

*In hindsight, it looks like the WSJ editors did do some judicious editing of my
original letter—the domestic economy, while not all peaches and cream, did not get
out of control and thus an incorrigible American public did not seem to care about the
Reagan-esque query.*

A month after Business Week had published my letter in defense of "outsourcing", I took up the mantra with The Wall Street Journal. I was responding to Douglas A. Irwin, who had written an op-ed piece, which said that outsourcing benefited America. My only issue was with the Paul Craig Roberts quote that he had used.

1/28/04: Letter to *WSJ*—Re: Douglas A. Irwin's "'Outsourcing' Is Good for America"[7]

I am a first generation immigrant from a third world country, which is contributing to the "good" of America as a major supplier of "outsourced" services. Consequently, I was distressed by Mr. Irwin's reference to Paul Craig Roberts' comment that said "The United States will be a Third World country in 20 years." I hope that I did not migrate to this country twenty years ago to come full circle with my economic destiny twenty years from now. As one who grew up in a caste conscious society, I get a sense of déjà vu when I hear some Americans gripe about the migration of our white-collar service sector jobs to third world countries. It seems to me that these same Americans had no qualms about a similar loss of our blue-collar manufacturing sector jobs back in the eighties? We not only survived that transformation in our economic paradigm, but it proved to be a successful model for the rest of the developed world to follow. I am confident that, in the long run, American innovation will similarly trump this current paranoia over "outsourcing".

* * *

It appears that the cry over outsourcing gradually died down following the election and Corporate America went back to running efficiently without the feeling of guilt.

On the same day that I was "outsourcing" my pearls of wisdom to the WSJ, I was also trying to lift the fog from the minds of the Post's editors. Peter Feaver had implied in a Post column that we needed to go easy on the "Intel" investigation. I suggested that we could not afford a "strike out" in this department, and we needed to "bring it on" ASAP.

1/28/04: Letter to *The Post*—Re: Peter Feaver's "Fog of WMD"[8]

California's criminal statute has a three strikes law, which puts away repeat offenders for life. In the past few years, U.S. intelligence has struck out twice, first with the 9/11 catastrophe and then with the fake call on Iraq's WMD. The first "intel" failure cost nearly 3000 American lives, while the second "intel" failure has so far cost over 500 American lives. Western intelligence has become the laughing stock around the world, wherein a despot living in a cave tens of thousands miles away can plan sophisticated, simultaneous attacks on our homeland, and yet another tyrant living equally far away can pretend to possess weapons of mass destruction that he no longer had? Yet Mr. Feaver says "let us have a full investigation into the intelligence failure (though let us not expect one during a presidential campaign)." Since when did post-9/11 national security take a back seat to presidential politics? So even as we struggle to come out from under the "fog of WMD", we can ill afford a third "intel" failure. I am therefore suggesting that President Bush's reaction to such an investigation should be to "bring it on"!

*   *   *

Notwithstanding Mr. Feaver's concerns, President Bush appointed the Silberman-Robb Commission in February 2004. It was officially known as the "Commission on the Intelligence Capabilities of the United States Regarding Weapons of Mass Destruction" and its report is expected early in President Bush's second term.

My rants on the subject of Pakistan's "serial nuclear proliferation" activities always fall on deaf ears at the WSJ and the Post. It seems to me that the national media has been reluctant to challenge the Pakistani government's blatant duplicity, which I highlight in this letter.

2/6/04: Letter to *WSJ*—Re: WMD Breakthrough & Pakistan's Dr. Strangelove[9]

In your passion to conclude, "The Bush strategy is working" in "WMD Breakthrough", it appears that you did not compare notes with your neighborly contributor Irfan Husain, who was more circumspect in "Pakistan's Dr. Strangelove". While you acknowledge, "All of that changed with the Bush policy of challenging terrorists and the states that support them after 9/11", Mr. Husain reveals that "Khan's secret contacts with North Korea began to emerge, including a report that he visited Pyongyang 19 times between 1997 and 2002." However, both of you concur on the complicity of Pakistan's military in the proliferation of its nuclear know-how. Your emphatic assertion that "No doubt the Pakistan military, of which General Musharraf is the ranking member, was aware of Mr. Khan's business, or at least turned a blind eye to it" is matched equally strongly by Mr. Irfan's "Many believe that he is being made a scapegoat for successive governments and army administrations that have been party to the export of nuclear technology."

Any rationale individual would therefore conclude from a reading of both of your respected opinions that the government of Pakistan, even after 9/11/01, has continued with its policy of "serial nuclear proliferation" to rogue nations. In fact, two of its beneficiary nations constitute President Bush's "axis of evil". More importantly, Pakistan, although an ally, has indirectly challenged the post-9/11 Bush maxim "You're either with us or against us in the fight against terror." The implicit harm to our national security by Pakistan's betrayal is probably greater than any previously perceived harm from Iraq's WMD. It's about time that we as a nation held our core democratic values to be absolute and stopped differentiating between "good" dictatorships (in Saudi Arabia & Pakistan) and "bad" dictatorships (in the now-deposed Saddam's Iraq & North Korea). Mr. President, the time to change the status quo actually passed us by on 9/11/01, so when our intelligence finally has it right for a change, it's incumbent upon you to do the right thing as well!

*   *   *

It is my belief that, as long as Osama Bin Laden is on the run somewhere in Pakistan, neither the Bush Administration, nor the national media will confront President Musharraf on his government's complicity in the activities of their top nuclear scientist, A.Q. Khan. If President Bush does not solve the A.Q. Khan mystery in his second term, it is likely that Pakistan's nuclear proliferation activities might come back to haunt us?

As a Hindu, who grew up in India, I have lived through violence instigated by religious differences—we witnessed our share of Hindu-Muslim tensions that severely tested our faiths. Consequently, I have repeatedly tried since 9/11, to get the national media to downplay the focus on Islam when they report on the war on terrorism.

2/13/04: Letter to *The Post*—Re: Charles Krauthammer's "The Other Shoe"[10]

Since 9/11 I have read in the mainstream media scores of times about "radical Islam", "Islamic fundamentalists", and now a new reference to "Islamism" from Mr. Krauthammer. Even if one were to ignore the offensive nature of such characterizations, which unfairly targets the religion as opposed to its misguided practitioners, wouldn't it be more appropriate to talk about "radical Muslims" and "Muslim fundamentalists". I don't know what Mr. Krauthammer had in mind when he wrote, "…because the seemingly high-tech West lacks the diabolical and methodical will that Islamism brings to the war"? Again, I doubt Islam or "Islamism" has anything diabolical about it. We have undoubtedly experienced horror at the hands of Islam's perverted interpreters, but must we keep countering that with this rather callous disregard for the religion itself? Let the healing process begin!

*   *   *

In 1998 after India conducted several underground nuclear tests, The Wall Street Journal had editorialized[11] that India often exhibited a "holier than thou" attitude. As an Indian-American, I was intrigued by that comment at the time—wondering what exactly they might have meant. With this letter to the Post, I felt that I was reflecting a similar opinion to what the WSJ editors might have meant back then? Since 9/11, I had been sensing a "holier than thou" attitude being displayed towards Muslims by several media pundits.

With no intention of appearing "holier than thou" at the present time, I would posit that an attitudinal adjustment might be required on the part of some in our media towards Islam.

Election season was upon us. After Senator Kerry had won the first round of Democratic primaries in early 2004, the pundits immediately started scrutinizing his post-Vietnam tolerance for war.

2/23/04: Letter to *The Post*—Re: Joshua Muravchik's "Kerry's Inner Dove"[12]

From a voter's perspective, Joshua Muravchik should realize that it is better to have served in actual combat and then turned into a dove, than to have never seen battle and yet turn out to be a rabid hawk!

*   *   *

More importantly, Senator Kerry's Vietnam war record and post-Vietnam anti-war activities were exploited by a Veterans organization called "Swift Boat Veterans for Truth" to more or less derail his presidential bid. Just like his father had refused to denounce those salacious "Willie Horton" commercials in his 1988 presidential campaign, President Bush declined to chastise the tactics of the Swift Boat veterans. This political calculation—from a man who had never been in a combat zone aside from Thanksgiving Day 2003 in Baghdad—went a long way in getting President Bush reelected.

I could probably crow until the cows came home on the subject of marginal tax rates, but the WSJ editorial page favors only one direction for those rates—down! I have tried on several occasions to engage them in an objective discussion about the relevance of an optimal rate—below which the top marginal tax rate cannot fall—but they refuse to oblige.

2/25/04: Letter to *WSJ*—Re: Thomas Sowell's "Low Taxes Do What?"[13]

I agreed with almost everything Thomas Sowell had to say in his "Economics for Dummies" style discourse. My minor disagreement related to the perception that he leaves behind on the issue of marginal tax rates. When President Reagan implemented "tax cuts for the rich", the 70% top marginal tax rate of 1981 was reduced to 28% by 1988. And, yes, "the federal government collected more tax revenue in every year of the Reagan administration than had ever been collected in any year of any previous administration." However, like that other law of microeconomics relating to diminishing returns, President Clinton's tax hikes of 1993, proved that we had long since breached the equilibrium point between federal revenues and the top marginal tax rate. So despite the Clinton tax hikes, federal revenues continued to rise throughout the Clinton administration as well. Even your editors would concede that given the size of the federal budget, there is an optimal rate beyond which the top marginal tax rate cannot fall? What this optimal top rate should be continues to be a valid point of discussion, and the Bush II tax cuts should help resolve in this decade?

*   *   *

Revenue collection by the federal government has fallen for three consecutive years since the Bush tax cuts were first enacted in 2001. Government spending has gone up every year for three consecutive years since 2001. Any wonder we are back to budget deficits. I have presented empirical data in an article entitled "The Truth About Taxes and Spending" later in this book.

President Bush might be under the illusion that he is emulating Reaganomics. However, aside from the matching budget deficits, there are many other important economic factors that do no line up with the Reagan economy of the 1980s. During the Reagan presidency, the dollar strengthened to a record high in 1984, gas prices tumbled to a record low in 1986, and job creation was robust throughout—each one of these measures has gone exactly the opposite way in the Bush first term.

President Bush started on his moral values campaign early on with what I called "The Passion of the Right" agenda. I pointed this out to the Post, based on several of their own front-page headlines, in one crazy week in late February.

2/28/04: Letter to *The Post*—Re: The Passion of the Right[14]

A rather controversial movie opened earlier this week on Ash Wednesday. This movie is not half as scary as the real life drama, which has been concurrently unfolding in Washington. On Wednesday the Post headlined on its front page, "Bush Backs Amendment Banning Gay Marriage". The next day, the Post reported that "Bush Opposes Additions to Gun Bill". Then, yesterday, the Post informed us "Passage of the Unborn Victims of Violence Act was backed by the White House and President Bush's conservative supporters." Today, Saturday February 28, we learned that "President Bush yesterday dismissed two members of his handpicked Council on Bioethics—a scientist and a moral philosopher who had been among the more outspoken advocates for research on human embryo cells." I have seen "The Passion of the Christ" and I have newfound respect for its director, Mel Gibson. However, it's the real life Washington drama, "The Passion of the Right", which petrifies me!

*   *   *

Understandably, The Post took a pass—but it was the selling of this very agenda that helped President Bush greatly expand voter turnout of his base, which helped him get reelected! It will be interesting to see how many of these social issues will actually be pursued by President Bush in his second term.

The missing labor force in the Bush first term was no myth—my son actually did a high school project on this subject in the summer of 2003, and was among select finalists chosen to present his findings at the Maryland Junior Science and Humanities Symposium in February 2004. His project even won the fourth place prize at this event.

3/6/04: Letter to *The Post*—Re: Job Growth Near Standstill In February[15]

Your front-page headline, "Job Growth Near Standstill In February", has actually been the theme song through much of the Bush presidency. In fact, the hypothesis that "…hundreds of thousands of people stopped looking for work" was the subject of a Senior Research Project conducted by my son under the auspices of Drs. Lawrence Mishel and Jared Bernstein at the Economic Policy Institute in DC last summer. By analyzing trends in unemployment to the employment population (EPOP) ratio and the labor force participation rate (LFPR) in three similar recessionary periods of the past three decades, they estimated that approximately two million people were unaccounted for in last summer's unemployment rate. These "missing" people, representing roughly 1.4 percent of the actual labor force, drop out of the work force as they become "discouraged" and stop looking for a job. Since the Department of Labor expects you to be looking for a job to be classified as unemployed, these "missing" people are never reported in the unemployment rate. It is quite apparent from your report that the February "unemployment rate held steady at 5.6 percent" for the same reason. The Bush economy is not only unable to create new private sector jobs, but it continues to discourage workers from looking for these jobs!

*   *   *

President Bush barely managed to break even in job creation in his first term. If we don't count the "missing labor force", the jobs that were created were more or less equal to the jobs that were lost in his first term. Going into his second term, President Bush has not had the robust job growth that is typical at this point in an economic recovery. It's apparent that tax cuts and low interest rates are not in and of themselves creating new jobs.

President Bush therefore has to do something about the "deficits that don't matter", the trade deficit which keeps on increasing, the undervalued dollar, and the high price of gas—all of which are putting a damper on the US economy and job growth.

9/11 was clearly front and center in people's minds when they opted to reelect President Bush for a second term. The Democrats failed to effectively countermand Karl Rove's 9/11 strategy. Despite the perpetrator of 9/11 not being captured "dead or alive", as the President had promised, a majority of the American public believed that he deserved another term. If 9/11 had happened in President Clinton's first term, I can't imagine he would have been reelected had he not brought its perpetrator to justice prior to the election?

3/7/04: Letter to *WSJ*—Re: Is 9/11 an Issue?[16]

Is 9/11 an issue? You bet it is! By all means, let the Republican National Committee use "the defining event of George W. Bush's Presidency" as the centerpiece of his reelection campaign. If the Democrats had any chutzpah, they would grab this RNC bait and respond immediately with a "Where in the world is Osama Bin Laden?" ad campaign. After all, the mastermind behind the 9/11 attack remains at large despite the Bush Administration's manhunt of the past two and one-half years. One could reasonably argue that we can never be safe until this monster is brought to justice? In the ultimate, however, irrespective of Osama's whereabouts, the President did use the defining event of his presidency to prosecute a broader "war on terror". Come election day, the American public will determine whether he has made adequate progress in its prosecution to grant him another term?

*　　　　*　　　　*

President Bush managed to make 9/11 an effective political issue in his first term to set and promote his foreign policy agenda. Since the WMD fiasco in Iraq has more or less paralyzed the Bush Doctrine, the President's second term foreign policy agenda won't be able to milk the terror cow as well as before.

Despite all the lies about "war and recession", and constantly playing on our fears, and failing the Reagan "better off" test in most people's minds, President Bush won reelection—because for Job No. 1 in the first term, he "chose to defend America every time."

3/12/04: Letter to *The Post*—Re: E. J. Dionne Jr.'s "Job No. 1 for Bush"[17]

Let's grant the Bush Administration that the NBER is wrong and that they "inherited a recession". Then, 9/11 did soon follow, while we were still in 2001. Most of the major corporate "financial scandals" unfolded by the summer of 2002. President Bush has had between two to three years to fix the "serious blow to our economy" caused by what he often refers to as this "trifecta" of shocks. At the end of the day, people are going to get tired of the excuses, and ask themselves "Are we better off than we were four years ago?" It doesn't take a rocket scientist in Pasadena, or the NASCAR dad in Atlanta, or the national guardsman in Mobile, or yet "manufacturing communities like Youngstown and Cleveland" to figure out the answer that we all feel in our gut. Now, it would be telling, if the President's poll numbers went up after yesterday's terror attacks in Spain. Because those negative ads will only make us feel more conflicted—and, it's a shame that they will play on our fears, and not raise our hopes?

*   *   *

But that was then and this is now—Job No. 1 for the second term will have to be the bread and butter domestic issues, since "defending America" in Iraq has not gone exactly as planned during the first term.

It appeared to me that most of the rest of the world believed that the "global war on terror" was a misnomer—how does a community of nations win a prolonged conflict against a shadowy network of violent irrational groups?

3/18/04: Letter to *The Post*—Re: Dana Milbank's "Opinion of U.S. Abroad Is Falling, Survey Finds"[18]

Dana Milbank reported that a recent survey by the Pew Research Center showed that a majority of the people in the Britain, France, Germany, Russia, Turkey, Morocco, and Pakistan believed that the war in Iraq had hurt the war against terrorism. So why would predominantly Muslim countries be in agreement with Western European nations on this issue? In fact, we were the only surveyed country whose majority mindset was on the fringes of this bell curve of popular world opinion. There are two possible explanations for this anomaly. The first one relates to the premise for the preemptive war, which was primarily waged on our conviction that Iraq possessed of weapons of mass destruction. When no WMD were found, it was natural for these rational foreigners to conclude that the war had been "unnecessary". Moreover, the increasing cycle of violence, which has taken hundreds of innocent Iraqi lives in the past few months, is seen as counter-productive in the larger war against terrorism. A second explanation for our contrary view on the efficacy of the "war against terror" lies perhaps in the rather illusive objective that this phrase itself implies to most foreigners. The American Heritage(r) Dictionary defines "war" as "a state of open, armed, often prolonged conflict..." It also defines "terror" as "violence committed or threatened by a group to intimidate or coerce a population..." At the end of the day, most rational people, as the Spanish electorate showed last Sunday, don't have the stomach for prolonged conflict against irrational groups that are prone to violence. They probably think it's time to preempt the Bush Doctrine and "give peace a chance".

*   *   *

In a post-9/11 world, would former Beatle John Lennon, a New York resident for almost a decade prior to his death, still have crooned, "All we are saying is give peace a chance"? It's kind of ironical that President is being forced to "give peace a chance" with the other two members of his "axis of evil", since Iraq has yet to turn out as expected.

When in doubt, we blame France—that's as American as cussing, which also doubles up for "French" in the U.S. of A. In order to better represent the geo-political and economic realities of the 21ˢᵗ century, I believe that France should give up its seat on the UN Security Council to Germany. However, we do have a relationship with France that dates back to the days of the American Revolution—so let's "se réconcil-ier" with the imbeciles!

3/21/04: Letter to *WSJ*—Re: Au Revoir, France; We're Cutting the Cord[19]

It is easy to do the popular thing, like you did in your March 16 "Letters to the Editor" segment, with six letters dumping vitriol all over France. We should definitely be concerned that the results of the recent Spanish elections might send the wrong message to Al Qaeda. But then, shouldn't we have been equally anxious a year ago when our Iraq policy was causing the biggest post-WWII rupture in, what Mr. Colombani referred to as, "the historical alliance between the U.S. and Europe"? What kind of a message did this fracture in our strategic trans-Atlantic partnership send to Osama Bin Laden?

9/11 had managed to isolate Bin Laden's Al Qaeda and coalesce nations worldwide, including several anti-western third world ones, behind our subsequent "war on terror" strategy. History will soon judge whether President Bush's willingness to pursue a preemptive strike on Iraq, at the expense of a fractured "old Europe", was the right thing to do? In the interim, as the world's leading democracy, we should be more troubled by the recent Pew Research Center finding that the majority—in nations such as Britain, France, and Germany on the one side of, and Russia, Turkey, and Morocco on the other side of, the continental divide—believe that the war in Iraq has hurt the war on terror. So I would venture to suggest that our national interests would be better served, not by cutting the cord, but by striking a more conciliatory note with our old friends across the pond.

*   *   *

It appears like President Bush took the advice of more sensible people in his clique because making up with "old Europe" was on top of the agenda at the start of the second term. Well begun, as the saying goes, is half done!

The proverbial stuff really started to hit the fan after Richard A. Clarke, who used to be counterterrorism coordinator in the Bush Administration, came out with his book in March 2004. His exposé followed two months on the heels of Ron Suskind's "Price of Loyalty", which was based on Treasury Secretary Paul O'Neill's two-year tenure in the Bush Administration. But unlike the O'Neill experience, the White House was ready to counter the Clarke tome with their spin machine. I wrote to the Post to highlight some of the facts, which I believed bolstered Clarke's version of events.

3/22/04: Letter to *The Post*—Re: Richard A. Clarke's memoir[20]

The White House is living up to the old saying, "the best defense is to go on the offense". So I wasn't surprised to see Barton Gellman's front page report on Richard A. Clarke's memoir appear at the same time as Condoleezza Rice's editorial page piece entitled "9/11: For The Record". But facts are a stubborn thing, and no amount of spin can change them. It might be worthwhile to highlight a few of these:

- Candidate Bush, appearing in the GOP debate on CNN's Larry King Live on February 15, 2000, was asked "What area of international policy would you change immediately?" and he replied, "Our relationship with China." Barely three months into his presidency, a U.S. Navy EP-3E Aries II spy plane collided with a Chinese Air Force F-8 fighter jet in international waters over the South China Sea, and was forced to land on China's Hainan Island. The ensuing drama gripped the nation for several weeks. One can presume then that it was not only Iraq, as claimed by Richard A. Clarke now and by former Treasury Secretary Paul O'Neill a few months ago, but also China, which was far ahead of Al Qaeda on President Bush's foreign policy agenda in early 2001.

- If President Bush did consider the Al Qaeda threat real, when he took over the reigns from President Clinton, why did he demote his counter terrorism coordinator from a cabinet level position to a staff level one? More importantly, after 9/11, why did he not elevate the position back to cabinet rank?

- Condoleezza Rice states "Because of President Bush's vision and leadership, our nation is safer", then why does he shy away from spending more than an hour with the 9/11 commission to tell them and the American people all about it?

*   *   *

Sadly, the Bush Administration did to Richard A. Clarke what conservatives claim the Clinton Administration used to do its tormentors—attack the messenger! Nonetheless Mr. Clarke's message was a sobering one. Eventually, Ms. Rice did spend ample time with the 9/11 commission.

Also, it appears that China has moved up in the list of priorities for the Bush second term. One can only hope that the Bush Administration does not indulge in petty trade wars with China, but evaluates the totality of the U.S.-China relationship and the relevance of a decades old engagement strategy in the post–Cold War and post–9/11 eras.

Despite the flak that he was taking in the media for his Iraq policy, President Bush tried to find humor in the missing WMD. At the 60th annual dinner of the Radio and Television Correspondents' Association on March 24th, he put on a slide show in which he appeared to be looking for WMD under furniture in the Oval Office. I was simply flabbergasted, so I let my feelings be known to the Post.

3/25/04: Letter to *The Post*—Re: Jennifer Frey's "George Bush, Entertainer In Chief"[21]

Despite having no family member serving in the military, I was simply appalled by President Bush's sense of humor. 571 American soldiers have so far been killed over those WMD, which he now jokes about in such a cavalier fashion. As a self-proclaimed "War President", one would have expected a little more tact from our commander in chief, especially concerning WMD, which were his primary justification to lead us into this preemptive war.

*   *   *

We have gone from a President Clinton, who used to apologize a tad too often, to a President Bush, who has apologized for nothing. But then if a President can't name a single mistake that he might have committed during his presidency, it is unlikely that he has anything to apologize for?

After he had locked the Democratic nomination, Senator Kerry was all over the media. The Wall Street Journal editorial page expressed some faux concern about this overexposure. However, in the final analysis, Senator Kerry was not as overexposed as he was overrated by the media and pundits alike.

3/28/04: Letter to *WSJ*—Re: Daniel Henninger's "Skiing As News: Is John Kerry Overexposed?"[22]

I must have missed the "face plant" on Fox because over on NBC they had John Kerry doing a rather graceful "Look Ma, no hands" glide down a steep hill! Daniel Henninger maybe thinking over exposure, but there are at least some of us experiencing a "Johnny, we hardly knew ye" type of revelation? First our man straddles a Harley, then a power play on ice, and now the dude's snowboarding—what's next? Playing in a rock band—wait a minute—been there, done that! There is only one four-letter word that can describe John Kerry, and its spelt S.T.U.D. So while candidate Kerry might inexplicably garner Mr. Henninger's sympathy, he can only have my envy. As the kids are wont to say, "Rock on, dude"; to which I am tempted to add, "you might be President, one day?"

*   *   *

Whether he still might become President some day—I believe that this is highly unlikely? After the 2000 election drama I had thought, "Gore in Four" was a possibility, until Gore bowed out. The truth is that the American public has become very unforgiving of losing presidential candidates. The days of Adlai Stevenson and Richard Nixon style reruns are most likely over.

In the early spring of 2004, The Bush Administration was strongly against some of its key officials testifying before the 9/11 Commission. President Bush's National Security Advisor, Condoleezza Rice, went on "60 Minutes" and put on a very lackluster performance.

3/29/04: Letter to *The Post*—Re: Dana Milbank and Walter Pincus' "Rice Defends Refusal To Testify"[23]

Your report concludes with Ms. Rice's incredulous answer, "That's the wrong way to look at it" to what had been a very pertinent question on "60 Minutes" from Mr. Ed Bradley. It related to the fact that there have been, as you report, "more terrorist attacks in the 30 months since Sept. 11 than in the 30 months prior." Frankly, Mr. Bradley should have followed up with, "What's the right way to look at it, Ms. Rice?" Ironically, Ms. Rice would have liked us all to see it the way she was spinning it, and not what the empirical data of the past 30 months has established.

*   *   *

It was quite apparent that Mr. Bradley had not been tough enough in his follow-up questions to Ms. Rice. It probably gave her the courage to agree to appear before the 9/11 commission.

It was only a couple of days later that President Bush flip-flopped on the issue of Dr. Rice testifying before the 9/11 Commission. I found this ironical given that the Presidential campaign was in full gear, and President Bush had been pounding on Senator Kerry for his inability to stick with a consistent position on any given issue.

3/31/04: Letter to *The Post*—Re: Mike Allen and Dan Eggen's "President to Let Rice Testify About 9/11" & Dan Balz's "Bush Scores Points By Defining Kerry"[24]

There is a lot of irony in the fact that these two cover stories were juxtaposed next to each other on your front page. On the one hand, Dan Balz reports that President Bush has been running ads for the past month to define Senator John Kerry as a flip-flopper. On the other hand, Mike Allen and Dan Eggen report that "President Bush reversed himself yesterday" regarding Dr. Rice's public testimony before the 9/11 Commission. In the meanwhile, Richard Clarke's underlying charge, that the Bush Administration's invasion of Iraq undermined the war on terrorism, was brought to the forefront again today. As I write this, five more U.S. marines were killed in Fallujah today. NBC News reports that the number of people killed worldwide in March 2004 as a result of terrorist acts is almost 25% of the total number of such deaths since 9/11. At some point of time, the Bush Administration will have to step back and rationally review its "eye for an eye" foreign policy, which is making all of us blind to the realities of the war on terrorism.

*   *   *

Ironically, a foreign policy review appears to have been forced upon the Bush Administration—by the facts on the ground in Iraq and the reality of continuing threats posed by North Korea and Iran—towards the end of the President's first term.

This was a classic case of OOPS! Republican Senator Mitch McConnell wrote an op-ed piece in the Post *and made some startling revelations.*

4/7/04: Letter to *The Post*—Re: Mitch McConnell's "Needs a U.S. Push"[25]

George Santayana, the great American philosopher had warned, "Those who ignore history are doomed to repeat it." By his own admission, Senator Mitch McConnell writes that "Since 1948 Egypt has received more than $59 billion in U.S. foreign assistance." Then Mr. McConnell goes on to add that this assistance has secured "Not greater freedoms", "Not greater tolerance", and "Not greater economic opportunity" in Egypt. By any measure, we have spent at least as much money in Iraq in little over a year, and we expect to establish Iraq as a model for democracy in the Middle East?

*   *   *

After 9/11 we have also been providing Pakistan $600 million annually in aid, and the most notable progress that they have made towards "democracy" is consolidating the power of General Musharraf by amending the constitution to "legitimize" his unelected governance. More significantly, soon after President Bush got reelected, General Musharraf announced that he was breaking his promise to surrender his military title (per the revised constitutional provision) and would continue to remain in control of the Pakistani Army as well.

This certainly was not an auspicious start to President Bush's "freedom and democracy" agenda for the second term. One can only imagine how other Muslim nations must be snickering at this double standard—we continue to conveniently look the other way when democracy starts backsliding in the various allied "Stans" of central and south Asia—that makes us tolerate dictatorships, which "support" us in the war on terrorism. It won't be too long before China and Russia start promoting their own cabal of dictators that they will claim to be indispensable to their respective national security interests.

Post-9/11 events have convinced me of the need for eternally divided govern-ment i.e., the party that controls the White House should never control the Congress at the same time. But unfortunately, this concentration of power will continue through at least 2006. And, we will continue to be ruled by people who never make mistakes and who never need to apologize.

4/12/04: Letter to *The Post*—Re: Dan Eggen's "Memo Not Specific Enough, Bush Says"[26]

As our first MBA president, Mr. Bush should know well enough that CEOs are expected to make tough decisions based on incomplete information. Would an Aug 6, 2001 PDB headline, such as "Bin Ladin Determined To Strike in US—World Trade Center & Pentagon Targeted", have been specific enough for the President to act? It's time someone in the Administration stepped up to the plate and took responsibility for events that happen on their watch. We are tired of the finger pointing—from their past attempts to back-date the recession, to current efforts to blame their pre-9/11 anti-terrorism policy on every branch of government save the executive. For the Bush Administration, it looks like the proverbial buck did stop in the Oval Office…of the Clinton Administration!

*   *   *

It sounded like his "dog ate the memo", when President Bush was vacationing on his ranch back in August 2001? But seriously, it seemed like President Bush wanted that famous August 6, 2001 PDB to specifically say "Bin Ladin Determined To Strike in US—World Trade Center targeted on 9/11/01 at 8:46:40 AM EST, Pen-tagon targeted on 9/11/01 at 9:37:46 AM EST", in order for him to have pre-empted those attacks? After all, preemption did become his doctrine!

Little over a year after the fall of Baghdad, the WSJ editorial page editors came out with a doozy—they recommended that the President be provided with "the option of using a highly precise, low-yield weapon that strikes a specific target than the Armageddon alternative that prevailed during the Cold War."

4/13/04: Letter to *WSJ*—Re: Rethinking Armageddon[27]

The worst possible outcome of the war on terrorism is not about a fear of being prepared for Armageddon. Based on the way the war in Iraq is progressing, our primary concern should be the beginnings of a great religious divide? With the Iraq war being increasingly viewed as a coalition of Christian nations occupying an Islamic country, it has become imperative for us to more actively engage non-Christian nations, such as China and India, in Iraq. The only way these two Asian giants might be willing to consider helping us in Iraq would be if the entire operation were brought under the control of the United Nations. The sooner we turn over Iraq to the UN, the sooner we can re-focus on the real war on terrorism by taking a hard look at its root causes. And, when we do, we will recognize that they point to culprits such as Egypt, Saudi Arabia, Syria, Iran, and Pakistan. If we are going to gain any credibility in the Islamic world, we have to stop coddling Islamic dictatorships in friend and foe countries alike. It's only by establishing economic opportunity linked with democratic principles that have been adapted to the nuances of Islamic law; can we hope to win the hearts of the Muslim people worldwide?

*   *   *

Nearly nine months after the WSJ editorial page made that recommendation, it is quite clear from the insurgency raging in Iraq that we are faced with a serious problem. Not only is there an inter-religious (Christian-Islam) divide between the occupier and the occupied, but also an intra-religious split (Sunni-Shia) amongst the occupied. In this complicated scenario, use of "a highly precise, low-yield weapon" can only inflame a highly volatile situation beyond the breaking point.

The new realities on the ground in Iraq at the start of President Bush's second term make my China and India option less realistic. Instead, I think President Bush must convince Egypt, Jordan, Kuwait, Pakistan, Saudi Arabia, and Turkey to provide a multinational Sunni Muslim army to quell the Iraqi insurgency.

Nearly a year after he had declared "Mission Accomplished" in Iraq, things had not been going swimmingly. With his Administration being pounded with all sorts of revelations, President Bush decided to hold one of his rare press conferences—at the end of which, he seemed to leave more questions unanswered than before the event?

4/15/04: Letter to *The Post*—Re: President's press conference[28]

I am hoping someone on President Bush's staff might help clarify a few items that were not adequately addressed at his press conference:

1. Candidate Bush asserted back in the 2000 presidential debate with Al Gore that he would not use our military in "nation building", which is what they are actually doing in Iraq now. So did he not mean what he said as a candidate?

2. Again, candidate Bush had also opined, "If we're an arrogant nation, they'll resent us." Can President Bush clarify why a majority of the world's people, who loved us so dearly immediately after 9/11, now resent us for the most part?

3. After barely 200 days in office, President Bush took a 30-day vacation that concluded about 10 days prior to 9/11. How many times did the principals meet during his vacation to discuss all the alerts being put out by the NIE (National Intelligence Estimate)?

4. President Bush stated at his press conference, "I don't want to sound like I have made no mistakes. I'm confident I have…maybe I'm not as quick on my feet as I should be in coming up with one." Now that he has had time to think about it, can he get the White House to release a statement confessing to at least the one mistake?

5. President Bush also said at the press conference, "That's what Mr. Brahimi is doing. He's figuring out the nature of the entity we'll be handing sovereignty over." So President Bush trusts a United Nations representative, Lakhdar Brahimi, to figure out what this Iraqi "entity" is, while an insurgency is still raging, and we then blindly transfer power—all inside three months? This is neither Vietnam, nor Somalia…this is a recipe for disaster!

*   *   *

To-date, President Bush has been unable to confess to any mistakes that he might have committed during his presidency. Notwithstanding my skepticism at the time, transfer of sovereignty proceeded on schedule.

The weekend after the President's press conference came Bob Woodward's "Plan Of Attack".

4/18/04: Letter to *The Post*—Re: Bob Woodward's "Plan Of Attack"[29]

After reading the first installment of Bob Woodward's "Plan Of Attack" this morning, I couldn't wait to see what he had to say later on "60 Minutes". I came away appalled by the cavalier attitude portrayed by President Bush when it came to the subject of war in Iraq. Mr. Woodward's book confirms earlier accounts by Bush's former Treasury Secretary, Paul O'Neill, and his former counterterrorism czar, Richard Clarke, that the President was obsessed with Iraq very early in his term. It appears that President Bush might have committed impeachable offenses, based on the following information revealed by Mr. Woodward:

- President Bush approved the re-routing of $700 million of funding, appropriated by Congress for Afghanistan, towards an "Iraq war plan", which he asked General Myers to develop as early as November 21, 2001.

- When General Myers was asked about an "Iraq war plan" in May 2002, he flatly denied it.

- At President Bush's request, Vice-President Cheney and General Myers disclosed "TOP SECRET NOFORN" information to Prince Bandar bin Sultan, the Saudi ambassador, regarding our Iraq war plans on January 11, 2003—two days before the President had even alerted his own Secretary of State.

- President Bush, himself, was not convinced Iraq's WMD were a "slam dunk" as professed by CIA Director, George Tenet, but he still allowed Secretary of State, Colin Powell, to perpetuate the WMD myth to the United Nations.

- President Bush continues to violate the principle of "separation of church and state", by constantly invoking God and a "higher calling" in the implementation of his foreign policy, with which he seeks to "free" the world of selective dictators through the use of preemptive military action!

*   *   *

Bob Woodward's revelations made me even more convinced that "divided government" is what we desperately required. Where was the independent counsel when you really needed one? Alas, how did a respected Secretary of State allow his reputation to sink to "foggy bottom"?

As expected the counter-attack by the conservative media soon followed. The WSJ editorial page gave Mr. Limbaugh room to vent, even though he confessed to not having read the book.

4/22/04: Letter to *WSJ*—Re: Rush Limbaugh's "Woodward at War"[30]

I personally heard Rush Limbaugh admit on his radio show yesterday that he wrote his article, entitled "Woodward at War", on Sunday evening after the "60 Minutes" piece with Bob Woodward had aired. He confessed to not having read the book. Nevertheless, the Journal's editors rushed Mr. Limbaugh's piece to print in what appears to be a "Plan Of Attack" by conservatives to counter Simon and Schuster's PR campaign for Mr. Woodward's book. Why would your esteemed editorial page engage in such petty politics, when the White House itself designated "Plan of Attack" as required reading? Or were you guys in on that master plan, too? I have been reading your paper for almost 18 years, but only in recent years has your editorial page let right wing politics consistently trump your conservative ideology.

*   *   *

The WSJ editorial page, which turned intensely partisan during the Clinton presidency, continued to lose its grip on objectivity during the Bush term. With their timing of the Limbaugh piece, they gave new meaning to the phrase "Rush to Print". Needless to add that my letter lay in "limbo" and never saw light of day until now.

It is important to understand that when I wrote this letter to the Post about the
"Saddamization" of Iraq nine months ago, the insurgency was still in its infancy.

4/25/04: Letter to *The Post*—Re: Robin Wright's "U.S. Moves to Rehire Some From Baath Party, Military"[31]

After reading Robin Wright's report, one wonders if the U.S. administrator of Iraq, L. Paul Bremer, might extend his "re-Baathification" strategy to include a "humbled" Saddam Hussein at some point of time in the near future. Outrageous and heretical as this suggestion might seem, we might recall that during the 1980s Iran-Iraq war, the Reagan Administration not only supported Saddam Hussein but also supplied him with some of the raw materials for his chemical and biological programs. With the current situation in Iraq spiraling out of control, Mr. Bremer could conceivably seek the assistance of a "de-programmed" Saddam Hussein to restore law and order in the country? The Bush Administration could justify this action on several grounds:

- Without WMD, Saddam Hussein is no longer a threat to the United States or his neighbors

- Saddam Hussein is the only one who can prevent Iraq from breaking up into parts à la Yugoslavia

- Saddam Hussein is our best containment-cum-insurance policy against a virulent Iran

- Saddam Hussein was never aligned with Al Qaeda, which is our real enemy

- Re-Baathification, with Saddam Hussein back in the saddle, provides us the quickest, cleanest, and most inexpensive exit strategy out of Iraq

If one thinks this is a far-fetched scenario, which patriotic American would have believed even six months ago that we would resume business dealings with Libya's Moammar Gaddafi!

*   *   *

Today, the insurgents are reigning "fire and brimstone" in Iraq. It appears like only the specter of "Sodom" can prevent Iraq from becoming a "Gomorrah"? As far as the U.S. is concerned, elections in Iraq amount to a Hobson's choice—they will indirectly transfer control of the Iraqi government to the Ayatollahs in Iran. One can only hope that this does not turn out to be déjà vu all over again for the United States as in—"Iranian Revolution Part Deux: An ironical end to the twenty-five year Iran-Iraq War"!

President Bush made deliberate choices, albeit three decades apart, on Vietnam and Iraq. Now, he needs to privately reconcile the consequences of those disparate choices. Just as privately, Senator Kerry must consider his election defeat to President Bush as a blessing in disguise—because now he does not have to resolve the complicated situation in Iraq?

4/27/04: Letter to *The Post*—Re: John Kerry's medal controversy et al.[32]

Senator Kerry should have realized that his primary campaign mantra "bring it on" would sooner or later run into the "Anything Goes School of Political Maiming" mastered by the Bush dynasty? It never ceases to amaze me that leading Bush Administration officials, including the President and Vice President, who never served their country in actual combat, are the ones who wear their patriotism most visibly on their sleeve (i.e. jacket lapel). The answer to the McCarthy era question posed by E. J. Dionne Jr. "Have you no sense of decency, sir?" is redundant. The more pertinent observation is that these guys entered politics because it was their last and only refuge. The sad irony is that if the situation in Iraq does not get better soon, Kerry will be the one who will have to face déjà vu all over again—in dealing with Bush's "Vietnam" for most of his first term!

*   *   *

Notwithstanding my ire at the ugliness of the campaign, I believe it will be a phenomenal foreign policy achievement, if President Bush and his "band of neocons" succeed where President Johnson's "best and the brightest" policy wonks and President Nixon's "madman theory" proponents tried and failed—i.e., to impose a system of government upon a nation against the inherent inclination and history of its people?

When the Abu Ghraib scandal broke, with an initial report on CBS' "60 Minutes II" on April 28, 2004, I missed it. But when those gruesome pictures appeared in the Post a few days later, I could have screamed, "Mayday, Mayday, Mayday!" This might appear to be a theme in this book, but for some karmic reasons the Bush presidency seems to encounter pivotal events around the month of May. In 2001 the fall-out from the EP-3E incident in the South China Sea was barely subsiding when Senator Jim Jeffords decided to quit the GOP giving control of the Senate to Democrats. In 2002 there was a buzz in Washington concerning pre-9/11 intelligence and "about what the President knew and when did he know it". In 2003 the President made that infamous "Mission Accomplished" pronouncement on Mayday itself. Now, it was Abu Ghraib in May 2004…

5/3/04: Letter to *The Post*—Re: Iraqi prisoner abuse[33]

If there were any doubts before, I think they have been laid to rest—this is the beginning of the end! A picture is worth a thousand words, and there is nothing that can be said from our side, which will placate the Muslim world. The irony is that without WMD, our primary justification for toppling Saddam became his brutal regime. On what grounds can we now justify our continued presence in Iraq? Although I previously disagreed with the Bush Administration's decision to rush the transfer of sovereignty by June 30th, I am now inclined to believe that it couldn't happen a day too soon.

*   *   *

No one will disagree that Abu Ghraib fundamentally altered international opinion about President Bush's Iraq venture. More critically, it inflamed the insurgency, which has only become worse every month since then? Whether we can ever completely overcome the stigma of Abu Ghraib is highly doubtful? Along with Camp Delta at Guantanamo Bay and the prison at Bagram Air Base, these three facilities have become an embarrassment to the United States. It's about time President Bush opened up all three of them completely to inspection by Human Rights organizations such as Amnesty International and the International Committee of the Red Cross.

I am getting increasingly convinced that old-line conservatives are more sensible than their neoconservative counterparts. In fact, as regular conservatives get older, they seem to get wiser—Barry Goldwater proved that over the years. George Will, John McLaughlin, William Buckley, and Brent Scowcroft's collective wisdom, on the frailties of President Bush's foreign policy, speaks for itself.

My biggest issue with recent neoconservative doctrines—such as the Bush Doctrine and the Reagan-era Kirkpatrick Doctrine—is that in their implementation, we compromised our fundamental values. The Reagan Administration supported authoritarian and rebel regimes around the world in its effort to topple the totalitarian "evil empire". One of these regimes came back to haunt us—the Mujaheddin of 1980s Afghanistan, pretty much morphed into the Taliban, which then later hooked up with Al Qaeda. Osama Bin Laden was a U.S. ally in the 1980s under the auspices of the Kirkpatrick Doctrine. In fact, until he betrayed the elder Bush by invading Kuwait in 1990, Saddam Hussein was also a strong U.S. ally.

So when conservative pundit, George Will, called for "reassessing comforting doctrines in face of contrary evidence", it made me feel vindicated.

5/4/04: Letter to *The Post*—Re: George Will's "Time for Bush to See The Realities of Iraq"[34]

Every time I give up hope on the "right", they live up to the literal meaning of the word. George Will's illuminating piece on Iraq must have the White House in blather? As a "brown-skinned" American, I would like to point out that the world's largest democracy, India, is a "brown-skinned" nation. However, the British, who occupied India for over one hundred fifty years, helped create a "culture of democracy" before granting India its freedom. Quite ironically, it was a "conservative" British Prime Minister, Winston Churchill, who was very skeptical of India's survival as a democracy. In any case, Mr. Will is right when he warns that the Bush Administration must consider "reassessing comforting doctrines in face of contrary evidence" in Iraq. We cannot hope to establish even a "McDemocracy" via our "drive-thru" occupation and a namesake "transfer of sovereignty" to an Iraqi entity, which remains undefined eight weeks prior to the event.

*   *   *

Undoubtedly, the Bush Doctrine is similarly flawed, in that it continues to support authoritarian regimes in the Muslim world—where ever it has proven convenient to the U.S. With the case for WMD turning out to be an "air ball" as opposed to a "slam dunk", the case for democracy in Iraq should be as important as, if not more, in Egypt, Kazakhstan, Pakistan, Saudi Arabia, and Uzbekistan.

When the Times sought the resignation of Donald Rumsfeld a few days later, I suggested that President Bush proactively fire him instead.

5/7/04: Letter to NY *Times*—Re: Donald Rumsfeld Should Go[35]

"A picture is worth a thousand words", and each one of those horrific pictures is screaming for justice. Donald Rumsfeld's Defense Department is also guilty on two major procedural counts: both, the President and Congress, first learned about this prisoner abuse through the media. At least, that is what they seem to suggest? In any case, no amount of apologies from our side will placate the Muslim world. The irony is that without any WMD to show, our primary justification for the Iraq war changed to the toppling of Saddam Hussein's "brutal regime". Now, we have lost claim to the "brutality" argument as well. Your hope is that "the world is waiting now for a sign that President Bush understands the seriousness of what has happened." If he does, indeed, the President should not be "demanding the resignation of his secretary of defense" as you ask—but instead, he should go ahead and fire him! Justice delayed is justice denied—the future of the Bush Doctrine itself is at stake.

*   *   *

At the end of the day, President Bush did what he is wont to do when the media tests his resolve. Invariably when it comes to a choice between loyalty and competence, the President will err on the side of loyalty. So President Bush not only looked the other way, with regards to the Defense Department's abject failure of leadership in the Abu Ghraib scandal, but he asked Secretary Rumsfeld to stay on as Defense Secretary for his second term. "So there, you can go and stuff it!" was the President's implied message to the venerable Gray Lady.

A few days later, George Will, my newly discovered paragon of virtue, got into the act.

5/11/04: Letter to *The Post*—Re: George Will's "No Flinching From the Facts"[36]

With respect to George Will's first axiom "When there is no penalty for failure, failures proliferate"—is exactly why Secretary Rumsfeld's verbal acceptance of responsibility with no commensurate penalty (his resignation) has no meaning. If Rumsfeld had gracefully and promptly quit, most Americans would be asking "why"? Now as more devastating and dreadful facts unfold, more and more of us are going to wonder "why not"?

As far as the Bush Administration's response to the events at Abu Ghraib is concerned, it has to be a powerful combination of symbolism and substance. By immediately appointing either an Arab-American or an American of the Muslim faith to his Cabinet, President Bush would send a strong message not only to the Middle East but also to the entire Muslim world. And, to prove his commitment to Iraqi democracy, President Bush should sanction a trial of the Abu Ghraib accused by Iraqi jury, which can be selected jointly by Paul Bremer and the Iraqi Governing Council.

*   *   *

Mr. Will had not directly ask for Secretary Rumsfeld's resignation because he had probably assumed that the Secretary would do the right and honorable thing. In any case, Mr. Will did end his article with a Charles De Gaulle axiom, "The graveyards are full of indispensable men." Apparently, President Bush did not think much of that French axiom because he did not dispense with his Defense Secretary. And unfortunately, my suggestion for religious diversity in his cabinet did not see light of day in the Post either.

Whilst all this was going on, the WSJ editorial page was trying to pump up the economy like they often do when their supply side principle is at stake.

5/12/04: Letter to *WSJ*—Re: Help Is Wanted[37]

Your May 10 editorial, "Help Is Wanted" is an economic snapshot, which does not see the forest for the trees. The stock market, which is a leading indicator of economic performance, has been on a downward trend since the beginning of the year. The collective market indexes, unlike your editorial page, have already discounted robust GDP and job numbers. Edwin LeFevre's tape—that never lies—is apparently more concerned with the $7.5 trillion national debt, a $0.5 trillion annual budget deficit, a $0.5 trillion annual run rate on the trade deficit, a record $40 per barrel price of crude, and a negligent Fed that should have begun hiking interest rates back in January. So unbeknownst to you, the title of your editorial provides a metaphorical double entendre regarding the true state of the economy?

*   *   *

In retrospect, while everything I wrote in this letter was true, they were right as well. By the end of 2004, after three years of job losses, the Bush economy finally created 2.23 million jobs. However, it was still about 170,000 jobs shy of a net job gain during his first term. The stock market, which had lost significant value in the first two years of the Bush presidency and seemed to gain it all back in 2003, performed marginally well in 2004. The Dow Jones Industrial Average gained about 3.6% in 2004.

On the down side, however, by year-end "help was wanted" in a number of other areas of the economic spectrum. The dollar was trading at an all time low against the Euro, and at five-year lows against most major currencies. The price of crude oil had soared to $55 a barrel in mid-October and was still trading in the mid-forties by year-end. With the Fed having hiked rates at a snail's pace in the second-half of 2004, inflation was rearing its ugly head, so we were not quite out of the economic woods going into 2005.

Charles Duelfer, Head of the Iraq Survey Group, was yet to come out with his final report to complete the humiliation of the "Iraq-has-WMD-and-in-time-we-will-find-it" crowd. Nonetheless, the WSJ editorial page put its stock in the likes of Gazi George, a former Iraqi nuclear scientist under Saddam, who was quoted by them as saying, "I'm sure they're going to find more once time passes."

5/18/04: Letter to *WSJ*—Re: Roadside Sarin[38]

Your editorial "Roadside Sarin" scrapes the bottom of the WMD barrel in its effort to resurrect the original justification for the Iraq war. There may be but a handful of countries in the world that do not have "warehouses full of commercial and agricultural chemicals". Given the Bush Administration's experience with the Iraqi National Congress leader, Ahmed Chalabi, I hope they do not heed your advice and put much stock in Gazi George. The President appears to have moved past WMD to focus on the reconstruction effort. I think it would behoove your editorial page and other like-minded conservatives to do the same.

*   *   *

Needless to say, Gazi George's assurances turned out to be as reliable as Ahmed Chalabi's. Mr. Chalabi's elaborate deception of the current Bush Administration reminded me of how the Kuwaitis duped Congress to act against Iraq's occupation of their country in 1990. None other than the Kuwaiti Ambassador's daughter had been coached by a global PR firm to offer sham testimony before Congress prior to the Gulf War. In both instances, the U.S. government was manipulated into military action—for the families of American soldiers who lost their lives in these wars, this cannot be very reassuring news.

Meanwhile an insurgency was raging in Fallujah, and the neoconservatives were screaming for blood. I tried to put the situation in perspective with a comparison to the 1980s Sikh insurgency in India, which was crushed with decisive military force. The Indian government paid heavily for this action, and it took a long time for the wounds to heal.

5/23/04: Letter to *The Post*—Re: Lewis E. Lehrman and William Kristol's "Crush the Insurgents in Iraq"[39]

Lehrman & Kristol offer the example of President Lincoln's persistence during the American Civil War of 1861–64, and then advise President Bush that "decisive military blows" must be "struck against violent opposition" in Iraq to realize "strategic success" in the global war on terrorism. I would grant that President Lincoln's tenacity of purpose, and not the actual case of the American Civil War, was the point of comparison.

A more apt situational comparison to the Fallujah insurgency would be the occupation in the early eighties of the Golden Temple (Sikhism's holiest shrine) in Amritsar, India by radical Sikhs, who were seeking an independent Sikh homeland. India's then Prime Minister, Indira Gandhi, ordered "decisive military action", which killed the leader of the radical Sikh faction and did great damage to the Golden Temple. Less than five months later, her own bodyguard, who happened to be a Sikh, assassinated Ms. Gandhi. A backlash against the Sikh community immediately ensued in parts of India, but the movement for a Sikh homeland gradually abated over the next decade. "Strategic success" in this case recently culminated with the appointment of India's first Prime Minister of the Sikh faith.

The larger point to be made with the India example is that striking hard at the insurgency in Fallujah might achieve a "decisive tactical victory" in the short term, but it will need to be sustained with a Lincoln-esque tenacity of purpose to guarantee "strategic success" in the long term. The American Civil War lasted four long years, and Reconstruction went on for much longer. Do we have what it takes to persevere in Iraq for the long haul? Recent events in Iraq and at home have cast serious doubts whether we can, as President Kennedy promised, "pay any price, bear any burden, meet any hardship, support any friend, oppose any foe to assure the survival and the success of liberty."

As the presumptive Democratic nominee, Senator Kerry made a major foreign policy address, in which his vision seemed to be on target for the problems in the Middle East.

5/30/04: Letter to *The Post*—Re: Glenn Kessler's "Kerry Says Security Comes First"[40]

John Kerry's preference for security over democracy appears to be the fashionable position to take in the post-9/11 era. It seems foolhardy to explicitly state one's view in this regard, especially in what Kessler calls "dealing with Pakistan, Saudi Arabia, Egypt, China and Russia." However, Senator Kerry is on target when he says, "You look at Egypt and Saudi Arabia and you have governments who like us and people who don't. In the case of Iran, you have a government who doesn't and people who do." So one would naturally expect that we would aggressively push for democracy in Iran? We don't have to opt for another "flowers and sweets" type of pre-emptive thrust in Iran, but nevertheless assist its citizens in a different sort of "popular revolution".

Also as an Indian-American, I am dismayed that India did not figure prominently in Senator Kerry's foreign policy vision. With India's recent change towards a left-of-center government, and an ongoing domestic backlash over outsourcing of jobs to India, one would have hoped that Senator Kerry had something to say about India? Entrepreneurial Indian-Americans have created thousands of high-skilled domestic jobs in the high-tech sector within the past decade. Yet it is the outsourcing of relatively low-skilled jobs to India that garners all the headlines. Ironically, outsourcing makes American companies more efficient and profitable, which in turn helps our domestic economy in the long term. If Senator Kerry were to see the forest for the trees, he would engage India as a long-term strategic partner of the United States and pursue economic, political, and military relationships with this rising Asian power to the mutual benefit of both nations.

*   *   *

With the end of the Cold War and the collapse of the Soviet Union, U.S. foreign policy quickly adjusted to expand NATO into Eastern Europe. However, in the post-9/11 era, I think we ought to make major re-alignments in the Asia-Pacific region as well. It seemed to me that Senator Kerry had missed an opportunity to differentiate himself from President Bush.

When an op-ed piece by Pakistan's dictator, General Musharraf, appeared in the Post, I literally saw red. I let off some steam, while quoting facts, but they never ran my letter. I must confess that, while I did read about the "the lesser of two evils" quote in press coverage from the subcontinent in the immediate aftermath of 9/11, I have been unable to source it on the Internet in recent searches.

It's also important to understand the Indian perspective on the global war on terrorism. The Indian government believes that it has been fighting terrorism in the state of Kashmir since 1989. This was the year that the Soviets withdrew from Afghanistan and left behind an army of unemployed jihadists, who then quickly redirected their efforts towards Kashmir—with unabashed support from Pakistan, who in turn claims these jihadists are "freedom fighters".

6/1/04: Letter to *The Post*—Re: A Plea for Enlightened Moderation[41]

Is it the policy of The Washington Post's editorial page to give dictators, albeit, newly "benevolent" ones who are also allies of the United States, valuable space to pontificate? In the immediate aftermath of 9/11, President Bush offered the likes of General Musharraf an escape clause, by stating that the United States would pursue nations that "continue to harbor terrorists". It is a well-known fact that Al Qaeda had been harbored by Afghanistan's Taliban regime, which in turn was actively supported by Pakistan and its military throughout the 1990s. In fact, "the militancy that was sparked in Afghanistan", which General Musharraf now bemoans, "was instead allowed to fester for a decade" by none other than Pakistan. Even as we speak, a similar militancy continues to incubate in thousands of "madrassas" across Pakistan. General Musharraf told his nation in a speech, shortly after 9/11, that in agreeing to cooperate with the United States, he was "choosing the lesser of two evils"! It amazes me that the Post sees it fit to give General Musharraf a voice, even as his country continues to harbor our number one enemy—Osama Bin Laden? I wonder if Moammar Gaddafi is sharpening his quill in anticipation.

*   *   *

Despite the fact that Osama Bin Laden might be still somewhere inside Pakistan, President Bush continues to reward Pakistan for its "cooperation" in the war on terrorism. In mid-June, he designated Pakistan as a major non-NATO ally, which probably ruled out a meaningful strategic relationship with India for a long time to come. At year's end, General Musharraf responded to President Bush's generosity by going back on his promise to step down as Army Chief. Apparently, he believed that Pakistani security was enhanced when he as a non-elected official held, both, the President and Chief of the Army, positions.

Meanwhile, President Bush thinks he will be more successful in bringing democracy to Iraq, which has never really experienced the concept before, than urging Pakistan to restore democracy, which it enjoyed as recently as five years ago. Any wonder why they hate us—could it be because our foreign policy is illogical and inconsistent.

Ronald Reagan was President when I first came to America in 1983. Those were the "Morning in America" days. I actually liked President Reagan, even though I didn't particularly agree with all his policies. So when he passed away on June 5, 2004 I felt like eulogizing him, while simultaneously distinguishing his legacy from that of our current President. Much to my dismay, the Post chose not to share my letter with its readers.

6/6/04: Letter to *The Post*—Re: Tribute to President Reagan[42]

Alas, the Great Communicator has "slipped the surly bonds of earth to touch the face of God." I am reminded of a couple of his other quotes, which are even more relevant today. In his 1989 farewell address to the nation, President Reagan said, "America is respected again in the world and looked to for leadership." What a difference the past couple of years have made to that legacy? Then in his 1992 address to the Republican National Convention, Ronald Reagan uttered these pearls of wisdom, "And whatever else history may say about me when I'm gone, I hope it will record that I appealed to your best hopes, not your worst fears, to your confidence rather than your doubts." Yes, sir, you most certainly did and for that alone you will be sorely missed!

*   *   *

Later in the summer, I built on this letter and submitted a full-fledged tribute as an op-ed piece to the Post. It was entitled, "The Relevance of Remembering Reagan" and will appear later in the book, since the Post declined to run it as well.

Amongst all the things that were going on in mid-2004, the unfolding genocide in the Sudan had not received any attention in the mainstream media—until the Post editorialized about it.

6/20/04: Letter to *The Post*—Re: As Genocide Unfolds[43]

While you make an impassioned plea regarding events unfolding in the Darfur province of the Sudan, I have yet to see a single front-page story in any of the national newspapers or even a news item on the evening newscasts of the broadcast networks relating to this unfolding genocide? Unfortunately, the average American's attention can only be grabbed by a headline or a sound bite. Until then, I suspect, it will be difficult for a President in the midst of an election cycle to get distracted by world events, which haven't even appeared on the American radar. Sadly, we could be headed for a Rwandan-type déjà vu?

*   *   *

It would be another month before the U.S. Congress passed a resolution labeling the situation in Sudan's Darfur region as "genocide". And, President Bush finally put out a statement on September 9, 2004 saying, "we have concluded that genocide has taken place in Darfur."

However, at the start of his second term, President Bush surprisingly went silent on the subject of Darfur.

In the early summer, the 9/11 Commission put out a preliminary report, which was being spun by partisans on both sides to their advantage. The Bush Administration was trying hard to convince the American public about a pre-9/11 link between Al Qaeda and Iraq. Meanwhile, I continued to harp on Pakistan's pre-9/11 links to the Taliban, which used to harbor Al Qaeda in Afghanistan. Why was that "collaborative relationship" any less significant than the one that the Bush Administration was trying to establish between Saddam and Al Qaeda?

6/22/04: Letter to *The Post*—Re: E. J. Dionne's "9/11 Credibility Gap", Richard Cohen's "Grand Delusion", Walter Pincus and Dan Eggen's "Al Qaeda Link To Iraq...", et al[44]

E.J. Dionne brings into question the Bush Administration's "credibility" and Richard Cohen infers that Cheney and Bush were "delusional" about Al Qaeda's pre-9/11 link to Iraq. Meanwhile, Walter Pincus and Dan Eggen report that 9/11 Commission member, John Lehman, might have been confused over similar sounding names in Saddam's Fedayeen and Al Qaeda. While we seem to be going to great lengths to either establish or disprove a pre-9/11 link between Al Qaeda and Iraq, we know for certain about a "collaborative relationship" that existed among the Taliban, Al Qaeda, and Pakistan's Inter Services Intelligence prior to 9/11. Isn't it ironical that the only three countries (Saudi Arabia, Pakistan, and the U.A.E) that had pre-9/11 diplomatic ties with the Taliban remain "allies" of the United States? In fact, Pakistan's pre-9/11 support for the Taliban and its post-9/11 nuclear proliferation activity (vis-à-vis its top scientist, A.Q. Khan) has done more damage to our interests than Saddam Hussein ever did. The recent award by the Bush Administration to Pakistan of the status of major non-NATO ally, while Osama Bin Laden may still be hiding inside Pakistan, is a travesty of justice!

*   *   *

In typical Bush fashion, Pakistan got rewarded for its incompetence—its inability to find Osama Bin Laden, the founder of Al Qaeda, who was known to be hiding somewhere in Pakistan since his escape from the Tora Bora mountains in December

2001. And yet, the Bush Administration was simultaneously justifying its Iraq War on the basis of some tenuous link between Saddam and Al Qaeda?

One of the hit movies of the summer of 2004 was Michael Moore's "Fahrenheit 9/11", which steamed up not only the box office, but also a lot of conservatives across the country. Surprisingly, some liberals had a few qualms as well. Richard Cohen of the Post was one of them.

7/1/04: Letter to *The Post*—Re: Richard Cohen's "Baloney, Moore or Less"[45]

Richard Cohen in denouncing Michael Moore's "assault on the documentary form" makes a cavalier assumption that the average Joe is as politically well informed as the pundit class? Even if Moore's documentary implies that the case against President Bush rests largely on "guilt by association", it's up to the American public to determine that. Mr. Cohen might be surprised to know that very many people, who do not read the newspapers or watch TV news programs on a daily basis, do go to the movies and this documentary will be their primary source of political information.

*   *   *

The brouhaha only helped "Fahrenheit 9/11" make box office history for a documentary and in January 2005 it picked up the People's Choice Award for Favorite Motion Picture of the year. However, Michael Moore's attempt to influence the presidential election by acquiescing to show "Fahrenheit 9/11" on Pay per View the night before election day failed miserably.

The day after July 4ᵗʰ, I wrote in a letter to the Post that Senator Kerry ought to get more assertive and propose definitive solutions on Iraq.

7/5/04: Letter to *The Post*—Re: John F. Kerry's "A Realistic Path in Iraq"[46]

John F. Kerry puts the cart before the horse by suggesting "It is only by pursuing a realistic path to democracy in Iraq…Only then can we heal the wounds between our allies and ourselves." President Bush has repeatedly said that he has asked our NATO allies and the UN to become more involved with the new sovereign Iraq. Apparently, they have not been very forthcoming with their assistance? It is therefore necessary for Mr. Kerry to distinguish himself from President Bush by asserting, "As your President, I will heal the wounds between our allies and us. I guarantee that I will get NATO and the UN involved in the peacekeeping operations and the reconstruction in Iraq. I promise to draw down US military forces in Iraq within the first year of my presidency." While making this case to the American people, Mr. Kerry needs to boldly combine "realism and idealism"; only then will he be able to convince us that his foreign policy can "win the war on terrorism around the world"?

*   *   *

On Friday, August 6ᵗʰ Senator Kerry in an interview on National Public Radio said, "I believe that within a year from now, we could significantly reduce American forces in Iraq, and that's my plan." The Post never published my letter, but Senator Kerry somehow seemed to have got the message.

When the bipartisan Senate Committee on Present Danger editorialized in the Post, I had to let them know that their religious qualification of terrorism needed to go. Sadly, the Post did not run my objection.

7/20/04: Letter to *The Post*—Re: Joe Lieberman and Jon Kyl's "The Present Danger"[47]

I am loath to point out that the Committee on Present Danger is going to have a very hard time in its third incarnation, if it does not redefine its mission to exclude the religious element. The committee must de-emphasize the "Islamic" nature of the terrorism, even if it is blatantly obvious. Recent history has proven that it is impossible to "win" religious wars even when identifiable nation states engage in them. The half-century old India-Pakistan row and the decades old Israel-Palestine conflict, while purportedly over disputed territories, are in reality pitting Hinduism vs. Islam and Judaism vs. Islam at their core. In the current war on terrorism, we are dealing with transient network cells that cross-pollinate across international boundaries, which is a major problem in itself. Why then do we want to make it harder by associating these with a major world religion? It might seem naïve to wish away the religious component behind this terror threat, but the only way to succeed is to stop our effort from being viewed as a modern-day crusade.

*   *   *

History has proven time and again that wars, which are based on religious differences, last for the longest time. Neither side is ever willing to concede that they are the "children of a lesser God". The real "present danger" is the western world's consistent reference to "Islamic fundamentalism", which only fuels the anger of the Muslim world. If the war on terrorism is ever to be won it has to be divested of its religious inferences.

The 9/11 Commission Report turned out to be the hot new read of the summer and quickly ranked #1 on several national bestseller lists. Based on the Post's extensive coverage at the time, I thought that the 9/11 Commission had seemed reluctant to make the buck stop at a unique individual or office.

7/23/04: Letter to *The Post*—Re: 9/11 Commission Report[48]

The question becomes "In its effort to issue unanimous findings, did the 9/11 Commission Report hold back in its criticisms of either the current or previous executive branch of government?" It is relatively easy to assign blame on "institutional failures" but the buck has to stop somewhere. One gets the feeling that the 9/11 Commission expects that the American public will deliver its verdict anyway, on the current Administration's pre-9/11 governance, in the upcoming general election. However, the Post's coverage of their Report indicates that the 9/11 Commission has left a lot to be "read in between the lines" as follows:

- 7 of 10 'operational opportunities' that were missed in detecting the 9/11 plot occurred in the first nine months of the Bush Administration.

- The 1995 'legal wall' memo was a non-issue in the summer of 2001 and probably dredged up by Attorney General Ashcroft to deflect attention from his department's conduct prior to 9/11, including his own deafening silence to the then Acting FBI Director's warnings on the terror threat.

- The departing Clinton Administration had about three months after the bombing of the USS Cole to retaliate against Al Qaeda. It would have taken at least as long to fully investigate the incident before any action could be realistically taken. It was therefore the incoming Bush Administration's responsibility to have followed up on this matter.

- President Clinton's 1998 cruise missile attacks on Bin Laden's camp in Afghanistan and the chemical plant in the Sudan were roundly condemned by the Republicans, and were used as a slur (à la the million dollar missile at a fifteen dollar tent) by the Bush campaign in 2000. This action, in fact, was justified and based on 'slam dunk' intelligence provided by the CIA. If Bin Laden had been killed with these strikes, 9/11 might never have happened?

• The Bush Administration's inaction against Iran, despite evidence that there was a "collaborative operational relationship" between Iran and ten of Al Qaeda's 9/11 hijackers, is a violation of the Bush Doctrine.

The ultimate measure of safety is the Bush Administration's own color-coded system, which has never fallen below the yellow (elevated) level. We have yo-yoed between yellow and red (high) since the schema was introduced shortly after 9/11. Just because we are now aware of our threatened condition does not make us any safer than we were prior to 9/11. If we were really safer, then the 9/11 Commission should have recommended that the alert level be reduced by at least one level below where we started!

*   *   *

In the ultimate, the 9/11 Commission seemed eager to recommend solutions without a complete analysis of the problems. If heads don't roll, for paradigm-shifting events that were caused by a breakdown in our national security apparatus, then I would dare to suggest that problems have not been fully analyzed? Consequently, when the Bush Administration talked about us "being safer, but not safe"—they were indulging in an inane play with words, which had no conclusive meaning.

Vice President, Dick Cheney, had told Tim Russert, moderator of NBC's "Meet the Press", in an interview on March 16th 2003, just three days prior to the start of the war, "Now, I think things have gotten so bad inside Iraq, from the standpoint of the Iraqi people, my belief is we will, in fact, be greeted as liberators." This preposterous statement, so close to the launch of "shock and awe", was based on the intelligence gathered from the likes of Iraqi expatriates, Dr. Ahmed Chalabi and Professor Kanan Makiya. Dr. Chalabi, who was the special guest of Mrs. Laura Bush at the January 20, 2004 State of the Union speech, was subsequently unceremoniously dumped by the White House as the situation in Iraq started to turn sour. Nonetheless, our friends at the Journal's editorial page were still strongly backing Chalabi, and editorialized about it on August 11, 2004. I simply wondered what Chalabi was doing in Iran?

8/11/04: Letter to *WSJ*—Re: The Chalabi Fiasco Continues[49]

Your editorial does not address the glaringly obvious question, "What is Ahmed Chalabi doing in Iran?" Unless he is negotiating with Iran, on behalf of the Bush Administration, to forgo its nuclear program—his presence in Tehran can only be viewed as threatening to the continued stability of Iraq and hence counter to the immediate interests of the United States?

∗   ∗   ∗

It was long after this letter was written that I learned about some of the conspiracy theories involving Dr. Chalabi. One of them had him as the mastermind of a grand plan in cahoots with the Ayahtollahs in Iran to use the United States to topple Saddam Hussein and then install a Shia government in Iraq. Irregardless of who the planner might have been, the plan has pretty much unfolded along those lines. In fact, it kind of meshes with what I had alluded to earlier in the book—with the Shia in control of Iraq's government, Iran will have finally won the Iran-Iraq War after 25 years.

President Bush needs to turn this situation to the advantage of the United States by cultivating the evolving Shia oil power structure as represented by Iran-Iraq to counter the mature Sunni oil consortium symbolized by Saudi Arabia-Kuwait-U.A.E. Given that Venezuela's Hugo Chávez has been threatening to turn off the spigot, we could use a more stable alternative supplier.

Any reader, who has noted the ratio of letters relating to Bush foreign policy as opposed to Bush economic policy, will recognize how smartly the Bush Administration had removed the spotlight away from the domestic economy going into the 2004 election. Conservatives, such as Robert Novak and the WSJ editorial pages, were painting the unemployment picture like it was as good as in the Clinton years. I pointed out that their frame of reference was disingenuous to say the least?

8/12/04: Letter to *The Post*—Re: Robert Novak's "Uncertain Trumpet"[50]

Robert Novak writes, "Furthermore, the July unemployment rate is 5.5 percent—a low rate and exactly what it was in July 1996 when Bill Clinton was seeking reelection." When this statement is read at face value it is true, but it does not paint the entire picture. I have seen it mentioned recently at least a couple of times in The Wall Street Journal editorial pages as well. What they don't tell you is—when Bill Clinton assumed office in January 1993 the unemployment rate was 7.3%, and he had created over 9 million new jobs by mid-1996. Whereas, when George W. Bush assumed office in January 2001 the unemployment rate was 4.2%, and as of July 2004 he still shows a net loss of over 1 million jobs. Mr. Novak should realize that when he blows the same "uncertain trumpet" as his Republican colleagues, it only produces noise.

*   *   *

Job growth continues to be lackluster at the start of President Bush's second term. He will need to combat various economic factors that are often at odds with each other. For example, a weak dollar typically affects imports because consumers have to pay higher prices for foreign goods. Despite a dollar that has weakened through much of Bush's first term, however, imports have boomed and our trade deficit has exploded. This might suggest that business incentives to promote exports are not necessarily going to further crimp the greenback. The challenge will be then to lift the value of the dollar at the same time as revving up our export engine. This would be a state of nirvana—a stronger dollar would help the travel and tourism industries at home while business investments favoring export growth would create more jobs.

In October 2003 Army Lieutenant General William G. "Jerry" Boykin, while in uniform, told an evangelical Christian group that Islamic extremists hated the United States "because we're a Christian nation." With reference to a Somali war-lord, he went on to say, "Well, you know what, I knew that my God was bigger than his. I knew that my God was a real God, and his was an idol."

When the Defense Department's Inspector General, who was charged with investigating General Boykin's behavior, issued his report the Post editorialized that "the findings completely miss the point."

8/23/04: Letter to *The Post*—Re: Missing the Point[51]

I would dare to suggest that it is the Post's editors who are "Missing the Point"? I have read on numerous occasions that Karl Rove's strategy for President Bush's reelection entails courting the base—made up of "evangelical Christians". Rove has apparently concluded that getting four million more votes from this base will win George W. Bush another term? If this logic were true, does it not explain why Secretary Rumsfeld would avoid chastising General Boykin's for his "bigoted remarks"!

*   *   *

In retrospect, I think my letter nailed this one on the head—so I wish the Post had published my letter at that time. We have since learned that the evangelical Christian base turned out in even larger numbers for President Bush then Karl Rove had wanted. More importantly, both, Secretary Rumsfeld and General Boykin, continue in their jobs in the Bush second term.

The reference to the "seven fat years" in this letter is a play on the title of WSJ Editor Robert Bartley's book on the Reagan presidency.

8/29/04: Letter to *WSJ*—Re: Health and Poverty[52]

Your editorials entitled "Health and Poverty" and "Poor Statistics" bring out an interesting "karmic" fact—in the past couple of decades, the poverty rate has risen primarily during both the Bush presidencies. After bottoming out in 1989, at the end of the first "fat seven years" under President Reagan, the poverty rate climbed steadily until 1993. It then resumed a steady decline during the second "fat seven years" under President Clinton through 2000. We have now seen the poverty rate rise again every year since 2001. War, recession, little or no job growth, increased poverty, etc.—can anyone convince me that "The fault, dear Brutus, is not in our stars"?

*   *   *

Like I have said before, I was a strong believer in the inevitability of the Bush family "karma", until President Bush blew my theory out the water by getting reelected. Nevertheless, the poverty statistic is a fact—poor people could not catch a break in either of the Bush Administrations. Let's hope President Bush does better by them in his second term—it would be the Christian thing to do.

When your stars are aligned, nothing can go wrong. Despite this "mother of all flip-flops", President Bush escaped with little or no damage. Although he backtracked shortly after, he was probably right about the difficulty in winning a war against an ambiguous enemy.

9/1/04: Letter to *NY Times*—Re: Flip-Flop-Flipper

President Bush yet again confirmed the old adage that "there is many a slip between the cup and the lip", when he told Matt Lauer on the "Today" show on Monday, "I don't think you can win it." It being the war on terrorism, which has become President Bush's raison d'être for reelection, given that everything else (economy, Iraq, foreign policy, etc.) is a losing proposition for him as reflected in most opinion polls? President Bush thus committed this "mother of all flip-flops" on the signature issue of his campaign—winning the war on terrorism. Then, barely twenty-four hours later in a speech to the American Legion, President Bush flipped his position back to what he had expressed originally to Larry King a few weeks ago—that, in fact, we can win this war on terrorism? So the President has one-upped Senator Kerry to become a flip-flop-flipper!

✳   ✳   ✳

On a more serious note, President Bush's winning the war on terrorism is analogous to President Johnson's winning the war against poverty. If one believes that we did win the latter war and are now living in a "Great Society", then one can most certainly believe that we will win the war on terrorism, and the entire Middle East will become a "Great Democratic Society"!

The Republican philosophy has evolved substantially from what it used to be in the days of Ronald Reagan. This became quite evident at the Republican National Convention in 2004 and came across plainly in President Bush's acceptance speech.

9/3/04: Letter to *NY Times*—Re: Mr. Bush's Acceptance Speech[53]

President Bush's 21st century version of "The New Deal" is centered in the GOP's "firm belief that the only thing we have to fear is fear itself." By harping on the tragedy of 9/11 and the war on terrorism through most of his acceptance speech, President Bush is appealing to, what Ronald Reagan once characterized as, "our worst fears as opposed to our best hopes." I suppose President Bush has determined the only way to achieve "catastrophic success" at the ballot box is by instilling a "frightened optimism" in our collective psyche?

*   *   *

Thus an opportunistic pessimist replaced yesteryear's eternal optimist, whose perpetually cheerful demeanor had brought us a classy "Morning in America" campaign. In stark contrast, President Bush, by constantly recycling the fear that average Americans associated with 9/11, rode a terror wave back into the White House.

On the heels of the Republican Convention came the Labor Day weekend, after which is the traditional start of the "real" Presidential campaign. Over this week- end, I broke my nearly twenty-month hiatus from submitting regular op-ed articles to national publications. In fact, over the summer I had already put together a few pieces that I wanted to share with a wider audience during the midst of a crucial Presidential contest. Despite my "best hopes", the Post editors declined to publish any of the articles that I sent them in the week following Labor Day.

In any event, after hearing President Bush's acceptance speech at the Republican National Convention, I not only wrote the above letter to the Times, but also sub- mitted—an op-ed article, which I had drafted earlier in the summer—to the Post. In it, I remembered President Reagan quite fondly. However, I concluded with a sharp distinction between his way of looking at America's future and President Bush's markedly different approach.

9/4/04: Op-Ed submission to *The Post* entitled, "The Relevance of Remembering Reagan[54]"

It seems kind of ironical to be "remembering" Reagan, who was gradually deprived of this very faculty during a long final journey into, what he himself had called, the "sunset of his life". Nonetheless, some memories from the Reagan years have as much significance today as they had when the Gipper was battling the "Evil Empire". When I came to the United States in 1983, it was undoubtedly a glorious "morning in America". The country had climbed out of a long recession, the economy was growing once more, jobs were being created in large numbers, interest rates were falling, inflation had been tamed, and times were looking pretty darn good. President Ronald Reagan had made it all happen in a little over two years at the helm.

In the foreign policy arena, however, "dawn" was not yet on the horizon. In fact, with Reagan's introduction of Pershing II missiles in Western Europe, the infamous Doomsday Clock had moved to within three minutes of mid- night by 1984. This was the closest reading for this symbol of nuclear catastro- phe since 1953, when the world had been but two minutes away from the apocalypse. Nevertheless, Reagan firmly believed in finding "peace through strength", so he significantly boost defense spending in furtherance of this goal. He boldly denounced the Soviet Union as the "Evil Empire" and called for a futuristic missile defense system that was derided as "Star Wars" by the media. Even though "Star Wars" never saw light of day, Reagan had also made a rather prophetic judgment about the fate of the "Evil Empire". In March 1983, he proclaimed, "I believe that communism is another sad, bizarre chapter in human history whose last pages even now are being written." In retrospect, it seems to me that some of these fundamental presidential visions have a gestation period of eight years before their fruition. Both, Kennedy's desire to put a man on the moon and Reagan's death wish on the "Evil Empire", took a little over eight years to fulfill. In 1991 the Soviet Union ceased to exist!

Much has already been written about Reagan's innate optimism and his omnipresent sense of humor, which was often self-deprecating and never offensive. In addition to having a sense of humor, Reagan was humble enough to recognize that he was not infallible. He did not hesitate to take responsibility, when a truckload of explosives slammed into the marine barracks in Beirut and killed 241 American soldiers. He told the nation, "If there is to be blame, it properly rests here in this office and with this president. And I accept responsibility for the bad as well as the good." The significance of this mea culpa was that it occurred barely eleven months before he was up for reelection. In the middle of his second term, when the Iran-Contra scandal was unraveling, Reagan proffered this gem of an apology, "A few months ago, I told the American people that I did not trade arms for hostages. My heart and my best intentions tell me that *is* true, but the facts and evidence tell me it is not." Clinton got lambasted for his tortured definition of "is", but Reagan's "is" turned out to be a redeeming use of the present tense given the circumstances.

After a decade long struggle with Alzheimer's disease, alas, the Great Communicator finally "slipped the surly bonds of earth to touch the face of God." But I would be remiss if I did not mention another couple of his quotes, which have even more relevance to the Presidency today. In his 1989 farewell address to the nation, President Reagan said, "America is respected again in the world and looked to for leadership." What a telling difference the past couple of years have made to that legacy? Then in his 1992 address to the Republican National Convention, Ronald Reagan uttered these pearls of wisdom, "And whatever else history may say about me when I'm gone, I hope it will record that I appealed to your best hopes, not your worst fears, to your confidence rather than your doubts." Given the post-9/11 culture of fear that has been allowed to permeate our lives, one would hope that with the passing of the Great Communicator, a new dawn will soon be ushered in, so that

Ronald Reagan's America can once again aspire to being that "shining city upon a hill"!

*   *   *

If one might have wondered prior to reading this article, what is the relevancy of a Reagan eulogy in a book on the Bush presidency, I trust that doubt has vanished. I would hope it might also help President Bush adjust his modus operandi during his second term.

One of the issues that was definitely flying below the public's radar in the 2004 election was the runaway government spending that had occurred on President Bush's watch. There had been no let up since my "wake-up call" to President Bush in a letter, which was published by the WSJ on January 27, 2004. Now, if one still believes that supply side economics actually helped increase revenues in the federal coffers, or one just assumed that Democrats were the really big spenders, then the following article will be quite revealing.

9/4/04: Op-Ed submission to *The Post* entitled, "The Truth About Taxes and Spending[55]"

It was actually President John F. Kennedy, a liberal Democrat, who first proposed tax cuts on marginal income tax rates. In 1964, the top marginal tax rate was reduced from 91% to 77% and then to 70% the following year. The top rate fluctuated in the 70% to 77% range until President Reagan, a conservative Republican, dropped it to 50% in 1982, and then again to 28% by 1988. Interestingly, the Bureau of Economic Analysis (BEA) reports that federal individual tax receipts as a percentage of GDP were 9.05% in 1982 and fell to 8.23% by 1989. So much for supply side theory, which postulates that tax revenues are boosted in the long term because of the incentives that marginal rate cuts provide to top rate filers?

It should also be noted that from 1961–80, a Democratic-controlled Congress managed federal outlays such that the average annual budget deficit was a paltry $24 billion during this entire period. By contrast, from 1981–1997, the average annual budget deficit was an eye-popping $178 billion. It so happens that Republicans took control of the Senate twice (in 1986 and again in 1994) during this period and they have been in control of the House of Representatives since 1994. This awkward fact belies the popular myth surrounding the GOP as the party of deficit hawks.

Nevertheless it was a Republican President, George H.W. Bush, who led the way to fiscal sanity with a courageous hike in the marginal tax rates in 1990, and he was soon followed by Democratic President Clinton with equally bold tax hikes in 1993—these helped build a surplus of nearly a half-trillion dollars in the federal coffers from 1998–2001. Here's the kicker: the BEA reports that federal individual tax receipts as a percentage of GDP actually rose from 7.61% in 1993 to 10.11% by 2000.

The economic record of the past 40 odd years indicates that there has to be an optimal number for the top marginal tax rate. No one believes in a top marginal tax rate as high as 91%, and facts have shown that we cannot support a top marginal tax rate as low as 28%. At least not at the current level of committed federal spending on various government programs, which only continue to expand at a rate that is always higher than the rate of inflation. In any case, the top marginal tax rate had been at 39.6% from 1993 through 2000. President George W. Bush's tax cut plan of 2001 dropped this top rate to 38.6% in 2002, and then a revised tax cut plan in 2003 further reduced the top marginal rate to 35% in 2004. During this same period, runaway government spending has once again produced massive budget deficits. We have gone from a $236 billion budget surplus in 2000 to a $374 billion budget deficit in 2003, and the projected 2004 budget deficit is estimated at $500 billion.

To put all of this in perspective, we need to take a look at yet another indicator, which is the measure of federal revenues as a percentage of GDP. Per the Office of Management and Budget records, federal receipts, which were at 19.6% of GDP in fiscal 1981 when Ronald Reagan became President, had sunk to 17.6% of GDP in fiscal 1993 when President George H.W. Bush left office. In fiscal 2000, which was President Clinton's final year in office, federal receipts peaked at a record 20.8% of GDP—the highest in fifty years. Yet, only four years later they reached a nadir of 16.6% of GDP—the lowest since 1959. Any wonder then that federal individual tax receipts as a percentage of GDP also fell to 7.4% in 2003, the lowest level since 1966.

It should be quite apparent by all of the evidence presented so far that today's top marginal tax rate is not optimally in sync with the rate of government spending. We cannot eat our cake (cut taxes) and have it too (increase spending) when it comes to the long-term economic health of the nation. No one likes to raise taxes; yet we must ensure that revenues are in alignment with spending. The simple truth is that the average of the top marginal rate over the past ninety years (1913–2002) has been approximately 61%! With today's top marginal rate roughly 26 points below that ninety-year average; one would conclude that supply-siders have won their argument on a principle, which has not been entirely corroborated by the facts?

*   *   *

It should surprise no one that President Bush has turned out to be the most profligate spender since President Johnson's concurrent escalation of the Vietnam War and launching of his "Great Society" programs. In just his first term, President Bush one-upped LBJ by launching a major Medicare initiative, two "nation-building" wars, and three huge tax cuts. Yet to come, a manned exploration of Mars, privatization of Social Security, and the making all of his tax cuts "permanent". I don't expect the WSJ editorial page to renew my "wake-up call" to President Bush in his second term because they favor at least two of the three "yet to come" initiatives that I have mentioned.

Since government spending was out of control and tax cuts had dramatically reduced federal revenues, I kept wondering how long the Federal Reserve would be asleep at the wheel. The Federal Funds rate had been pegged at an unsustainably low 1% for almost a year. When I wrote the first draft of this article in mid-June 2004, the Fed had yet to begin its rate hikes, the first of which then occurred on June 30th. So in mid-June, I had wondered if the Fed Chairman was "fed-up", which was meant to be a pun to indicate that a series of quick rate hikes was required to ward-off inflation. Disappointingly, "Greenspan Fed-Up?" got a thumbs-down by the Post.

9/4/04: Op-Ed submission to *The Post* entitled, "Greenspan Fed-Up?[56]"

Since 2001, President Bush's tax cuts and runaway government spending have pushed the federal budget deficit to an all-time high. Both, the Congressional Budget Office and the Office of Management and Budget, estimate that the federal budget deficit for the current fiscal year will be in the $500 billion range. Even if "deficits don't matter", as Vice President Cheney is wont to say, the simultaneous effect of tax cuts, burgeoning government spending, and precipitously low interest rates over a prolonged period is bound to have an adverse effect on the economic recovery.

While the fiscal side of economic policy is beyond Mr. Greenspan's control, he certainly manages the monetary side of the equation. A popular measure of inflation in days gone by used to be the price of gold. The price of gold shot up 20% in 2002, another 20% in 2003, and then hit a 14-year high of $425 in January 2004. Also, the dollar's persistent weakness during the same period has further exacerbated the upswing in oil prices, which hit an all-time high of $42 a barrel in early June 2004. Thus, the window of opportunity, for Mr. Greenspan to make a "preemptive strike" on inflation, might have already passed. Both, the Producer Price Index and the Consumer Price Index, have each risen at an annualized rate of 4.8% in the first half of 2004. Mr. Greenspan will be thus forced to push the brakes hard on his protracted easy money policy with several rate hikes before the end of this year. But will these rate hikes be too little, too late?

Mr. Greenspan was accused of waiting too long to cut interest rates at the end of the previous recession in 1991? Although the Fed had lowered the Federal Funds rate from 8.25% at the start of that recession in June 1990 to 6% at the end of that recession in April 1991. When the Fed was finally done with rate cuts, it maintained the Federal Funds rate at a thirty-year low of 3% for sixteen months from October 1992 through January 1994. The annualized real GDP growth rates during the corresponding five quarters were 4.5%, 0.5%, 2.0%, 2.1% and 5.5% respectively. In January 1994 the Fed suddenly began a series of nine rate hikes, doubling the Federal Funds rate from 3% to 6% in little over a year. Mr. Greenspan made a preemptive strike against his old nemesis, despite the annual rate of inflation in 1993 being a mere 2.8%.

So who clipped the wings of the old hawk? In the current scenario, the Fed began a series of eleven rate cuts in January 2001 and dropped the Federal Funds rate from 6.5% to a forty-year low of 1.75% by the end of that year. During this entire period, we were deemed to be in a recession but the National Bureau of Economic Research would not officially confirm this fact until mid-2002. Nevertheless, Mr. Greenspan continued his easy money policy by hacking away at interest rates once again in November 2002 and July 2003, by which time the Federal Funds rate stood at a 45 year low of 1%!

In the meantime, GDP grew at annualized rates of 7.4%, 4.2%, 4.5%, and 3.0% in the past four quarters from July 2003 though June 2004. It is therefore quite apparent that the U.S. economy is firing on all cylinders. So we now have—a robust economy, a Congress that is spending money like there is no tomorrow, soaring energy prices, a weak dollar, and inflation that has already penetrated into the producer pipeline and is now seeping into the consumer channels as well. Despite all of these warning signs—we have a Federal Reserve that is asleep at the wheel of our economic destiny.

With data so overwhelming, it might be fair to ask, "Has Greenspan lost his touch?" If the Fed does move aggressively to reign in inflation during the latter half of 2004, will it stifle economic growth? On the other hand, if Greenspan continues to move with "a slow hand", will soaring inflation negate growth anyway? How will the old maestro finagle monetary policy in the face of this impending dilemma without causing an economic crisis? The political brouhaha notwithstanding, "Fasten your seat belts, it's going to be a bumpy ride!"

*   *   *

Chairman Greenspan was not as "Fed-Up" as I thought he should have been. The Fed began a measured pace of rate hikes (25 basis points at a time) in June 2004 and the Federal Funds rate was upped five times through the end of President Bush's first term to 2.25%. As expected, annual inflation in 2004 was 3.35%, which was the highest since the 3.44% in 2000, and it seemed to be headed further up at the start of President Bush' second term.

In this fourth piece in the series, I wanted to highlight the fact that nobody in the Bush Administration was asking the most potent electioneering question of all time—"Are you better off than you were four years ago?" The GOP's revered icon, Ronald Reagan, had introduced this very pertinent query into our quadrennial lexicon in his 1980 campaign against Jimmy Carter.

9/4/04: Op-Ed submission to *The Post* entitled, "Four More Years?[57]"

With the presidential election less than four months away, this would be a good time to put the Bush Presidency through the Ronald Reagan litmus test. This test has become the gold standard since that conservative icon introduced it in 1980, when he ran for President against Jimmy Carter. The test asks a simple question of the American people, "Are you better off than you were four years ago?"

Every President is usually gauged by his performance on two main fronts: domestic and foreign policy. This article will not cover the foreign policy aspects of the Bush presidency. On the domestic policy front, a good measure of performance is the state of the economy. Since different people's responses can be rather subjective, I decided to objectively analyze actual empirical data on the economy. I looked at several different economic categories and compared their values at the start of the Bush term (January 2001) to their corresponding values in June 2004.

The Fed blessed the Bush economy with thirteen rate cuts, which started in January 2001 and ended in June 2003, bringing the Federal Funds rate to its lowest point since 1954. From a business standpoint, banks have been lending money at their lowest rates in over thirty years. Mortgage rates have remained at historic lows through the Bush Presidency fueling a housing boom that has pushed home ownership to a record 68%. After a mild recession in 2001, economic growth was sluggish in 2002, but picked up to a more robust 3.1% in 2003. Despite an easy money policy, inflation was surprisingly contained through the first three years of the Bush term, as increased consumer spending was countermanded by lackadaisical business investments.

However, the Bush Administration's honeymoon with the Fed might finally be over. The war with Iraq has kept the price of gas at elevated levels for a prolonged period. Despite robust GDP growth, the unemployment rate remains stubbornly high, and the Bush presidency is still short by over one million jobs. The combination of tax cuts and uncontrolled government spending has sent the federal budget from a surplus to a deficit during the Bush Presidency. Our national debt will be approximately $7.3 trillion dollars by the end of fiscal 2004. A key leading indicator of economic performance has always been the stock market. In the three and one-half years of the Bush presidency, the Dow Jones Industrial Average has been almost flat, and the tech-heavy NASDAQ is still down over 25%. I have captured all of these key statistics in the table below:

Economic Category[58]	1/2001	6/2004	Comments
Federal Funds Rate	5.98% avg.	1.03% avg.	Lowest since Nov 1954
Bank Prime Rate	9.05% avg.	4.00% avg.	Lowest since Mar 1972
10 year T-bond yield	5.16% avg.	4.73% avg.	Down 8.3%
30 year FHMLC rate	7.03% avg.	6.30% avg.	Mortgage rate down 10%
Housing Starts SAAR	1.60 million	1.97 million	5/2004 number, up 23%
Inflation Rate annual	3.76%	3.04%	Avg. latest 12 mos. Down 19%
Price of Texas Crude	$29.58/barrel	$38.02/barrel	Up 29%
Average Price of Gold	$265/ounce	$392/ounce	Up 48%
U.S. Retail Gasoline Price	$1.46/gallon	$1.86/gallon	Up 27%
Annual real GDP growth	3.7% in 2000	3.1% in 2003	Over previous year; down 16%
Unemployment Rate	4.2%	5.6%	1.1 million less non-farm jobs
Index of Help Wanted	77	39	Down 49%, '87=100
Federal Budget Balance	+$236 billion	-$375 billion	Fiscal year-end 2000 & 2003
U.S. National Debt	$5.67 trillion	$6.78 trillion	Fiscal year-end 2000 & 2003

Economic Category[58]	1/2001	6/2004	Comments
Dow Jones Industrial Avg.	10578 (1/22)	10435 (6/30)	Down 1.35%
NASDAQ Index	2758 (1/22)	2048 (6/30)	Down 25.7%

When all is said and done, the Bush economy has been a mixed bag. Based purely on the supply side nature of the stimulus (tax cuts) to the economy and the concomitant increases in government spending and national debt, one would be tempted to judge it as "déjà voodoo all over again" in the classical Reagan tradition. However, President Reagan created eighteen million new jobs. President Bush does not have a lot to hang his hat on to, when it comes to economic performance? Quite simply, the "feel good" factor is missing, and that is a key ingredient when the Average Joe is mulling that succinct Reagan query, "Am I better off than I was four years ago?" More tellingly, one never hears any official of the Bush Administration or the Republican party ask that question in any public forum. It is like they are afraid to hear the answer!

*   *   *

No one really asked the question on a sustained basis during the 2004 campaign, not even senior leaders from the Democratic Party. Amazingly, thanks to the GOP's superior positioning and messaging strategy, the average Joe was more hung up on the war on terrorism than in his individual well-being. The rest as they say is history.

This is the fifth and final article from my "Labor Day Weekend of Love" series. I had noticed for the longest time that there were six key elements in a presidential candidate that contributed heavily to the candidate's winning potential. So I decided to do some research and see how my "six counts of presidential calculus" played out. My model performed rather well with past contests, so I used it to forecast the outcome of the 2004 presidential election.

For the record, President Bush won the 2004 Electoral College by 286-251 over Senator Kerry—my model had Kerry tipping Bush by approximately the same margin[i]!

9/4/04: Op-Ed submission to *The Post* entitled, "Six Counts of Presidential Calculus"

With the recent passing of Ronald Reagan, I was overwhelmed by the bipartisan affection for this President. It made me wonder, "What made this man tick?" Upon further analysis, I determined that we inherently use six counts to get the measure of a President. These six qualities, which I metaphorically refer to as the "six C's of separation", are: Character, Charisma, Confidence, Chemistry, Communicability, and Camera-friendliness. These "C" notes determine whether a President or presidential candidate is making music to our ears, and it is with these "C" strokes that they paint us a vision.

To validate my hypothesis on these "six C's of separation", I decided to grade the candidates of the past six presidential contests using the afore-mentioned six criteria. Not surprisingly, I was able to confirm the Electoral College results going back to 1980 fairly accurately. In order to do this, I used a five-point scale (E=Excellent for 100 electoral votes, G=Good for 75 electoral votes, S=Satisfactory for 50 electoral votes, P=Poor for 25 electoral votes, and F=Failure for 0 electoral votes) to rate competing candidates on each of the six

---

i.   My six counts of presidential calculus, originally compiled back in July 2004, showed Kerry winning by a margin of approximately 50 electoral votes. However, back then, I had selected Kerry as the winner on the "charisma" count. Even if this were true back in July 2004, I suspect that President Bush and Senator Kerry were tied at a "satisfactory" charisma level by election time. If all the other counts held true as originally forecast, President Bush then wins the Electoral College by an approximate count of 300 to 275! The real life result had President Bush winning by 286 to 251.

criteria. I awarded "winner-takes-all" points for a candidate who obtained a higher rating in any particular category, and I split points equally for similar ratings in any specific category. While we do have a total of 540 electoral votes in the U.S. presidential election system, my model is only a predictor of candidate performance. Thus, it is theoretically possible for a candidate to win 600 electoral votes, in my model, by scoring an unmatched E in all six categories. In fact, this was the case in 1984, when Ronald Reagan swept Walter Mondale 600 to 0 in my model and by 525 to 13 in real life. Also, grades in a particular category were awarded on the basis of my perception of the candidate's performance around the time of the actual election. Thus, it was possible for Reagan to score a "G" for "Character" in 1980, and then an "E" for "Character" in 1984. My justification being that we came to know Ronald Reagan's character far better in 1984, after he had served four years as President.

In any case, I first looked at the most closely contested presidential election in recent memory by analyzing the two main candidates in the 2000 contest:

Category	Bush	Gore
Character	G (75)	S (0)
Charisma	S (50)	S (50)
Confidence	S (0)	G (75)
Chemistry	G (75)	S (0)
Communicability	P (0)	G (75)
Camera-friendliness	S (50)	S (50)
"SIX-COUNT" TOTAL	250	250

It should come as no surprise that we had such a squeaker in 2000, when Gore won the popular vote by over a half-million votes but lost the Electoral College by 266 to 271 to Bush.

When I analyzed the 1996 match-up, my six-count model gave Clinton a 400-175 victory, while the actual 1996 Electoral College score was 379-159. By considering the 1992 race as a two-man race between Bush-Clinton, I got a similar result in all categories as in the 1996 Clinton-Dole contest. The actual 1992 Electoral College score was 370-168 in favor of Clinton. In the 1988 match up between Bush-Dukakis, I had Bush handily defeating Dukakis by 400-150, close to the real life score in which Bush won 426-111. The final historical test of my six-count model was the 1980 Carter-Reagan duel. My six-count total of 550-75 in favor of Reagan was slightly off the mark from his actual victory, which he pulled off with a 489-49 tally.

The true test of the efficacy of this model will come after the results of the 2004 presidential election. Based on my current understanding of the two prime contenders, I have rated them as follows:

Category	Bush	Kerry
Character	E (100)	G (0)
Charisma	S (0)	G (75)
Confidence	S (0)	G (75)
Chemistry	G (75)	S (0)
Communicability	S (0)	G (75)
Camera-friendliness	G (75)	G (75)
"SIX-COUNT" TOTAL	250	300

With Ralph Nader in the race, Kerry's advantage per my model could be adversely affected. In any case, based on my *six counts of presidential calculus*, it appears that we have another tight race ahead of us. The news coming out of Iraq in the next two months will have a direct impact on President Bush's confidence, communicability, and camera-friendliness. If the news is good, the six-count total will swing dramatically in his favor, and if the news is bad, President Bush will be sent home to Texas!

*   *   *

My six-count model intentionally disregarded the most obvious C—content, which usually breaks along party lines. Nonetheless, President Bush's content (message) in 2004 had unusual crossover appeal.

So the presidential campaign was upon us. While the Republican National Convention had been going on in New York, a ghastly hostage crisis was brewing half a world away in Russia. The day after the RNC concluded on September 2nd, a horrible massacre of Russian school children occurred in Beslan. All manner of editorial pages across the country condemned this appalling action by Muslim terrorists. The Journal wanted "the vast majority of Muslims who condemn terrorism speak out publicly." I politely pointed out why this was unlikely to happen.

9/7/04: Letter to *WSJ*—Re: The Children of Beslan[59]

"Communism lost ground during 50 years of the Cold War" because, when all was said and done, it was largely a battle of ideologies—dominated by mind games that were played out over the years amongst the various "chess players" that occupied the corridors of power at the Kremlin, the White House, 10 Downing Street, et al. During the Cold War, absence of religion was our big fear—we believed that the godless communists would not hesitate to destroy us? But they did not—because hate, the core driver behind violent response, was fundamentally lacking. They, the communist masses, might have envied us, but they did not hate us.

In the war on terrorism, it is the preponderance of religion that is our biggest apprehension. Given that some of these Muslim radicals have exhibited a "go for broke" mentality, how can we expect to make any progress with the ideological struggle to win their hearts and minds, while we continue to fight them in the streets of Baghdad? We have also seen Israel's "eye for an eye" strategy escalate into a never-ending cycle of violence in the Middle East. Do you really expect "the vast majority of Muslims who condemn terrorism speak out publicly" under these circumstances?

∗ ∗ ∗

President Bush needs to not only remove the religious component from the war on terrorism, but he also needs to rethink his "axis of evil" philosophy. Since the "evil empire" was godless, the evil reference was apt. Thus, North Korea could still belong to an "axis of evil". However, Iran is an Islamic Republic and it can only hurt our cause by referring to it as evil. A value judgment that breaks along religious lines is fraught with danger. Besides, it is in our long term interests to reconcile with

Iran—their people do not hate us and are likely to forgo "The Great Satan" moniker as reconciliation progresses.

Democrats, either out of sheer naiveté or uncommon decency, never seemed to cap-italize on the fact that President Bush had failed to bring Osama Bin Laden to jus-tice more than three years after the 9/11 attacks. When the selfsame fact eluded Maureen's keen mind, I felt obliged to point it out.

9/16/04: Letter to *NY Times*—Re: Maureen Dowd's "Pre-emptive Paranoia"[60]

Maureen Dowd forgot to mention one of the most critical issues that has pretty much shadowed the Bush presidency—the perpetrator of 9/11—Osama Bin Laden. Another "vast left-wing conspiracy theory" would have us believe that Osama has been held in captivity by U.S. forces in Pakistan for some time now, and that he will be produced for the world to see as an "October sur-prise"—thus sealing Bush's re-election? So, in yet another instance of pre-emptive paranoia, the Democrats have refused to capitalize on another broken Bush promise—to deliver Osama "dead or alive". In the meantime, we are expected to continue to believe that President Bush will keep us more secure, even as the man behind 9/11 continues to haunt us from his cave half-a-world away!

*　　　　　*　　　　　*

As was widely anticipated, Osama Bin Laden did turn out to be the "October surprise" of the 2004 presidential election. However, it was a surprise that was not orchestrated by the Bush Administration, but one of Bin Laden's own making. On October 29, 2004 just days before the election, Osama Bin Laden released another one of his infamous video taped messages. In it, he warned the American public, "Your security is in your own hands." The fear implied in the message dovetailed nicely with the theme of the overall Bush campaign.

On a fine September day, three different columnists and the Post editors opined about Bush foreign policy. I saw a common thread weaving through their articles—the need for consistency in our relationships with the Muslim world.

9/21/04: Letter to *The Post*—Re: Broken Promises, Rejecting Turkey And the Future, et al.[61]

Pakistan could very well become the next Turkey, if it undertook similar "dramatic economic, political and social reforms" to use Fareed Zakaria's eulogy to a real NATO ally? But then, per Richard Cohen, Washington has chosen to "settle for a pro-American strongman such as Pakistan's Pervez Musharraf." It is ironic that President Bush is compelled to tolerate General Musharraf's various flip-flops, even as he tries to convince the rest of the world that the U.S. does not have, what George Will calls, "dubious dreams about Iraq."

*   *   *

If by the end of this book, readers are tired of hearing the words consistency, convenience, and core values, my book would have achieved its purpose. The key is for someone to get the message across to the Bush Administration, so they can get it right in the second term.

Barely five weeks prior to the election, Al Hunt of the Journal opined that neither Bush nor Kerry had convinced the American public regarding their claim to the job. I tried to disavow President Bush's claim by citing the "better off" test.

9/24/04: Letter to *WSJ*—Re: Albert Hunt's "Neither Guy Has Made the Sale Yet"[62]

Per your own paper's poll, President Bush has failed the Ronald Reagan litmus test for reelection. Not only do a majority of the people believe that the country is worse off than it was four years ago, but they also believe the country is still moving in the wrong direction. So with an approval rating under 50% this close to the election, the prospects of a second term for President Bush seem unlikely. If he does win, I would think that "The fault, dear Brutus, is not in our stars, But in ourselves" and we would deserve what we get.

*   *   *

As it turned out we will have to live with "fear more years". The Daily Mirror, a London tabloid, put out a sarcastic front-page headline on November 4, 2004 "How can 59,054,087 people be so DUMB?" with reference to President Bush's reelection. It made news around the world. However, it looks like President Bush had the last laugh, when official U.S. election results, reported a couple of months later, had Senator Kerry closer to the "DUMB" people total with 59,028,109 votes.

Following the first Presidential debate, the liberty vs. security theme became a topic for discussion. "Vladimir" as in Vladimir Putin had been mentioned in the debate.

10/2/04: Letter to *The Post*—Re: The Truth on Russia[63]

A key "Truth on Russia" dawned on me during the first Presidential debate. When President Bush referred to President Putin as "Vladimir", I finally realized the extent to which our President is willing to tolerate the erosion of liberty at the expense of security. As the popular saying goes, "charity begins at home". Since 9/11 we have seen a slow but steady degradation of our core democratic values at home, which makes it harder for us to be the moral beacon for fledgling democracies worldwide. President Bush's poor performance in the debate is a direct result of his alienation from real people in real surroundings on the campaign trail. His behavior is thus becoming increasingly autocratic and therefore even more indulgent of dictatorial regimes—Saudi Arabia, Egypt, Pakistan, and now, Russia—which are supportive of his "war on terror". Unfortunately, this indulgence carries a long-term cost that might be harder for us to bear than any perceived short-term gains.

*   *   *

After their first meeting in June 2001, President Bush had said about Putin, "I was able to get a sense of his soul." My gut reaction at the time was—"Wait a minute; I thought godless communists didn't have a soul?" I sense that President Bush, in his dealings with the ex-KGB holdover from the Soviet era, maybe violating a cardinal Reagan principle—trust but verify! President Bush cannot afford to let Russia slide back into empire mode.

It never ceases to amaze me how quickly the media had condemned President Clinton for "lying" about sex. Yet when we learned that President Bush had essentially lied about Iraq's WMD capabilities, programs, "program related activities", and what have you—in most of the media's viewpoint, he only "misled" us because his actions were not deliberate.

Well, on October 5, 2004 the Times editorialized, "The foundation for the administration's claim that it acted on an honest assessment of intelligence analysis—and the president's frequent claim that Congress had the same information he had—has been steadily eroded by the reports from the Senate Intelligence Committee and the 9/11 commission."

10/5/04: Letter to NY *Times*—Re: The Nuclear Bomb That Wasn't[64]

How egregious does the fault have to be, before some brave soul in the media will come forth and boldly state that several members of the Bush Administration, have not "terribly misled", but downright lied to the American public in making their case for war against Iraq? And, knowing what they know now, why can't anyone one of them (Bush, Cheney, Rumsfeld, Powell, Rice) have the courage to apologize to the American public for some of their more blatant mistakes? Like Senator Kerry said during the first debate, one can be "certain and wrong". However, if none of them is willing to make an AA-type of acknowledgement that they have erred, the Iraq situation is only going to get worse before it can get better. Eventually, the Bush Administration must recognize that we all want it to get better—the sooner, the better!

*   *   *

I failed in my attempt to get the Times to make the leap of faith from "misled" to "lied" because they never published my letter. The whole effort reminded me of a bumper sticker that I had seen during the Presidential campaign, "When Clinton lied, nobody died!"

After Charles Duelfer of the Iraq Survey Group presented his preliminary report to the Senate Armed Services Committee on October 6, the Times noted that UN sanctions had worked. I went a step further to point out that it was the Clinton Administration, which had enforced those sanctions and the attendant inspections in Iraq.

10/7/04: Letter to NY *Times*—Re: The Verdict Is In[65]

You forgot to mention that President Clinton has also been absolved by Mr. Duelfer's report. While Clinton had called for regime change back in 1998, he did not foresee the need to preemptively strike Iraq to bring it about. The sanctions and inspections enforced during the Clinton Administration had pretty much rid Iraq of WMD!

*   *   *

The Bush Administration's humiliation on WMD was complete, when the Post headlined a front page story on January 12, 2005 "Search for Banned Arms In Iraq Ended Last Month". The White House Press Secretary admitted at a press briefing the same day that "there no longer is an active search for weapons." President Bush said later that he had appointed a panel to investigate "why the intelligence about Iraq's weapons was wrong."

I also wrote to the Post on the same day to suggest that the Presidential candidates talk about how they would seek to prevent such flawed intelligence from being used in the future in the making of critical foreign policy choices.

10/7/04: Letter to *The Post*—Re: Weapons That Weren't There[66]

Your editorial is right in seeking answers from the presidential candidates about the justification of a preemptive war that is based on intelligence, which later turns out to be seriously flawed. However, now that we have undertaken one, it is more important to understand how these candidates would seek to remedy the situation, so that it never happens again? Also, since our system of government is based on truth, the whole truth, and nothing but the truth, it is critical that the President first apologize to the American people and the international community for this horrendous mistake, even if he still believes that the war was justified. It is an acute embarrassment to find out that Saddam Hussein's government had been largely telling the truth about its WMD capability just prior to the war. Finally, with Al Qaeda now firmly ensconced in Iran and several parts of Iraq, we might have just been better off (i.e. safer) with a stable dictatorship in Iraq (similar to the ones in Egypt, Pakistan, and Saudi Arabia). Because, even if we do manage to leave Iraq in a relatively stable manner, Iran and Al Qaeda won't let it last for long—which will eventually make America even less safe than it was prior to 9/11!

*   *   *

There is much to contemplate in this letter so I really wish the Post had run it. In any case, President Bush could never apologize for having taken the nation to war on false premises. From a political standpoint, it would be tantamount to admitting that American soldiers had died because of a mistake—which was supposed to never happen again after Vietnam?

George Will turned out to be "right" about the direction in which America leaned.
So I am the one who is now "seeing red and feeling blue" after the last election.

10/10/04: Letter to *The Post*—Re: George Will's "Why America Leans Right"[67]

George Will's "Why America Leans Right" left me unconvinced. If one looks at the electoral map of the United States, the major population centers along the east coast, the west coast, and in the Midwest, for the most part, still "sing the blues" of liberalism's heydays. Despite the expanse of the south, the plains, and the Rocky mountain states, conservatives like Will tend to "see red" where they must? More significantly, conservatives keep harping on the fact that America has become this large canvas of red states—as if our democracy is now assigning one vote per square mile as opposed to one vote per person. Isn't it ironical that the America, which supposedly leans right, voted in a majority for the liberal Al Gore and the left-wing radical Ralph Nader in the last general election? The proof of the ideological pudding, Mr. Will, lies in the ballot box, which has tilted to the left in the past three presidential elections.

*   *   *

It should be noted that the general media's persistent use of the infamous "sea of red" map is the single most disingenuous illustration of the "one person, one vote" principle of our representative democracy that I have ever seen. I hope that Democrats will counter this misrepresentation in people's minds with something more meaningful?

David Broder in a column on October 10, 2004 in the Post, said that the ulti-mate "enforcers of accountability" would be the American people—because they con-trolled the ballot.

10/10/04: Letter to *The Post*—Re: No Accountability[68]

David Broder's "No Accountability" misses an important aspect pertaining to the culture of the Bush Administration. It's a Cosa Nostra like expectation of loyalty at the expense of the truth. This expectation has resulted in high-rank-ing Administration officials such as Treasury Secretary Paul O'Neill, Counter-terrorism Czar Richard Clarke, and CPA Administrator Paul Bremer to speak honestly only upon leaving their respective jobs within the Administration. Their behavior has been akin to the critical defections, which we used to see out of the old Soviet Union, and which helped reveal the true state of affairs behind the Iron Curtain. One can expect a similar unraveling from Secretary of State Colin Powell and Secretary of Defense Donald Rumsfeld, among others, if President Bush were to lose his reelection bid next month. I suspect that these forthcoming revelations will have a cathartic effect on our foreign policy, which will go a long way to assuage all of our Allies, and stabilize the situation not only in Iraq but also vastly improve the prospects for peace in the greater Middle East. However, this happy outcome is entirely dependent on the voters, who Broder rightly refers to as the "enforcers of accountability."

*   *   *

The American people opted for more of the same—so one can expect the Cosa Nos-tra style to continue for another four years. One can only hope that President Bush does not also keep chipping away at our civil liberties in the name of security.

The folks at the Journal weren't too thrilled that Senator Kerry had been dismissive of Poland's contribution to the war in Iraq. The Journal editorial page seemed to forget that this country's heritage is steeped in "old Europe". If the "the Muhlenberg Vote" of January 1795 had gone the other way, they could be working for "Die Wall Strabe Journal" today? But seriously, the fundamental difference—that I have with the Bush Administration, the Wall Street Journal editorial page, and neoconservatives in general—is why do we need to discard old friends in trying to make new ones?

10/13/04: Letter to *WSJ*—Re: Kwasniewski on Kerry[69]

Your fundamental argument—"isn't whether we'll have allies, but which ones they'll be"—is flawed. While Kerry erred in slighting the Poles, your continual denigration of the French and Germans is also misguided. We all should realize that, for the first time since the end of WWII, we have a fractured western alliance. In this regard, the terrorists have already gained a significant moral advantage. It's great that we attracted countries from Eastern Europe into our coalition, but this should never have occurred at the expense of "old Europe"? So ultimately, whoever occupies the Oval office come January, they need to bring back not only France and Germany, but also win over China, India, and Russia as committed members of the "coalition of the willing". Only then, can we expect to succeed in Iraq—and, by extension, start winning the global war on terrorism.

*   *   *

In the ultimate, diplomacy is as much about style as it is about substance—so the Bush Administration should end its "my way or the highway" style of dealing with other nations, especially when they happen to be allies from whence a lot of America's forefathers came.

What intrigues me greatly is how would conservatives have dealt with Abu Ghraib had it happened on a Democratic President's watch? In fact, how would these conservative pundits have reacted to 9/11, or launching of a war on false pretences (WMD), or the inability to find Osama Bin Laden—if any of these events had transpired under the leadership of a Democratic commander-in-chief?

10/15/04: Letter to *The Post*—Re: Remember Abu Ghraib?[70]

There are two primary reasons that Abu Ghraib did not come up during the presidential debates:

- As a society we have proven time and again that we find it very difficult to openly discuss or castigate such mind-numbing behavior that has its origins in revered authority figures or institutions. It took several years, following the discovery of child abuse within the Catholic Church, before any sort of redress and justice was achieved.

- Both candidates would not have had the courage to say anything, which could have been even remotely construed as "anti-troops", so close to the general election.

Nevertheless, it is incomprehensible that either the three moderators or the general public at the second debate did not bring up this subject. Although, as a people, we seem to have been through four of five stages of grief—denial, bargaining, anger, and despair—without having "accepted" our collective responsibility for these "cases of torture and homicide in Iraq and Afghanistan". In any case, we the people have been delinquent in not being appropriately outraged, a good part of the media still seems to be in denial, and our government appears to be biding its time until the election is out of the way.

*   *   *

On January 16, 2005 the Washington Post reported, "Former Army prison guard Spec. Charles A. Graner Jr. was sentenced to 10 years in a military stockade Saturday for his role in abusing Iraqi prisoners at the Abu Ghraib prison." It remains to be seen if there will be more convictions further up the chain of command?

I "put out" an early warning on Putin, which I hoped that the Post would pick up. This letter provides a succinct synopsis of the problems with Bush foreign policy, in general, and warns about the likelihood of a new Cold War.

10/19/04: Letter to *The Post*—Re: Today's editorials[71]

"The Rape of Belarus" highlights the major contradictions that have plagued the Bush Administration's foreign policy. Bush's signing of the Belarus Democracy Act, while giving Putin a pass as the Russian President continues to promote a slow restoration of the old "evil empire", is short-sighted. President Bush must soon realize that there is no healthy trade-off between real security and true democracy in the long term. Our problems in the Middle East are compounded because of his duplicitous foreign policy, which tolerates certain friendly dictators in Egypt, Pakistan, and Saudi Arabia—while it justifies the removal of others, such as Saddam Hussein in Iraq, in the guise of liberty for the Iraqi people and security for the rest of the world. This situation has become all the more unbelievable because neither are the Iraqi people truly free, nor is the rest of the world really more secure.

More critically, President Bush needs to immediately get off his theological high-horse at home, if he has to credibly deal with the mullahs in Iran. As David Ignatius points out in "Counter-Errorism", President Bush said in the last debate, "I believe that God wants everybody to be free." Even if this were true, the world does not need to hear it from the President's mouth. Tomorrow, Iran's Ayatollah Khameini might state, "We believe that Allah does not want everybody to be free." So there is no strategic advantage in bringing God into the debate—our founding fathers were wise—we should trust them on this one. Finally, it would be a shame if President Bush's policies were to undo the single most important victory of the 20th century—the collapse of the "evil empire". Bush better indicate to Putin really soon that he better not plan on becoming the new BOSS (Backdoor Organizer of Soviet States). As Mr. Ignatius quoted, "Those who cannot remember the past are condemned to repeat it." President Bush needs to wake up and smell the coffee—due to his intransigence; its aroma might not be coming only from the war on terrorism, but also from a new Cold War!

*   *   *

My instincts about Russia seemed to be right on the money as several incidents—the jailing of Russian tycoon Khodorkovsky, the sale of Yukos, the cancellation of gubernatorial elections in Russia's 89 regions, and Putin's support for Viktor Yanukovych in the Ukraine election—in the coming months would establish.

The next time they meet, President Bush better look President Putin in the eye again—because it is confession time and Putin needs to really "bare that soul".

William Safire wrote about "the year of fear" and "forgot" to mention its creator—I couldn't let him forget that! If there was one single reason to "fear more years", it was the abhorrent conduct of Vice President Cheney during the presidential campaign. The quote below was outrageous but he plainly got away with it.

10/20/04: Letter to *NY Times*—Re: William Safire's "The Year of Fear"[72]

William Safire conveniently forgot the Master Fear Monger, who started it all back around Labor Day—Vice President Cheney came up with this mother of all zingers, "It's absolutely essential that eight weeks from today, on Nov. 2, we make the right choice, because if we make the wrong choice then the danger is that we'll get hit again and we'll be hit in a way that will be devastating from the standpoint of the United States."

Also, if President Bush had privatized a portion of Social Security on his first day in office back in 2001, seniors would be losing approximately 22% of their privatized investment based on the value of the S&P 500 index as of yesterday.

*   *   *

If nothing succeeds like success, then (with apologies to the Great Yogi) nothing frightens like fear. "Big time" Cheney proved yet again that he belonged to the "Anything Goes School" of campaigning. Lest we forget, the Vice President of the United States in the hallowed halls of Congress asked a Senator to perform the impossible task of fornicating with himself!

Among the many horrors that the Bush White House had wrought, Maureen Dowd failed to mention how its serial bungling had seriously degraded our super-power status.

10/28/04: Letter to NY *Times*—Re: Maureen Dowd's "White House of Horrors"[73]

The ultimate horror that Cheney's neocons have wrought is a serious undermining of our superpower status with this bungled invasion of Iraq. If Iraq doesn't turn out right eventually, a renewed belligerence by the other two charter members of Bush's "axis of evil" will make the threat of the old "evil empire" pale in comparison.

The other lesson for Bush is that he should have listened to his earthly father as opposed to a "higher" father. This is what has distinguished our system of government thus far—we let our faith guide our personal behavior but do not allow it to drive our professional actions—and, one hopes that it will continue to remain that way.

*   *   *

It seemed kind of ironical that we had a "faith-based" President in the White House at a time when we were dealing with an enemy, which was also fanatical about its faith. If one side does not back off on the public pronouncements of faith, the war on terrorism is going to turn into a religious war before one can say "holy crusades".

A few days before the election, I felt confident enough to submit one final humiliating op-ed to the Post. In it, I had Kerry over Bush by five to six points—what had I been smoking? President Bush's reelection taught me the lesson that I had been preaching without practicing—to keep my own faith out of my politics. I seriously believed that the Bush family karma would undo the Bush presidency and, like his father before him, George W. Bush would not be elected to a second term. Despite all the "karmic" factors highlighted in the article below, conservative values trumped my hope for a new "liberal mass" by over 3 million votes.

10/28/04: Op-Ed submission to *The Post* entitled, "Liberal, Mass.[74]"

As I watched the World Series game on the night of the total lunar eclipse, an old Bonnie Tyler number played inside my head. But the words that I kept hearing sounded very much like "a total eclipse of the Cards". By shutting out the St. Louis Cardinals in Game 4, the Boston Red Sox finally reversed the 86-year old "curse of the Bambino". Yet, the bigger story here is that 2004 can be now dubbed as the "Year of New England".

On January 27 Senator Kerry of Massachusetts came from behind to win the New Hampshire primary with a decisive 13-point victory over then perennial leader Howard Dean. Four days later on February 1, the New England Patriots beat the Carolina Panthers 32-29 in Super Bowl XXXVIII. On March 2nd Senator Kerry wrapped up the Democratic Party nomination for President by winning 9 of 10 Super Tuesday primaries.

The first October surprise of this election year was delivered when the wild card Boston Red Sox came from a 0-3 deficit to beat the New York Yankees 4-3 in the American League Championship Series. Some of us diehard political types noted the karmic significance of Boston (host city for Kerry's nominating convention) defeating New York (host city for Bush's nominating convention). Of course, the second October surprise soon followed when Kerry's hometown Red Sox went on to sweep the 2004 World Series in four straight. Meanwhile, the Super Bowl champions, New England Patriots, continued their winning ways with a 6-0 start in the 2004–05 NFL season.

With the "big dig" nearing completion, the road ahead can only be smooth. So I fully expect that on November 2nd the people will elect the next JFK as the 44th President of the United States! Again, in keeping with New

England's ascendant star, Senator Kerry should win by a margin of five to six points and herald the revival of a "Liberal, Mass."

*   *   *

Ouch! President Bush officially won 62,040,606 votes, which was 50.7 percent of the ballots cast, and Senator John F. Kerry got 48.3 percent, or 59,028,109 votes. President Bush received 11.5 million more votes than he had won in 2000, while Senator Kerry polled about 8 million more votes than Al Gore did in 2000. With a 60.7 percent turnout, the 2004 election had the largest turnout since 1968. Karl Rove deserves to be very proud. From what I have seen of Mr. Rove on TV, in a post-election appearance on "Meet the Press", he appears to be a very dignified, soft-spoken, and humble man. Congratulations!

Reality hit in the form of a new Osama Bin Laden video, which aired three days prior to the presidential election. The liberal masses had long been expecting Osama Bin Laden as President Bush's "October surprise", including an announcement from the White House saying that he had been captured. Nobody expected an "October surprise" from Osama Bin Laden, himself, in which he would deliberately remind us that he was still around. In fact, even threatening, "Your security is in your own hands." This letter was written to appreciate the graceful way in which both Presidential candidates handled this unexpected "October surprise".

10/30/04: Letter to *The Post*—Re: Dana Priest and Walter Pincus' "Bin Laden Warns U.S. Voters"[75]

We all need to express our heartfelt appreciation to both, President Bush and Senator Kerry, for their appropriate and measured responses to the Bin Laden tape. It would have been terrific if they had actually put their respective campaigns aside for a moment to make a joint appearance on TV to denounce this man and everything he represents. I am especially heartened that Kerry said, "As Americans, we are absolutely united in our determination to hunt down and destroy Osama bin Laden and the terrorists." The best thing that both candidates can do in the remaining hours of this campaign is not to mention this man, his video, or its message. In Bush's words, "Americans will not be intimidated or influenced by an enemy of our country." So Osama, can crawl back into his cave and count his days because his security is also in our hands!

*   *   *

Osama Bin Laden probably believed that he was delivering a coup de grace to President Bush. However, I think his foolish action—trying to influence the U.S. presidential race—backfired. Nobody would deny that Osama Bin Laden would have loved to see President Bush defeated. However, with his ill-timed video, Osama Bin Laden ensured that President Bush would get "four more years" to hunt him down.

It took me three weeks to "recover" from the outcome of the presidential election. I still find it hard to fathom that a U.S. presidential election was won because "moral values" were a primary concern—this is tantamount to admitting that more people voted their hearts not their minds. Also, by every measure, perception trumped performance—which is a tribute to the vastly superior election strategy of Karl Rove. I must say that all the jokes, about red and blue states that emerged as a result of this election, seemed to have a cathartic effect. However, I do hope that the red vs. blue dichotomy disappears by the next election because it bears the classical hallmarks of the North-South divide from the Civil War? It is kind of a shame that the southern states have not elected a northeastern liberal for President in the post-civil rights era.

In any event, with President Bush proudly proclaiming that he had gained political capital with his victory, I sensed that this President would become a spending machine. In his first term, he had burned away a large budget surplus to create a record budget deficit and increase the national debt to over $7.6 trillion by the time of his second inaugural. Now, he claimed political capital to spend as well—he appeared to be itching for a fight with the Democrats—he not only re-nominated all ten filibustered judges from his first term, he also nominated Alberto R. Gonzales for the Attorney General position. This was the same Mr. Gonzales, who as White House Counsel in President Bush's first term had redefined torture and questioned the applicability of the Geneva Conventions? The Washington Post immediately took up the question of "Mr. Gonzales's Record".

11/22/04: Letter to *The Post*—Re: Mr. Gonzales's Record[76]

Quite frankly, in a civilized society, it is hard to fathom any acceptable answer to Mr. Gonzales's revised "definition of torture". By the same token, he should be equally hard-pressed to defend his disregard for "the views of the uniformed military legal corps" with respect to the Geneva Conventions? Thus, by inference, the answer to your last question—whether Mr. Gonzales is qualified to serve as attorney general—is rather obvious.

*   *   *

The Post editors would finally answer their own question, originally posed in this editorial of November 22, 2004. They would ponder it further with another editorial entitled, "The Gonzales Record" on January 6, 2005. I happened to respond to that editorial as well. But they would finally reveal their position in an editorial entitled, "The Vote on Mr. Gonzales" on January 16, 2005.

With the U.S. election out of the way, everyone's attention soon turned to the Iraqi elections that were little over two months away. A lot of conservatives were of the opinion that if elections could be held in 80% of the country that would be good enough. David Ignatius of the Post highlighted some of the problems with this "80% solution".

11/23/04: Letter to *The Post*—Re: David Ignatius' "Dangers Of the '80 Percent Solution'"[77]

80-20 is a good rule of thumb in business, but a non-starter when it comes to democracy and nation building. We cannot realistically expect to exclude the Sunnis from the Iraqi election and hope that the outcome will be acceptable to anyone. Besides, Iraq is not only 20% Sunni. The Kurds, who make up 20% of the Iraqi population, are also largely Sunnis. More importantly, except for Iran, Iraq is surrounded by Sunni-majority nations such as Saudi Arabia, Jordan, Kuwait, and Syria. These countries have a vested interest in the result of the Iraqi election, and I am sure that they would not fancy another Shiite theocracy in their neighborhood? Ironically, this is WMD (W. Mandated Democracy) that the Bush Administration will have to "find" in Iraq—however long it takes!

*   *   *

Sadly, a large majority of the Sunni Arabs decided to boycott the Iraqi election—this did not bode well for the integrity of the democratic process or for the fledgling democracy in Iraq.

When neoconservative, Charles Krauthammer, piped in with a casual display of ignorance about the make up of the region, I knew we had a problem on our hands. It seemed to me that these conservatives were so hell bent on forcing democracy down Iraq's throat that they were quickly forgetting our recent history in the region.

11/26/04: Letter to *The Post*—Re: Charles Krauthammer's "A Fight for Shiites"[78]

Charles Krauthammer displays typical western ignorance—mistaking ethnicity with religion—the Kurds might not be Sunni Arabs, but they are nonetheless Sunni Muslims, who make up almost 40% of Iraq's population. Also, Mr. Krauthammer's claim, "It is their civil war", reflects the tired, imperial arrogance of an occupying colonial power wanting a quick out of a rapidly deteriorating situation largely of its own making. Justifying half-baked democratic elections in 21st century Iraq, by comparing it to a very different situation in 19th century America, is inherently disingenuous. Moreover, Mr. Krauthammer ignores the realpolitik of the region. Iraq is surrounded by Sunni nations—Jordan, Kuwait, and Saudi Arabia—who are our allies and, who might be uncomfortable with a Shiite government that is closer to Iran than its Arab brethren? Most importantly, the last time we left a Shiite government in charge (circa. 1979 Iran), it rapidly became an Islamic fundamentalist theocracy—which now openly harbors terrorists and continues to undermine the global war on terrorism!

*   *   *

Given President Bush's various pronouncements on Iraq, I trust there will be no question of the United States abandoning Iraq, if it came to a situation that Mr. Krauthammer so callously refers to as "their civil war".

Then that old bulldog at the Times, Mr. William Safire, got into the act. So I took it upon myself to give the Times a history lesson as well.

12/1/04: Letter to NY *Times*—Re: William Safire's "The Fourth Election"[79]

Democracy does not happen because elections take place, as we are currently witnessing in the Ukraine. Iraq is surrounded by Sunni Muslim nations, such as Saudi Arabia, Kuwait, Jordan, and Turkey—all allies of the United States—who will be as uneasy with a Shiite-ruled Iraq as they were with Saddam's regime. A quarter century ago we allowed a Shiite revolution to overthrow a friendly dictator, the Shah of Iran. We then sided with Sunni Iraq against Shiite Iran in their decade long war, which ended in a stalemate. Now, the outcome of the forthcoming Iraqi election should be pretty clear to everyone—Iran will come out the eventual winner—its Shiite theocracy will have succeeded in orchestrating a brilliant coup d'état! So we better be careful in what we press for—we could either suffer unintended consequences or outstanding success in a deliberate foreign policy tilt away from the Saudis?

*   *   *

With Bush back in the saddle, I was sensing a "quick-fix" approach to nation-building within the conservative punditry. By equating elections to democracy, it looked like they just wanted to tick-off another item on their nation-building check-list. Whatever happened to all their previous comparisons to American Reconstruction after the Civil War, and Japan and Germany after World War II?

The next day, another favorite columnist of mine, Thomas L. Friedman of the Times, wrote a really interesting piece. In it, he equated the "9/11 bubble" to the "dot-com bubble" and warned that President Bush was basically spending us in to bankruptcy. It made me wonder why Mr. Friedman had not written about this when the pre-election "year of fear" scenario was being touted by his Times colleague, William Safire. The Kerry side could have used some help at the time?

12/2/04: Letter to NY *Times*—Re: The 9/11 Bubble[80]

Good Lord, Mr. Friedman, if you had written about this "9/11 bubble" prior to November 2nd, Mr. Snow might not have been the only one looking for a job? I am sure those sensible Midwestern folk from Ohio might have seen just enough red—ink, that is—to join the rest of the blue states. President-elect Kerry would be deflating that 9/11 bubble as we speak. Instead, we are at the mercy of the "Chinese and other foreigners", who have the capacity to burst this 9/11 bubble when it suits them. My suspicion is that President Bush needs to make up with "Old Europe"—the masters of the mighty Euro—in a real hurry!

*   *   *

President Bush, without acknowledging a 9/11 bubble, has already indicated that he will make up with "Old Europe" early in his second term. It also appears that the Bush Administration has realized that the U.S. economy has become increasingly dependent on China. In this regard, there is demand for China to revalue its currency so as to alleviate problems with the U.S. trade deficit.

Then there is the larger problem with the U.S. current account deficit (simply, the difference between domestic investments and domestic savings), which has risen to over 5% of GDP—a growing percentage of our prosperity is being financed by foreigners! Most economists believe that by tackling our monstrous budget deficit, President Bush can augment domestic savings as well.

The entire A.Q. Khan affair is so ridiculous that it would make me laugh, were it not about such a serious matter. In the letter below, I suggested that it is quite likely that a quid pro quo exists between Pakistan's dictator, General Pervez Musharraf and its serial nuclear proliferator, A.Q. Khan.

12/5/04: Letter to *The Post*—Re: Robin Wright's and Peter Baker's "Musharraf: Bin Laden's Location Is Unknown"[81]

It has to either be plain old American naïveté about South Asian politics or the public face of our intelligence is in worse shape than I had imagined. Does anyone really believe that a renegade scientist could run a black market in nuclear technology without the knowledge of his government? More importantly, what are the chances for such high security materials to be transferred out of the country, when the nuclear program is not run by private enterprise and the government is not a democratically elected one?

Why is Pakistan really refusing "to allow U.S. or International Atomic Energy Agency investigators to interrogate Khan"? In all likelihood, Pakistan's premier scientist, Abdul Qadeer Khan, and President Musharraf have reached some sort of a quid pro quo arrangement that conceals the truth and protects them both. And, the truth is that Pakistan supplied critical nuclear expertise to the remaining two members of President Bush's "axis of evil". In the case of North Korea, this expertise was exchanged for missile technology, even after 9/11.

Finally, we can never convince the Muslim world about our commitment to democracy as long as we tolerate dictators in countries when it is convenient to us. As naïve as this may sound, our dedication to freedom and democracy has to be absolute. If we can push Putin on elections in Ukraine, we can most certainly press Musharraf to relinquish the uniform!

*   *   *

In my mind, the U.S.-Pakistan relationship is so transparent that I suspect it will collapse once Osama Bin Laden has been captured or killed. Any wonder then, why Osama Bin Laden has not yet been found—it would cost Pakistan roughly $600 million a year in U.S. economic and military aid! At some point of time, President Bush has got to realize that we can't keep propping up these dictators with *money. We have tried it several times before and it doesn't work—in fact, once the dictator has fallen, the concomitant fallout has proven more detrimental to our long-term interests.*

Ah! What would we do without the "Rummy Retort", as I now like to call the Defense Secretary's penchant for putting his foot in his mouth? The descendant of immigrants from "Old Europe" made a classical gaffe while answering tough questions from troops stationed on the ground in Iraq. In response to a Maureen Dowd column on the subject, I pointed out why Secretary Rumsfeld's logic might have been true when applied to Afghanistan, but was false in the case of Iraq.

12/9/04: Letter to *NY Times*—Re: Maureen Dowd's "Lost in a Masquerade"[82]

"As you know, you go to war with the Army you have." This statement was true when we invaded Afghanistan—because that was a retaliatory strike following the 9/11 attacks on our homeland. However, we made a preemptive strike on Iraq—a war of our choosing—much to the chagrin of the United Nations. A preemptive war should be launched, if at all, when we have an Army that is "required and necessary" to do the job.

✳   ✳   ✳

This Rummy Retort has spawned an industry of "(fill in your choice of noun) you have" suggestions. The irony is that "the President we have" asked "the Defense Secretary we have" to hang in there for four more years of Rummy Retorts!

This was my only attempt at a post-mortem on Senator Kerry's defeat. It was in response to a post-election op-ed piece in the WSJ by a pair of Democratic consultants. As a marketing guy, I noted that they had forgotten Marketing 101—on messaging! To my mind, Senator Kerry's defeat could be explained very simply—his campaign message was neither consistent nor clear. But I still voted for him as I explain why in the letter below.

12/9/04: Letter to *WSJ*—Re: Al From and Bruce Reed's "Get the Red Out"[83]

Upon reading the latest analysis from Messrs. From & Reed, I am convinced that the Democratic leadership has not recognized its basic problem. In order to "get the red out", the Visine needs to be crystal clear. President Bush's message, even though I did not buy it, was unambiguous. Notwithstanding the inflated charges of flip-flopping by the Bush team, John Kerry's message was not crystal. Despite not being able to see clearly into Senator Kerry's ball, I voted for him, because I believed that President Bush did not deserve a second term based on his performance in the first term. I suspect that even though several Bush supporters (especially in the red states) felt that the President's performance in the first term was inadequate, they read his crystal ball quite plainly and believed in the future it was forecasting. Only time will tell!

∗   ∗   ∗

I can recite President Bush's simple message in my sleep because I heard it several times a day, every day, throughout 2004—"I will choose to defend America every time!" If that message "ain't like red meat at a red state BBQ", I don't know what is?

In mid-December I got a call from The New York Times saying that they were going to publish one of my letters. This seemed to be an apt culmination to an effort that began almost two years earlier. I felt a tremendous sense of achievement that the venerable Times thought that my letter was "fit to print". Surprisingly, they made very few edits to a lengthy letter, which pushed the 150-word boundary.

I was piqued when President Bush awarded Presidential Medals of Freedom to the three prime architects of a largely botched operation in Iraq. I felt that the Bush Administration had reached a new nadir for delusional behavior.

12/15/04: Letter to NY *Times*—Re: David E. Sanger's "War Figures Honored With Medal of Freedom"[84]

How can one justify the awarding of the Presidential Medal of Freedom to what the President called, "three men who have played pivotal roles in great events"? CIA Director George Tenet came to the "pivotal" conclusion that Iraq's WMD was a "slam dunk" case. General Tommy Franks acquiesced with the Pentagon's "pivotal" estimates on required troop strength, which was sufficient to topple Saddam Hussein's regime but has proven inadequate to secure the peace. And, Iraq's Chief Civilian Administrator L. Paul Bremer made the "pivotal" decision to transfer sovereignty on a rushed timetable—which has left Iraq in a deteriorating security situation since his departure. The irony is that President Bush decided to award these medals of freedom, even before Iraq has taken its first real step to freedom—the holding of free and fair elections. It has consistently been this Administration's policy to declare victory and move on, even if the facts are at odds.

*   *   *

Since this letter appeared, people that I have talked to, including conservatives, agree with my assessment on at least two of the three awardees. General Tommy Franks gets a pass because he led the successful invasion of Iraq and toppled Saddam Hussein's regime in record time.

C. Raja Mohan wrote an op-ed piece in the Journal about the burgeoning rela-
tionship between the U.S. and India. I wish that all the positive things that he had
to say were true. I felt that there were still a number of sticking points preventing the
partnership from growing rapidly...

12/15/04: Letter to *WSJ*—Re: C. Raja Mohan's "'Old' Europe Make Way for New Delhi"[85]

C Raja Mohan fails to recognize an underlying element in "India's enthusiasm for the Bush administration." It's the very same reason that Israel has become the darling of neocons, evangelical Christians, and even Catholics in the United States—after 9/11, we joined Israel and India as nations that constantly face the threat of terrorism, which has its roots in radical Islam. Without wanting to put a damper on Mr. Mohan's optimism, I would like to point out that historically the Congress-led government in India has always leaned towards Russia. More importantly, the larger Indian populace has always been a little skeptical about the U.S. as ally—especially because of the unreliable partner that we have been to its archrival Pakistan. For President Bush, the road to New Delhi might well be through another "Old Europe" ally and common friend, Great Britain.

*   *   *

Frankly I see two headstrong democracies, the oldest and the largest, butting heads over foreign policy differences, much along the lines that I have written throughout this book. Now that India's economy has opened up, I can see the United States and India getting closer as economic partners—in the long run, probably developing even stronger economic ties than we have currently with China?

Whether we can make India a true political and military ally anytime soon is highly doubtful. Our post-9/11 tilt towards Pakistan, despite its links to the Taliban government in Afghanistan, did not go down well with the larger Indian population. Also, the recent rewarding of "major non-NATO ally" status to Pakistan, while Osama Bin Laden is still on the loose inside Pakistan, was also a jolt to India.

If the U.S. pushes for making India a permanent member of the Security Council, as it should be, then "Old Europe could make some headway for New Delhi." Although I do believe that we do not need to sacrifice Old Europe, in order to make new friends. Nevertheless, it is a strategic imperative for the United States to quickly re-align itself to the new realities in the Asia-Pacific region.

As I have written earlier, I think that Shia hegemony as a counter-balance to Sunni Arab supremacy—if allowed to proceed as a natural evolution of the new realpolitik in the Middle East—could benefit us in the long-term, without the need for another preemptive war in the short-term. This thinking formed the basis of my response to David Ignatius's column in mid-December.

12/18/04: Letter to *The Post*—Re: David Ignatius' "How Iran Is Winning Iraq"[86]

David Ignatius is right, in that, the Ayatollahs in Iran will succeed in taking control of Iraq through the outcome of a legitimate political process backed by the United States. What Saddam Hussein was unable to achieve, despite U.S. support during the 1980s Iran-Iraq war—the Iranians will now gain without having fired a shot—i.e. regional hegemony. From a strategic standpoint, this new Shia hegemony will offer a good counter-balance to the traditional Sunni Arab supremacy in this part of the world. Also, Middle East oil assets will become more evenly distributed between the Shia and Sunni factions causing Saudi Arabia to lose some of its clout within OPEC. After the Iraqi elections, by co-opting the Iranians to bring peace to Iraq, President Bush could effectively neutralize Syria, and thus find an early "exit strategy" out of Iraq. In return for our endorsement of their enhanced prominence in the Middle East, the Iranians must be willing to give up their nuclear ambitions. President Bush would be then left to deal with the last remaining member of his axis of evil, North Korea!

*   *   *

Seymour Hersh followed with a controversial article entitled, "The Coming Wars" in The New Yorker (issue dated January 24 & 31, 2005 and posted online on January 17, 2005). In it, he suggests that the Bush Administration has already got Iran in its sights as the "next strategic target". I can only pray that he is dead wrong!

*The Post editorialized that the Bush Administration was responsible "for the doc-
umented torture and killing of foreign prisoners." If this belief leads to a lawsuit
against the Bush Administration by Human Rights Watch, or Amnesty International, or the International Committee of the Red Cross, we could get the U.S.
Supreme Court involved in the case in relatively short order. The hypothetical question that I have posed below will then become very relevant—were the Supreme
Court to rule against the Bush Administration, what would the remedy be?*

12/23/04: Letter to *The Post*—Re: War Crimes[87]

You conclude your editorial with a poignant remark, "For now the appalling
truth is that there has been no remedy for the documented torture and killing
of foreign prisoners by this American government." If the U.S. Supreme
Court were to find that the Bush Administration was liable for these "war
crimes", how could it justify any longer the toppling of Saddam Hussein's
regime on the basis of his "war crimes", "torture chambers", etc? The only
remaining raison d'être for our occupation of Iraq will have vanished.

*   *   *

*Truth is stranger than fiction, per the old adage. But wouldn't it be "wicked cool",
as my teenagers are wont to say, if the Bush exit strategy from Iraq was necessitated
by a decision from the very same Supreme Court, which originally made his presidency possible? Hey, an idle mind maybe the devil's workshop, but an active mind is
an angel's warning!*

A great tsunami hit South Asia on December 26, 2004. When I heard some of the descriptions ("the sea has disappeared") and saw some of the amateur videos on the news, my mind immediately harkened back to an ancient Vedic concept called "Pralaya". It marks the end of a cosmic cycle and is accompanied by dissolution or cleansing, which is usually brought about by a great deluge.

In any case, the tsunami hit on a Sunday morning (Eastern time), and the death toll climbed quite dramatically every day in the first few days. The Post had banner headlines on Monday, Tuesday, and then Wednesday—but there was still no official response from President Bush. I was apoplectic, so I wrote a letter to the Post on Wednesday morning.

12/29/04: Letter to *The Post*—Re: John F. Harris and Robin Wright's "Aid Grows Amid Remarks About President's Absence"[88]

Talk about missed opportunities to show leadership—the U.S. reaction was not as much "stingy" as it has been painfully "subdued". While "actions may speak louder than words", the Bush Administration ought to know that diplomacy is as much about style as it is of substance. This tsunami hit South Asia while we were still celebrating Christmas. It has so far taken more than twenty times the lives we lost on 9/11. The hardest hit country, Indonesia, is not only a Muslim nation, but also a key U.S. ally. President Bush should have reflected a more palpable Christian spirit, especially during this season of giving, by taking a more visible and active role in this international crisis. It might not be too late?

*   *   *

At midday on Wednesday, President Bush finally appeared on national TV to make a statement. While the Bush Administration's subsequent response has been more than adequate, its initial reaction was quite baffling. My letter needs to be read in that context—because it reflects my ongoing concern about the Bush Administration's style. I am hopeful that they will follow the old motto, "Well begun is half done" in their second term?

This would be the second consecutive year that I ended the year writing about Pakistan. It was in response to a Post editorial, wherein they had lamented yet "another pass for Pakistan" from the Bush Administration.

12/31/04: Letter to *The Post*—Re: Another Pass for Pakistan[89]

It's time President Bush realized that the hand (Pakistan's Inter-Services Intelligence) that rocks the cradle (President Musharraf's government) rules the world (Pakistan). General Musharraf, A.Q. Khan, and the Taliban were beneficiaries of the ISI, which will not allow them to be compromised any further. As we all know, the Taliban provided succor to Osama Bin Laden and his Al Qaeda organization. As long as President Musharraf remains Army chief, the ISI ensures that A.Q. Khan remains protected, and that Osama Bin Laden is never captured "dead or alive". So while President Bush may "prefer expediency", it is not going to help him one iota as far as bringing the perpetrator of 9/11 to justice is concerned.

*   *   *

Unfortunately, General Musharraf continues to pull the wool over President Bush's eyes by perpetrating a charade with respect to "finding" Osama Bin Laden. I strongly doubt it is going to happen as long as a military dictatorship is ruling Pakistan.

And, this would be the second consecutive year that I began the year writing about the Bush economy to the Journal. They had started 2004 by touting 2003 as "Economy of the Year", and then they kicked off 2005 with a sarcastic reference to "that sluggish economy" of 2004? But they never compared apples to apples, so I did.

1/1/05: Letter to *WSJ*—Re: "That 'Sluggish' Economy"[90]

It's always fair to compare apples to apples, so your editorial would have made better sense if it had averaged real GDP growth rates across each four-year term for each of the recent Presidents. Thus, Reagan I averaged real GDP growth of 3.1%, Reagan II averaged real GDP growth of 3.8%, Bush (41) averaged real GDP growth of 2.1%, Clinton I averaged real GDP growth of 3.2%, and Clinton II averaged real GDP growth of 4.2%. Bush (43), through the third-quarter of 2004, is averaging real GDP growth of 2.4% in his first term. In the first three quarters of 2004, real GDP growth is averaging 4%, which is not "sluggish" by any standard. However, my "cursory comparative analysis" does show that the U.S. economy, in George W. Bush's first term, has not performed so robustly by its own recent historical standards?

*   *   *

My analysis revealed more than I expected—firstly, that the Clinton economy beat the Reagan economy on a term-to-term comparison, and secondly the "Bush karma" theory works when applied to the economy—both, father and son, gave us "sluggish" economic growth in their first term. Of course, in the case of the father, that sluggish growth denied him a second term. In the case of the son, he went to war and "chose to defend America every time", so the people gave him a pass on the economy. Needless to say, the Journal did not run my letter.

As the date for the Iraqi elections drew near, all manner of pundits were pontificating about whether they should be held as scheduled or postponed? Adnan Pachachi, who had served as Iraqi foreign minister and ambassador to the UN before the Baathist coup in 1968, in an op-ed piece in the Post called for a delay. After his piece appeared, the Bush Administration started to downplay the significance of the Iraqi elections from a turnout and participation standpoint.

1/2/05: Letter to *The Post*—Re: Adnan Pachachi's "Delay the Elections"[91]

Adnan Pachachi makes a good point, when he notes, "Elections were delayed in Afghanistan, but the results there gained wide acceptance from all political factions." Elections were held in Afghanistan almost three years after we toppled the Taliban regime, and we faced a relatively minor insurgency in Afghanistan during that time. It's been under two years, since we toppled Saddam Hussein's regime, and a major insurgency rages in several key regions of Iraq. President Bush again needs to make a vital choice—symbolic democracy before lasting security—in Iraq. It might be worth noting that he has acquiesced to stable dictatorships over people power in most of the Middle East—Egypt, Iran, Jordan, Kuwait, Pakistan, Syria, and Saudi Arabia.

*   *   *

Regardless of the outcome of the Iraqi elections, President Bush is going to be hard-pressed to live up to his promise for democracy throughout the Middle East. Nonetheless, these elections will be a turning point in the future of Iraq leading to either freedom and democracy, or chaos and civil war!

These two editorials in the Post could not have contrasted the character of the people of the Unites States more starkly from the persona of its government as represented by the Bush Administration.

1/4/05: Letter to *The Post*—Re: David Ignatius' "More Water Bottles, Fewer Bullets" & Richard Cohen's "Ugly Truths About Guantanamo"[92]

David Ignatius' "More Water Bottles, Fewer Bullets" gave me goose bumps, while Richard Cohen's "Ugly Truths About Guantanamo" made my skin crawl. Therein lays the stark dichotomy in our position in the world today. On the one hand, we are a compassionate nation that David Ignatius says wants "to become more connected with the world." On the other hand, we are an aggressive superpower that Richard Cohen writes "has raised itself above the law." Isn't it ironical that our government, represented by the Bush Administration, only talks about the compassion, which "we the people" practice? If we could only get the Bush Administration to "walk its talk" through a moral and consistent application of its foreign policy, and in consonance with international laws, there would be no "ugly truths" about the United States!

*   *   *

In its second term, if the Bush Administration focused on a foreign policy, which was based on our core values, and applied it consistently as opposed to conveniently, I think we would make remarkable progress—both, in the war on terrorism and our standing in the Muslim world.

Prior to his inaugural, none of President Bush's second term appointments caused as much controversy as the one for Attorney General. I tried to highlight my concerns by revisiting some historical facts that appeared OK when they originally occurred, but increasingly distasteful with the passage of time.

1/6/05: Letter to *The Post*—Re: The Gonzales Record[93]

One hopes that history will enlighten the minds of Senate Judiciary Committee members as they begin confirmation hearings for Alberto R. Gonzales as President Bush's new Attorney General. Patriotic Americans might have not been too perturbed with the incarceration of Japanese-Americans over six decades ago. With the passage of time, almost everyone agrees it was an abhorrent action that violated their constitutional rights, just as slavery violated the constitutional rights of African-Americans for almost a century after Independence.

Mr. Gonzales' redefinition of torture and obsolescing of some of the Geneva conventions with respect to the "war on terrorism"—are not only a perversion of our constitution, but also a willful disregard of international law. The character of a nation, and hence its people, is defined in times of adversity. It will be highly ironical, if the Senate allows a man who so debased American jurisprudence to head the Justice Department.

* * *

Ten days after I wrote this letter, the Post finally concluded in a January 16, 2005 editorial that Mr. Gonzales "does not deserve to be confirmed as attorney general."

In response to a Times article by Clyde Haberman entitled, "NYC; Queasy Feeling About a Decade With No Name", an Irish immigrant wrote in a letter to the Times about how good she felt about this decade (2000–2009) with no name. I did not share her optimism and you can see why.

1/10/05: Letter to *NY Times*—Re: Angela M. Hegarty's "Name That Decade (and Try to Smile)"[94]

I wish I could share Angela M. Hegarty's optimism. However, as a fellow immigrant, I am not too hopeful for a decade that will have borne eight years of the Bush Doctrine. I suspect the international community will still be seeing "red", and a lot of Americans will still be feeling "blue", until "our long national nightmare is over." So if it turns out to be a decade that we would rather forget, why even bother trying to name it?

*   *   *

In case one thinks that I am being too cynical about the Bush decade, let me present some facts. Why would anyone want to remember a decade that brought us the biggest crash in the U.S. stock market since 1929[95], 9/11—the first attacks on U.S. soil since Pearl Harbor, the biggest corporate scandals[96] since the formation of the SEC in 1933, the Afghan War, the Iraq war—which caused the first serious rupture in our trans-Atlantic alliance since World War II, the first Presidency since Herbert Hoover (1929–1933) to probably have a net loss of jobs[97], the largest budget deficits in our history[98], the largest trade deficits in our history[99], the highest price for crude oil in a generation[100], the highest price of gold in sixteen years[101], and the weakest dollar in five years[102]? I rest my case.

President Bush has pretty much followed the dictum of his hero, Winston Churchill, who had said, "Success consists of going from failure to failure without loss of enthusiasm." Failure to find WMD and failure to quell the insurgency did not seem to dull the Bush Administration's enthusiasm for conducting the Iraqi elections as scheduled. With the elections barely three weeks away, the Times weighed in on the subject, and I had to respond.

1/12/05: Letter to NY *Times*—Re: Facing Facts About Iraq's Election[103]

President Bush is actually faced with a Hobson's choice with regards to the Iraqi elections. If his primary objective is a stable, democratic Iraq—as he has maintained all along—then he needs to postpone the elections. If his primary objective is "to declare victory and begin pulling out American troops", he still needs to postpone the elections. There is no easy exit for the U.S. from Iraq and—notwithstanding the domestic political capital he has gained going into his second term—it is unlikely to happen on President Bush's watch?

*   *   *

I am glad that my Hobson's choice did not make it to print because President Bush ignored all his critics and the Iraqi elections were held as scheduled. Despite a boycott by a majority of the Sunnis, over 8.5 million Iraqis turned out to vote. A Shia-dominated coalition won nearly 48% and the Kurdish groups got over 25% of the votes cast.

The initial euphoria over the successful election started to die down as the parties struggled to form a government. Nevertheless, I can only hope that I am wrong about our exit from Iraq, and it does happen in President Bush's second term—that would be success no American would want to deny him.

In my final letter to the Times at the end of President Bush's first term—I offered a simple answer to the question often asked after 9/11, "Why do they hate us?"

1/18/05: Letter to NY *Times*—Re: Thomas L. Friedman's "Pop-Tarts or Freedom?"[104]

I thought about "Pop Tarts or Freedom", and it occurred to me that Mr. Friedman's answer to "Why they hate us?" is the same as President Bush's. While I agree with the President and Mr. Friedman that freedom can be the great equalizer, it still does not answer why Muslims cannot "want our jobs, not our lives" as Mr. Friedman wonders? To me the answer is simple—we need to adopt a consistent foreign policy that makes our core values, freedom and democracy, non-negotiable in our relationships with all Muslim nations without any exceptions!

*   *   *

My solution is entirely consistent with what President Bush had said, when he addressed the United States Chamber of Commerce at the 20th Anniversary of the National Endowment for Democracy in November 2003, "Sixty years of Western nations excusing and accommodating the lack of freedom in the Middle East did nothing to make us safe—because in the long run, stability cannot be purchased at the expense of liberty. As long as the Middle East remains a place where freedom does not flourish, it will remain a place of stagnation, resentment, and violence ready for export. And with the spread of weapons that can bring catastrophic harm to our country and to our friends, it would be reckless to accept the status quo."
Amen!

And, in my final letter to the Post at the end of President Bush's first term—I rec-ommended that the Bush Administration revisit the style vs. substance issue in its conduct of foreign policy.

1/19/05: Letter to *The Post*—Re: The Second Term Abroad[105]

Based on Ms. Rice's testimony before the Senate Foreign Relations Commit-tee yesterday, it appears that the Bush Administration recognizes at least half the problem—with Ms. Rice agreeing to at least fix the "style" part of their diplomacy. As the saying goes, "well begun is half done"? Now, if only, Ms. Rice would focus on the "substance" as well and adjust U.S. policy on Iraq (get the UN involved, even if it means apologizing to the world body), on North Korea (resume meaningful bilateral negotiations), and on Palestine (with Mahmoud Abbas legitimately elected, resume Camp David accords where President Clinton left off in September 2000). If the Bush Administration were serious about getting results, changes in these three regions would help it build a substantial legacy.

*   *   *

Two years earlier, when I had quizzed Bob Woodward about this very nuance in Bush foreign policy, I had suggested that its style was largely lacking. However, after seeing their Iraq strategy unravel, North Korea get ignored, and the state of Pales-tine remain a wishful dream—I would dare say that the Bush Administration's for-eign policy also needs substantive tuning. In the ultimate, if U.S. foreign policy is made more consistent with our core values, and the Bush Administration uses tradi-tional diplomacy to further policy goals, its Second Term might turn out to be a memorable "American Intifada"!

Notes:

[1] Robin Wright is the diplomatic correspondent for *The Washington Post*. Ms. Wright joined the Post as a staff writer in 2004. This report entitled "Bush Faces a Challenging Year: The Turn From War to Peace" appeared in *The Washington Post* edition dated January 1, 2004.

[2] *The Washington Post* editorial entitled "Silence on the Hill" appeared in its January 5, 2004 edition.

[3] Mike Allen was a White House correspondent for *The Washington Post* until December 2004. He now covers the Congress. This report entitled "O'Neill: Plan to Hit Iraq Began Pre-9/11" appeared in *The Washington Post* edition dated January 11, 2004

[4] Susan Lee is a member of *The Wall Street Journal's* editorial board. This op-ed piece entitled "Will Greenspan Seal The Bush Re-Election" appeared in *The Wall Street Journal* edition of January 12, 2004.

[5] Charles Krauthammer is a Post columnist. His column generally appears on The Post's opinion page on Fridays. This column entitled "A Modest Proposal" appeared in *The Washington Post* edition dated January 16, 2004.

[6] *The Wall Street Journal* editorial entitled "GOP Spending Spree" appeared in its *Review & Outlook* section of January 20, 2004.

[7] *The Wall Street Journal* editorial entitled "'Outsourcing' Is Good for America" appeared in its *Review & Outlook* section of January 28, 2004. Paul Craig Roberts, who is a senior fellow at the Hoover Institution, John M. Olin Fellow at the Institute for Political Economy, and research fellow at the Independent Institute, made the quoted comment at a Brookings Institution briefing, "Free Trade in the New Global Economy: A Discussion on the State of U.S. Trade Policy", on January 7, 2004.

[8] Peter D. Feaver is a professor of political science and public policy at Duke University. This op-ed piece entitled "Fog of WMD" appeared in *The Washington Post* edition dated January 28, 2004.

[9] *The Wall Street Journal* editorial entitled "WMD Breakthrough" appeared in its *Review & Outlook* section of February 6, 2004. Mr. Husain, a former civil servant in Pakistan, is a columnist for two Pakistani newspapers, *Dawn* and the *Daily Times*. Mr. Husain's op-ed piece entitled "Pakistan's Dr. Strangelove" also appeared in *The Wall Street Journal* edition of February 6, 2004.

[10] This Charles Krauthammer column entitled "The Other Shoe" appeared in *The Washington Post* edition dated February 23, 2004.

[11] *The Wall Street Journal* editorial entitled "Desert Blasts" appeared in its *Review & Outlook* section of May 13, 1998.

[12] Joshua Muravchik is a resident scholar at the American Enterprise Institute. This op-ed piece entitled "Kerry's Inner Dove" appeared in *The Washington Post* edition dated February 23, 2004.

[13] Thomas Sowell is the Rose and Milton Friedman Senior Fellow on Public Policy at the Hoover Institution. Mr. Sowell's op-ed piece entitled "Low Taxes Do What?" appeared in *The Wall Street Journal* edition of February 24, 2004.

[14] I came up with "The Passion of the Right" moniker long before Chris Matthews, host of MSNBC TV's "Hardball", aired a segment with the very same title on November 19, 2004.

[15] Washington Post Staff Writers, Nell Henderson and Kirstin Downey, wrote this front-page report entitled, "Job Growth Near Standstill In February", for *The Washington Post* edition dated March 6, 2004.

[16] *The Wall Street Journal* editorial entitled "Is 9/11 an Issue?" appeared in its *Review & Outlook* section of March 7, 2004.

[17] E.J. Dionne Jr. is a senior fellow in government studies at the Brookings Institution. He has been a Post columnist since 1993. His column appears on The Post's opinion page on Tuesdays and Fridays. This column entitled "Job No. 1 for Bush" appeared in *The Washington Post* edition dated March 12, 2004.

[18] This Dana Milbank report entitled "Opinion of U.S. Abroad Is Falling, Survey Finds" appeared in *The Washington Post* edition dated March 17, 2004.

[19] On March 16,2004 *The Wall Street Journal* editorial page published letters from six readers under the heading, "Au Revoir, France; We're Cutting the Cord".

[20] On March 22, 2004 *The Washington Post* editorial pages published an op-ed piece by President Bush's National Security Advisor, Condoleezza Rice, entitled, "9/11: For The Record". On the same day, the Post also ran a front-page

news report by national staff writer Barton Gellman entitled, "Memoir Criticizes Bush 9/11 Response".

[21] Jennifer Frey is a *Style* staff writer for *The Washington Post*. Her report, entitled "George Bush, Entertainer In Chief", appeared in the *Post* edition dated March 25, 2004. It covered the 60th Annual Radio & Television Correspondents' Association dinner, which was held the previous evening at the Hilton Hotel in Washington DC.

[22] Daniel Henninger is deputy editor of *The Wall Street Journal's* editorial page. He writes the "Wonderland" column, which appears on Fridays. This column entitled "Skiing As News: Is John Kerry Overexposed" appeared in *The Wall Street Journal* edition of March 26, 2004.

[23] Walter Pincus has been reporting on national security affairs for over 25 years at *The Washington Post*. Dana Milbank co-authored this front-page report, which appeared in *The Washington Post* edition dated March 29, 2004.

[24] Dan Eggen is a national staff writer covering the Justice Department for *The Washington Post*. Mike Allen co-authored this March 31, 2004 front-page report entitled, "President to Let Rice Testify About 9/11". Dan Balz is a national political correspondent at the *Post*. His front-page report entitled, "Bush Scores Points By Defining Kerry" also appeared in the March 31, 2004 edition of the *Post*.

[25] Senator Mitch McConnell (R-KY) is majority whip, serves as a senior member of the Appropriations Subcommittee, and serves as a senior member of the Agriculture and Rules Committees. His op-ed piece entitled. "Needs a U.S. Push" appeared in *The Washington Post* edition dated April 7, 2004.

[26] This front-page report, entitled "Memo Not Specific Enough, Bush Says", by Dan Eggen appeared in *The Washington Post* edition dated April 12, 2004.

[27] *The Wall Street Journal* editorial entitled "Rethinking Armageddon" appeared in its *Review & Outlook* section of April 12, 2004.

[28] This letter was in response to Dan Balz's front-page report entitled, "President Is Long On Resolve but Short on Details", which appeared in *The Washington Post* edition dated April 14, 2004.

[29] Bob Woodward is an Assistant Managing Editor at *The Washington Post*. The *Post* published excerpts from his book, "Plan Of Attack" over a five day period from April 18–22, 2004.

[30] Rush Limbaugh is a conservative talk-show host, whose three-hour program can be heard on 600+ radio stations across the country on weekdays. This op-ed piece entitled "Woodward at War" appeared in *The Wall Street Journal* edition of April 21, 2004.

[31] This front-page report, entitled "U.S. Moves to Rehire Some From Baath Party, Military", by Robin Wright appeared in *The Washington Post* edition dated April 22, 2004.

[32] This letter was written in response to an op-ed column, entitled "Stooping Low to Smear Kerry", by E. J. Dionne Jr. appeared in *The Washington Post* edition dated April 27, 2004.

[33] On April 29, 2004 CBS Television's "60 Minutes II" broke the story about Iraqi prisoner abuse at Abu Ghraib. On May 3, 2004 *The Washington Post* was among the first newspapers to publish actual photographs of Iraqi prisoners being abused by U.S. military personnel.

[34] This George Will column entitled "Time for Bush to See The Realities of Iraq" appeared in *The Washington Post* edition dated May 4, 2004.

[35] *The New York Times* editorial entitled "Donald Rumsfeld Should Go" appeared in its May 7, 2004 edition.

[36] This George Will column entitled "No Flinching From the Facts" appeared in *The Washington Post* edition dated May 11, 2004.

[37] *The Wall Street Journal* editorial entitled "Help Is Wanted" appeared in its *Review & Outlook* section of May 10, 2004.

[38] *The Wall Street Journal* editorial entitled "Roadside Sarin" appeared in its *Review & Outlook* section of May 18, 2004.

[39] Lewis E. Lehrman is a partner in the investment firm L.E. Lehrman & Co. William Kristol and Mr. Lehrman co-authored this op-ed piece, which appeared in *The Washington Post* edition dated May 23, 2004.

[40] Glenn Kessler is a staff writer for *The Washington Post.* His front-page report entitled "Kerry Says Security Comes First" appeared in its edition dated May 30, 2004.

[41] General Musharraf, President of Pakistan, wrote this op-ed piece entitled "A Plea for Enlightened Moderation". *The Washington Post* published it in its edition dated June 1, 2004.

[42] I can't remember if I wrote this letter in response to a *Post* editorial. In any case, it was my spontaneous reaction to the passing of President Reagan, who happened to be the President when I first came to the United States in 1983.

[43] *The Washington Post* editorial entitled "As Genocide Unfolds" appeared in its June 20, 2004 edition.

[44] E. J. Dionne's column entitled "9/11 Credibility Gap" and Richard Cohen's column entitled "Grand Delusion" appeared in the editorial pages of *The Washington Post* on June 22, 2004. On the same day, Post staff writers, Walter Pincus and Dan Eggen had a report, entitled "Al Qaeda Link To Iraq May Be Confusion Over Names" appearing on page A13.

[45] This Richard Cohen column entitled "Baloney, Moore or Less" appeared in *The Washington Post* edition dated July 1, 2004.

[46] Senator John F. Kerry (D-MA) was the presumptive Democratic nominee for president, when his article entitled, "A Realistic Path in Iraq" appeared in the editorial pages of *The Washington Post* on July 4, 2004.

[47] Senator Joe Lieberman (D-CT) and Senator Jon Kyl (R-AZ) are honorary co-chairmen of the Committee on the Present Danger. Their editorial entitled, "The Present Danger" appeared in the op-ed pages of *The Washington Post* on July 20, 2004.

[48] This letter was in response to the *Post's* extensive coverage of the release of the 9/11 Commission Report on July 22, 2004. The coverage was spearheaded by a front-page report entitled, "9/11 Panel Chronicles U.S. Failures" by Dan Eggen in *The Washington Post* edition of July 23, 2004.

[49] *The Wall Street Journal* editorial entitled "The Chalabi Fiasco Continues" appeared in its *Review & Outlook* section of August 11, 2004.

[50] This Robert Novak op-ed column entitled "Uncertain Trumpet" appeared in *The Washington Post* edition dated August 12, 2004.

[51] *The Washington Post* editorial entitled "Missing the Point" appeared in its August 23, 2004 edition.

[52] *The Wall Street Journal* editorials entitled "Health and Poverty" and "Poor Statistics" appeared in its *Review & Outlook* section of August 27, 2004.

[53] *The New York Times* editorial entitled "Mr. Bush's Acceptance Speech" appeared in its September 3, 2004 edition after the Republican National Convention in New York.

[54] My eulogy to President Reagan was written shortly after his passing on June 5, 2004. I made a spate of op-ed submissions to *The Washington Post* over the 2004 Labor Day weekend.

[55] I submitted an early version of this op-ed piece to *The Wall Street Journal* in May 2003. Needless to say, the empirical data on tax revenues do not support the core supply side principle. More importantly, spending under Republican Presidents has been historically a bigger problem than under their Democratic counterparts. Data for this article were gleaned from two popular websites http://www.economagic.com/ and http://www.taxpolicycenter.org/.

[56] Historical data on GDP, federal funds rates, PPI and CPI for this op-ed piece were gleaned from the http://www.economagic.com/ website.

[57] This op-ed piece was actually written in early July 2004 and hence the reference to the presidential election being "less than four months away".

[58] The historical data in most of these economic categories were gleaned from the http://www.economagic.com/ and http://finance.yahoo.com/ websites.

[59] *The Wall Street Journal* editorial entitled "The Children of Beslan" appeared in its *Review & Outlook* section of September 7, 2004.

[60] This Maureen Dowd column entitled "Pre-emptive Paranoia" appeared in *The New York Times* edition dated September 16, 2004.

[61] Fareed Zakaria is the Editor of *Newsweek International* and a political analyst for *ABC News*. *The Washington Post* editorial entitled "Broken Promises", Richard Cohen's column entitled "Coming Clean About This War", Fareed Zakaria's op-ed piece entitled "Rejecting Turkey And the Future", and George Will's column entitled "Dubious Dreams About Iraq"—all of which appeared in its September 21, 2004 edition.

[62] In December 2004, Albert Hunt resigned as executive Washington editor of *The Wall Street Journal*. For eleven years, he wrote its "People & Politics" column, which appeared every Thursday. This one entitled, "Neither Guy Has Made the Sale Yet" appeared in the September 23, 2004 edition of the paper.

[63] *The Washington Post* editorial entitled "Truth on Russia" appeared in its October 2, 2004 edition.

[64] *The New York Times* editorial entitled "The Nuclear Bomb That Wasn't" appeared in its October 5, 2004 edition.

[65] *The New York Times* editorial entitled "The Verdict Is In" appeared in its October 7, 2004 edition.

[66] *The Washington Post* editorial entitled "Weapons That Weren't There" appeared in its October 7, 2004 edition.

[67] This George Will column entitled "Why America Leans Right" appeared in *The Washington Post* edition dated October 10, 2004.

[68] This letter was in response to David Broder column entitled "No Accountability", which also appeared in *The Washington Post* edition dated October 10, 2004.

[69] *The Wall Street Journal* editorial entitled "Kwasniewski on Kerry" appeared in its *Review & Outlook* section of October 13, 2004.

[70] *The Washington Post* editorial entitled "Remember Abu Ghraib?" appeared in its October 15, 2004 edition.

[71] David Ignatius is an associate editor of *The Washington Post*. He writes about international affairs and business. His column generally appears on Tuesdays and Fridays. The editorial entitled "The Rape of Belarus", and David Ignatius'

column entitled "Counter-Errorism" appeared in the *Post* edition of October 19, 2004.

[72] William Safire had been a political columnist for *The New York Times* since 1973. This column entitled "The Year of Fear" appeared in *The New York Times* edition dated October 20, 2004. Mr. Safire wrote his farewell column for the *Times* op-ed page on January 24, 2005.

[73] This Maureen Dowd column entitled "White House of Horrors" appeared in *The New York Times* edition dated October 28, 2004.

[74] Liberal, Mass. was a metaphor for what I believed was going to be the reemergence of the liberal masses with the election to the presidency of the first Northeastern liberal since 1960, and another JFK to boot! However, the people's reluctance to change the Commander-in-chief in the midst of a war took precedence.

[75] Dana Priest covers national security for *The Washington Post*. Ms. Priest has been with the Post for 16 years, and has also been an analyst for *NBC News* since 2003. Dana Priest and Walter Pincus' front-page report entitled "Bin Laden Warns U.S. Voters" appeared in *The Washington Post* edition dated October 30, 2004.

[76] *The Washington Post* editorial entitled "Mr. Gonzales's Record" appeared in its November 22, 2004 edition.

[77] This David Ignatius op-ed column entitled "Dangers Of the '80 Percent Solution'" appeared in *The Washington Post* edition dated November 23, 2004.

[78] This Charles Krauthammer op-ed column entitled "A Fight for Shiites" appeared in *The Washington Post* edition dated November 26, 2004.

[79] This William Safire op-ed column entitled "The Fourth Election" appeared in *The New York Times* edition dated December 1, 2004.

[80] Thomas L. Friedman has been with *The New York Times* since 1981, and has been the paper's foreign affairs columnist since 1995. This column entitled "The 9/11 Bubble" appeared in *The Times* edition dated December 2, 2004.

[81] Peter Baker is the White House correspondent for *The Washington Post.* This front-page report co-authored by Robin Wright and entitled "Musharraf: Bin Laden's Location Is Unknown" appeared in the *Post* edition dated December 5, 2004.

[82] This Maureen Dowd column entitled "Lost in a Masquerade" appeared in *The New York Times* edition dated December 9, 2004.

[83] Al From is founder and CEO of the Democratic Leadership Council. Bruce Reed is president of the DLC and was President Clinton's domestic policy adviser. Their op-ed piece entitled "Get the Red Out" appeared in *The Wall Street Journal* edition dated December 8, 2004.

[84] David E. Sanger covers the White House for *The New York Times*. His report entitled, "War Figures Honored With Medal of Freedom" appeared in *The Times* edition dated December 15, 2004.

[85] C. Raja Mohan is professor of South Asian studies at Jawaharlal Nehru University in New Delhi. His op-ed piece entitled "'Old' Europe Make Way for New Delhi" appeared in *The Wall Street Journal* edition dated December 15, 2004.

[86] This David Ignatius op-ed column entitled "How Iran Is Winning Iraq" appeared in *The Washington Post* edition dated December 17, 2004.

[87] *The Washington Post* editorial entitled "War Crimes" appeared in its December 23, 2004 edition.

[88] John F. Harris is a staff writer for *The Washington Post*. This front-page report co-authored by Robin Wright and entitled "Aid Grows Amid Remarks About President's Absence" appeared in the *Post* edition dated December 29, 2004.

[89] *The Washington Post* editorial entitled "Another Pass for Pakistan" appeared in its December 31, 2004 edition.

[90] *The Wall Street Journal* editorial entitled "That 'Sluggish' Economy" appeared in its *Review & Outlook* section of December 30, 2004.

[91] Adnan Pachachi is a member of the Iraqi national assembly and heads the Iraqi Independent Democrats Party. Mr. Pachachi has served as foreign minister of Iraq, president of the governing council and chairman of the committee for drafting the Transitional Administrative Law. His op-ed piece entitled "Delay the Elections" appeared in *The Washington Post* edition dated January 2, 2005.

[92] David Ignatius' column entitled "More Water Bottles, Fewer Bullets" and Richard Cohen's column entitled "Ugly Truths About Guantanamo" appeared in *The Washington Post* edition dated January 4, 2005.

[93] *The Washington Post* editorial entitled "The Gonzales Record" appeared in its January 6, 2005 edition.

[94] Reader Angela M. Hegarty's letter appeared, under the heading "Name That Decade (and Try to Smile)", in *The New York Times* dated January 10, 2005. Ms. Hegarty's letter had been in response to Clyde Haberman's article entitled, "NYC; Queasy Feeling About a Decade With No Name", which had been published in *The Times* on January 4, 2005.

[95] The Dow Jones Industrial Average fell by 31.2% from President Bush's first day in office to its low point on October 9, 2002.

[96] Forbes.com's "The Corporate Scandal Sheet" lists 20 companies from Adelphia to Tyco, whose scandals became public starting in October 2001 and were steadily exposed through the summer of 2002. For a complete rundown see http://www.forbes.com/2002/07/25/accountingtracker.html.

[97] Per *The Heritage Foundation's* interpretation (http://www.heritage.org/Research/Economy/wm647.cfm) of the Bureau of Labor Statistics report of February 4, 2005 the U.S. economy had a net gain of 119,000 jobs in President Bush's first term.

[98] Per a *Reuters* report dated October 14, 2004, "The U.S. budget gap expanded to $412.55 billion in fiscal 2004, marking the Bush administration's second-straight record deficit, the Treasury Department said on Thursday."

[99] Per a *CNN Money* report dated February 10, 2005, "The Commerce Department reported that while the trade deficit narrowed slightly in Decem-

ber from November's monthly record, the deficit for the full year grew to $617.7 billion, up $121 billion from 2003, the previous annual record."

[100] Per a *CBS News* report dated October 18, 2004, "Crude for November delivery on the New York Mercantile Exchange hit $55.33 per barrel around noon in Asia, up 40 cents from its Friday settlement price." It went on to add, "The crude oil prices are the highest in a generation and while oil is around 80 percent higher than a year ago, they are still around $25 below the peak inflation-adjusted price reached in 1981."

[101] The *Merrill Lynch Investment Managers* report (http://mlimadviser.com.au/cms/public/mlim003951.jsp) of December 2004 entitled, "Gold Shines Again" began with a summary as follows, "In November 2004 gold reached a price of USD 455 per ounce, its highest level since 1988 after making an unsteady recovery from a low of about USD 253 per ounce in 1999.

[102] *The Economist* dated December 2, 2004 in an article entitled, "The passing of the buck?" reports, "Since mid-October the dollar has fallen by around 7% against the other main currencies, hitting a new all-time low against the euro and a five-year low against the yen." It goes on to add, "The real broad trade-weighted dollar has so far fallen by only 15% since early 2002, compared with a drop of 34% from its peak in 1985."

[103] *The New York Times* editorial entitled "Facing Facts About Iraq's Election" appeared in its January 12, 2005 edition.

[104] This Thomas L. Friedman column entitled "Pop Tarts or Freedom" appeared in *The New York Times* edition dated January 16, 2005.

[105] *The Washington Post* editorial entitled "The Second Term Abroad" appeared in its January 19, 2005 edition.

EPILOGUE

The Second Term—Second Thoughts

In a post-inaugural editorial, the Post noted that President Bush used the word "freedom" 27 times and the word "liberty" 15 times in his inaugural speech. It seemed quite apparent to me that President Bush was already looking to establish a legacy based on spreading democracy around the world. While I welcomed the noble objective, my only caveat was that it needed to be pursued consistently.

When President Bush invaded Iraq, "freedom" and "liberty" were not among his top priorities. In fact, he was primarily concerned with "WMD" and "terrorism", both of which had inundated his pre-election rhetoric, but neither of which rated a mention in his inaugural speech. Nonetheless, if President Bush is serious about moving beyond what the Post called "the rhetoric of freedom" and pursuing it consistently across the globe—however inconvenient it might be to do so with certain "allied countries"—not only would his legacy be established, but also the true American character would be rekindled, regardless of the actual outcome of his efforts.

One could say that President Bush's second inaugural speech was America's equivalent of Dr. Martin Luther King's "I have a dream" vision for the world. Although Dr. King's dream of a color blind society in America has yet to be fully realized, we never back-tracked on his stated goals, and have come a long way towards achieving them.

Just as my hopes were surging, twenty-four hours after President Bush's inaugural speech, the Bush Administration started back tracking on the freedom agenda. President Bush was quoted as saying, "My inaugural address reflected the policies of the last four years." Say what? So just like the first term began with a foreign policy faux pas with China, the second term started inauspiciously with a flip-flop on freedom. Alas, the more things change, the more they remain the same!

In any event, when President Bush delivered his inaugural speech, I sensed a compassionate move from Bush Doctrine I (the U.S. will act preemptively to rid the world of the "axis of evil") to Bush Doctrine II (the U.S. will promote democracy to make the world a "nexus of free will"). So I continue to hold out hope for "legacy" trumping "lunacy"—only time will tell!

*   *   *

Priorities for President Bush's Second Term

The population of the world can be divided into roughly four equal quadrants—Judeo-Christian, Hindu-Buddhist, Muslim, and Communist. A vast majority of the people that constitute the Judeo-Christian and Hindu-Buddhist quadrants happen to live in secular democracies. It would therefore seem natural for these quadrants to be more closely aligned, since they share similar economic and political value systems? One would hope that an alignment of this nature could become an ideal for peace and prosperity throughout the world. When I was a child, my father always fueled my ambition with one of his favorite lines, "not failure, but aiming low is a crime." So, in a utopian sense, I believe that President Bush's focus on freedom and democracy is an appropriate start to his second term—I would hope that he does not have any second thoughts, and I wish him Godspeed and success!

Having said that, I would like to caution President Bush not to get carried away with any illusions of a mandate from the 2004 election. Bush got reelected by a mere 2.46% margin over Kerry—it is the smallest margin of victory for a president's second term since the 22nd Amendment was ratified over fifty years ago. Bush's predecessor, Clinton, won reelection in 1996 by a 8.53% margin despite the presence of a strong third party candidate, Perot, who got 8.4% of the popular vote. If President Bush wants to know what "political capital" is really about—he should look back at Republican icons, Reagan, who got reelected by a 18.2% margin in 1984; Nixon, who was returned by a 23.2% margin in 1972; and Eisenhower, who won reelection by a 15.4% margin in 1956! In fact, even Bush's "guns and butter" spending counterpart, Johnson, capitalized on the Kennedy legacy and got reelected by a 22.6% margin.

With that dose of reality, I would like to conclude with what I consider to be the critical success factors—domestic and foreign—for President Bush in his second term. The infamous 3Gs—God, Guns and Gays—do not make my list. Somehow public debate on the 3Gs always seems to be driven by emotion (i.e., by appealing to people's hearts) as opposed to being influenced by reason (i.e., by debate amongst rational minds). Although, I do believe that the SLR—safe, legal, and rare—principle is more or less applicable to the governance of these 3Gs in our society as it should be in the case of abortion.

Without further ado, I would like to end these diaries by listing in random order a list of thirteen priorities for President Bush's second term:

1. The budget and trade deficits are in more urgent "crises" than Social Security so defer any personal accounts and tackle these deficits on a war footing. Personal accounts are a good idea—but we cannot afford the enormous costs associated with their implementation until the budget deficit is substantially eliminated and the national debt is significantly reduced. This can only be brought about if the President

scales back some of his tax cuts, in order to raise revenues quickly in the short term, while simultaneously reducing government spending on, both, discretionary and non-discretionary programs.

2. The strength of a nation is also reflected in the value of its currency, so the President must strive to restore the greenback's true worth by supplementing the Fed's belated, yet, wise monetary policy with equally sound fiscal and trade policies. A big step in this direction would require that the President pressure China into allowing its currency to float—this is a better alternative to imposing punitive tariffs on Chinese imports.

3. It is in the long term interests of any nation to have an independent judiciary, so the President should take the high road and strongly condemn those within his party, who would try to undermine it. This also implies that the President appoint judges that would appeal to a broad cross-section of the American public—consulting with the Democrats prior to making key nominations to the courts might be a way to go—and, it would simultaneously fulfill a belated first term promise to "change the tone in Washington."

4. Every year our children's performance in school falls further behind their counterparts in other developed and third world nations—so the President needs to fully fund his *2001 No Child Left Behind Act* by petitioning private sector sponsors, as required, to make it more effective. Other countries are catching up with our technological prowess, but we don't have to accelerate that process by falling rapidly behind? The President must solicit large corporate donors with appropriate tax incentives to get them to subsidize under-graduate and graduate studies in science and engineering across the country.

5. Notwithstanding the skepticism about global warming in conservative circles, a clean environment is not just a liberal fantasy—so the President must stop chipping away at the Clean Air Act and proactively recommend an acceptable alternative to the Kyoto protocols.

6. The President should recommend a sensible, long term energy policy that will not only reduce our dependence on foreign oil in the near term, but also eliminate it entirely by 2020. If limited, environmentally-friendly drilling in the ANWR can reduce our reliance on Mid-

dle East oil in this decade, so be it. Simultaneously, the President must recommend a progressive increase in our fuel-efficiency standards over the next decade, and also propose a progressive increase in the number of hybrid vehicles on the road through appropriate state-sponsored initiatives.

7. "Stop the genocide in Darfur" has become an embarrassing cliché, since the collective international community has been unable to act upon its stated intentions for well over a year now. President Bush, already constrained by the war on terrorism, needs to pressure Muslim allies in the region—Egypt, Saudi Arabia, and Turkey—to get more actively involved. They should immediately send in the required amount of peacekeeping troops into the Sudan under a UN resolution sponsored by the United States.

8. The Iraq war has more or less invalidated the efficacy of the Bush Doctrine—"shock and awe" was successful in rapidly toppling an "axis of evil" regime, but we have since then got mired in "block and tackle" operations in trying to secure the peace. The President must exploit the Shia nexus unfolding in the Persian Gulf, to counter-balance the predominant Sunni Arab influence in the Middle East, by altering U.S. policy towards Iran—whose people appear to be fed up with their theocracy?

9. With Mahmoud Abbas elected as President of the Palestine people, President Bush must take a more proactive approach to resolving the Israeli-Palestine issue by re-introducing President Clinton's final proposal of September 2000 as a starting point for discussion. The President's objective must be to establish a Palestinian state before the end of his second term.

10. An evil dictator rules North Korea, which has confessed to possessing WMD, and which is a threat to its neighbors as well as the United States—the President cannot indefinitely rely on the on again-off again six-party talks to resolve this looming crisis. It's time to get the UN to pass some meaningful resolutions and serve North Korea an ultimatum—which could unfortunately become the real decisive test for an already-weakened Bush Doctrine? But, how the President resolves this situation is going to determine our standing in the world and could make or break the Bush legacy?

11. The Cold War was winnable because the enemy was a "godless" evil empire—the "war on terror" cannot be won unless god is removed from the equation—the President must make U.S. policy towards Muslim nations uniformly consistent in order to win over the "hearts and minds" of the larger Muslim populace. I have covered the hypocrisy of U.S. foreign policy in this regard throughout the book.

12. The President must ensure that the Reagan legacy is preserved by not allowing Russia to slide back into "empire" mode—which means that the President must make Putin "put out" on domestic reform—by using more of the G8 type carrots in more western initiatives on the global stage. President Bush could get Russia involved in the European initiative to convince Iran to come clean on its nuclear program.

13. The unfolding alliance between China and India, which together represent a third of humanity, is a major strategic threat to the United States. It's time the President played his "strategic competitor" card more aggressively with China—from Tiananmen to Taiwan, and democracy to human rights—there are several trump cards to choose from. At the same time, the President must accelerate and enhance our engagement with India with the objective of making India an important strategic—economic, military, political, and technological—partner in the 21st century.

*   *   *

When the Age of Truth is at hand, the truth will ultimately prevail.

978-0-595-35898-4
0-595-35898-5